CONSCIOUS CHOOSING FOR FLOW

TRANSFORMING CONFLICT INTO CREATIVITY

*Toniola,
Wishing you Flow &
Curiosity in your life.*

HAYDEN D.M. HAYDEN

Copyright © 2014 Hayden D.M. Hayden
All rights reserved.

ISBN: 1497553857
ISBN 13: 9781497553859
Library of Congress Control Number: 2014906522
CreateSpace Independent Publishing Platform
North Charleston, South Carolina

Flow is the positive, dynamic, creative, forward-moving energy between people.

In order to consciously create Flow, we must have the ability to transform the destructive tension of conflict and disconnection into the dynamic energy of creativity and connection in the moment, in real time, and then consciously choose to use that ability. That's what this book is all about—how to consciously choose to create Flow. It's not about negotiation or conflict management; it's about transformation.

The Conscious Choosing logo represents human interactions that are in flow. Based on the yin-yang symbol, the two swishes signify the exterior forces on our life and our internal response to them. The red dot signifies the state of Flow that we can create when we are conscious of the meanings we create from events in our lives, and consciously choose the perspectives and actions that create results through our human connection.

ADVANCE PRAISE FOR CONSCIOUS CHOOSING FOR FLOW

I asked many people from various walks of life, that I know both professionally and personally, to read this book and give their honest evaluation of it's contents. My purpose in doing so was to provide you with a quick and efficient way to get a sense of what you will gain from reading it. You will notice that many of those whose comments follow are also mentioned in the stories and examples in this book and their experiences reveal the power of establishing and experiencing Flow in their lives. It is my hope that their comments will give you, the reader, the confidence and assurance that you too will benefit from the skills and awareness contained in this book. You can read the entirety of each person's response on our website at: www.ConsciousChoosing.com/Book.

"The tools and concepts described in this book can be applied in the real world. And they work! As a 52 year-old CEO of a privately held company with a strong track record, I wanted to learn something that would help my Leadership Team improve performance and have more fun together. Our team is using the contents of this book to address things we would have ignored in the past and it's making a difference... I am a believer."
—Phil Raimondo, President & CEO, Behlen Mfg. Co.

"A masterful work, heralding in a new era of heart-based human interaction. Hayden's approach for connecting with others in any situation or circumstance is mind-blowing in its simplicity and complete, utter effectiveness. Conscious Choosing for Flow is intuitive and natural - the way humans were intended to interact. Whether you want new and better results in your business, your personal relationships or any area of your life, this skill is the key to mastery, joy and achievement. You DO NOT want to pass up this life changing opportunity. Learn this skill NOW and improve your results. Period."
—Ron Hollenbeck, Senior Enterprise Analyst, IT Planning and Transformation Office, General Motors

"Conscious Choosing does something that most other "conflict management" books don't do. It takes the reader through specific, personal and professional examples, has the reader work those examples real time in a reflective manner, and enables the reader to draw from previous experiences thus setting them up for success to Consciously Choose a different approach next time! ... *Conscious Choosing for Flow* sets up the reader to first effectively recognize their current behaviors and intentions, and secondly to learn from those patterns. Then it takes the reader through the more difficult journey of making different choices by building up confidence and skill concurrently.

I highly recommend this read for a variety of populations such as managers, leaders, executives, and I see a specific application for people in service industries such as clinicians (doctors, nurses, nurse practitioners, physical therapists, etc.), sales, and hospitality to enable them to address specific situations directly and appropriately. The clear accountabilities are one of the many gems that *Conscious Choosing for Flow* highlights. Readers will leave their investment of read time with life skills that will not only advance their careers, but will also advance their personal relationships."
—Rhonda Hall, Senior Director, Organizational Effectiveness, Ascension Health

"Just as physicists search for a unified theory of everything, many leaders I coach and train search for a robust and simple theory for the interpersonal complexities that emerge whenever and wherever people work together. In *Conscious Choosing for Flow*, Hayden provides that theory and then explains how to make it a practice. This is an essential guidebook for leaders, aspiring leaders, anyone who wants to connect with colleagues in ways that work even when faced with deep adversity or conflict. I recommend keeping a second copy on hand because you'll want to pass it on!"
—Deb Palmer George, CEO, Palmer Solutions
"Helping leaders build thriving organizations."

"*Conscious Choosing for Flow* is a must read for anyone wishing to better understand themselves as well as their associations with others... Before I retired from the Federal Bureau of Investigation (FBI), I designed, developed and implemented the officer "Safety and Survival" and "Mental Mindset" programs at the FBI Academy in Quantico, Virginia. These programs were designed to help the "Violent Crimes Task Forces" of the FBI to deal with violent criminals in a safer manner. I have trained thousands of law enforcement officers worldwide in these techniques and I am totally convinced that if the skill presented by Hayden could be taught to the senior and mid-level management of law enforcement we could majorly change, for the better, how law enforcement officers are trained... Understanding and implementing the principles of *Conscious Choosing for Flow* will help them deal with conflicts in a way that will create "FLOW" within their lives which will result in healthier "Choices" for their life and environment."

—Philip P. Hayden, Ed.D., Retired Supervisory Special Agent, FBI, Presently the CEO of Corporate Global Solutions, an International Investigative Company

"In *Conscious Choosing for Flow*, Hayden has created a terrifically valuable resource for businesses everywhere that are struggling to achieve optimal results. What makes *Conscious Choosing for Flow* so valuable is not just the discussion of theory related to behavior and conflict, but the inclusion of valuable tools like the STAR process and Restorative Dialogue. Hayden works through the reasoning behind challenges we all face regularly in a patient in an understandable way, and shows us, with rich examples, how to use the many tools he has assembled in this most valuable toolkit.

But *Conscious Choosing for Flow* is much bigger than just running businesses effectively. The insights and tools discussed here can be applied to all of the interactions we have with other humans - spouse, children, parents, friends, even casual acquaintances like convenience store clerks... Hayden's

writing is clear and clean, and his text is very well documented. He takes us along a logical path through the explanation of how curiosity can help us overcome the more basic and instinctive fight, flight or freeze reactions... I have become acquainted with Hayden's concepts through the work he has done for our organization. I am truly grateful to him for having done the hard work of organizing and recording his knowledge in so useful a form."
—Todd S. Sorensen, MD, MS, President and CEO,
Regional West Health Services

"It's not always what you say, but how you say it ... the written word deepens the understanding and enlightenment of *Conscious Choosing for Flow* for me. Hayden has laid out the diagnosis, strategy and process for resolutions for everything from divorce to world peace. Good Job Hayden, its a life work and I am sure it will become the holy grain for all sorts of folks from business leaders to psychologist to marriage counselors, executives of state and hopefully standard curriculum for high school students, and a requirement for college degrees, its that big..."
—Jim Jamail, CEO, Jamail&Smith Construction,
a Texas Construction Company

"Where there are people, there is conflict. Organizational success depends on people working together to achieve common goals. Conflict gets in the way of teamwork and can derail an organization if not addressed. *Conscious choosing for Flow* is your tool kit for uncovering the root cause of conflict. You will learn how to uncover unmet needs, which fuel conflict and destructive behavior. By identifying common goals and together going forward to accomplish these goals, your organization will be on a path of mitigating conflict and maximizing teamwork and success."
—Tony Raimondo, Jr., Vice Chair of Behlen,
President of AG Division, Behlen Manufacturing

"Hayden outlines a process and a mindset that is not only transformational in any organization; it is also a recipe for successful and fulfilling personal relationships. I have personally witnessed how *Conscious Choosing For Flow* transforms an organization and propels it to even higher levels of success by employing this process throughout the organization. In addition, it transforms a culture in to one that is highly collaborative and authentic. In my own personal life *Conscious Choosing For Flow* is transforming my life by enriching each and every relationship."
—Keith G. Bushardt, Vice President,
Strategy and Consulting, KGB Group

"Conscious Choosing for Flow is the new operating system for anyone seeking to communicate with others in order to connect as human beings and achieve great things together. My team and I have had the opportunity to work with Hayden in his *Conscious Choosing for Flow* workshop with great success and this book ... is interesting, easy to read style allowed me to refresh in my mind the simple steps that transform conflict into connection by observing a situation and responding with curiosity instead of immediately having all the answers. Influenced by several different behavioral/communication disciplines, Hayden has created a process to guide in discovering what motivates another person, allowing us the understanding that results in meaningful collaboration. *Conscious Choosing for Flow* clearly demonstrates how important it is that we acknowledge and embrace the role that everyone's feelings and needs have in our ability to live, work and play with each other and the way to do it effectively."
—Hill Abell, CEO, Bicycle Sport Shop

"Often, when we discuss "soft skills," we talk about their importance while at the same time minimizing their impact –in our work lives and in our personal lives. Hayden has made the case for how we can consciously choose to use our soft skills in productive ways. With models, examples, techniques, exercises, comprehensive explanations, and a passionate call for making the world a better place, "Flow" takes us to places we never knew we could go before, and tells us what to do when we get there. This is a breakthrough piece of work."

—Tom Sechrest, Associate Dean for Academic Programs, The Bill Munday School of Business, St. Edward's University, Austin, Texas

"Hayden lays out the transformative power of curiosity and choice in a clear, compelling way. He translates each of his major ideas into action by providing intuitive tools that can be used immediately by the reader. If you're open to meaningful change, this book is a must read for sustainable growth in business and life."

—Tadd M. Pullin, Senior Vice President of Marketing and Planning, The Nebraska Medical Center

"In my 35 years in business, I have never experienced a communications consultant with the skill of Hayden... I have witnessed his ability to bring totally polarized individuals into useful and coherent conversation that results in mutual understanding and levels of trust otherwise thought impossible... His results have always been impressive to remarkable...

This book offers the ability to practice "Curious Questioning" and how to keep positive "Flow" of dialog and build "Connections" with others to gain understanding and resolve conflicts in a manner that brings people together in mutual understanding and trust...

As I read the book, it occurred to me that Hayden will be limiting his potential as a consultant as he is giving away all the things that he would otherwise be paid to teach under a consulting agreement... Upon further reflection, it became clear to me that when someone reaches the level of understanding and skill that Hayden has obtained, the only compassionate option is to give it away so others can benefit from it. Read this book!"

—Steven S. Martin, President & CEO, Blue Cross Blue Shield of Nebraska

"As a leader in Mfg. for over 50 years, I have interviewed 100's of candidates pursuing promotions or trying to get hired. I have always been curious about their thinking process, and I would hire those who seem to have a good thinking process. In *Conscious Choosing For Flow* Hayden has captured and presents a toolbox of thinking tools nicely package to strengthen leadership skills for those in a search to be among the best in their respective businesses and markets."

—TR Raimondo, Chairman & Coach, Behlen Mfg. Co.

"Hayden brings his wealth of experience, his insight and his genius to the fullest in *Conscious Choosing for Flow: Transforming Conflict into Creativity*. He masterfully synthesizes a broad knowledge in the area of Conflict, Leadership Effectiveness and Personal Growth into a very practical formula and playbook that we can all use. In the Worth Ethic commitment to work with Alpha Leaders, we face the opportunity to move Conflict into fullest Impact day... Hayden's work and wisdom will add immensely to our effectiveness ... Thank You Hayden!"

—Eddie Erlandson MD, EVP and executive consultant Worth Ethic Corporation; Kate Ludeman PhD, founder and president, Worth Ethic Corporation. Authors of *Alpha Male Syndrome and Radical Change, Radical Results*

"I appreciate Hayden's loyalty and his honoring the author of NonViolent Communication, Dr. Marshall Rosenberg... his work on empathy and reflective listening. All-in-all very simple, straightforward and difficult work that continues in a line of practitioners committed to being compassionate humans... Hayden's book moves us in that direction."

—Patrick F. Siebert, Student & Prodigy of Marshall Rosenberg, NVC Practitioner

"Hayden's new book *Conscious Choosing For Flow* is a thought provoking book. It will lead you to be more self-aware and also more aware of those around you in a positive way... a process for dealing with people when there is conflict. Questioning and curiosity is central to *Conscious Choosing for Flow* as it is to many things including selling, negotiating, discussing subjects like politics, parenting, coaching, and the obvious arena of education and the Socratic method of teaching. ... filled with anecdotes and experiential references, it is an enjoyable read. Knowing Hayden personally, I can say that he walks the walk and we are both better for it. Do an honest self-assessment and if you see any friction or stress in your life as a result of interactions with people in your life, this book may be helpful in increasing your personal enjoyment and satisfaction by offering a means of reducing tension and stress when engaging with others."

—Lou Heavner, Consultant, Industrial Solutions,
Emerson Process Management, Emerson Worldwide

"Hayden's book, *Conscious Choosing for Flow*, describes a structure and process for making sure any interaction, no matter what the conflict may be, is safe and respectful, while getting results that work for all parties involved. At Meals on Wheels we are committed to speaking and acting with compassion as we prepare and deliver meals to shut-ins. Since conflict can occur at the drop of a hat we want to make sure our compassion is maintained throughout any challenge that arises as we serve our thousands of clients every day. This book is a breakthrough in compassionate communication with the insights and awareness it explains and teaches to communicate in a manner that maintains compassion, no matter what the conflict. I recommend it to anyone wanting more compassion in their relationships and a way to communication that is safe and respectful with anybody."

—Dan Pruett, President & CEO,
Meals on Wheels and More, Austin, TX

"Hayden, thank you for professionally translating the "woo-woo" of this work into the acceptable application of the business world. The time has come for the business world to embrace words like "feelings and needs" as they relate to their "human assets." I have never experienced another book, workbook or methodology that pulls it all together like *Conscious Choosing for Flow*. This is an excellent resource for anyone in any type of relationship with another - at home and at work. You have artfully taken so many different components of communication and pulled it into a system for personal and business success. The world needs this book - with gratitude,"
—Alice Dendinger, SPHR Human Resource Consultant, Coach and Mediator

"*Conscious Choosing for Flow* is a breakthrough book on how to turn conflict into creativity while improving your home and work environment with others. Hayden has woven two tried and proven approaches, used in a select few areas in our world, for a simple and straightforward approach that can be learned and mastered by any company or individual for a better way forward... I learned the power of curiosity from Hayden during our work together and my approach to businesses has never been the same. My bottom line business results continue to increase and new possibilities reveal themselves to me as I use curiosity to discover new areas of growth and effectiveness in my world. Curiosity is a very powerful tool when used in your own life and business. If you don't read any other book this year, make sure you read *Conscious Choosing for Flow*. It will make a huge difference in your life and business."
—Paul J. Dunham, Dunham & Jones, Attorneys at Law, P.C.

"While seemingly a plethora of conjoined philosophies, it is not. Hayden nails it in this book by getting to the very soul of situational resolution. The information within these pages takes the reader on a simple, yet clever journey of self-development and introspective clarity. I found the book to be a rather personal explosion of "aha" moments. Knowing the information taught on these pages wasn't enough; living it was where my very being found a better way to be; I now look for it, listen for it, and reach for it, in every interaction of my life.

Conscious Choosing for Flow is insightful and life changing. Thanks Hayden, this book truly hit home."
—Jim Hansel, PhD, CEO, Garden County Health Services

ACKNOWLEDGEMENTS

Conscious Choosing's motto, *Creating Results Through Our Human Connection*, was adopted early on in the company's formation and has guided me and my relationships ever since. Without human connection and the collaboration with numerous, generous, hard working, and supportive people, this book would not have come to fruition. I am grateful to all who have believed in the cause and contributed to the development of the Conscious Choosing for Flow training and this book. This journey has been full of twists and turns, trials and tribulations, all of which created the opportunities for growth and development, and fine-tuning of the skills you will learn in this book. Thank you to those who partnered with me to build a world-class training program, organizations that sponsored pilot programs in the early days, trainers who provided valuable real-world feedback, and affiliates who have been strong advocates. I have been fortunate to work with many interesting and successful individuals and businesses, and appreciate those who have contributed by sharing their stories in these pages. And finally, thank you to my wife, Iwalani, who keeps me grounded while providing amazing support and encouragement as we live our life together in flow.

MY REQUEST OF YOU

I ask that you read this book with an open mind to explore and discover a new way of operating in the world, a way that works for you and those around you. Ultimately, it's your choice. People are just doing what they're doing in an attempt to meet their needs. It's *you* that has the power to choose your actions and your responses.

As you delve into these pages, it is my sincere hope that you come to a new level of understanding and gain new skill-sets to have the life you love and live it powerfully, no matter what the situation you find yourself in.

I invite you to visit the Conscious Choosing website, at ConsciousChoosing.com, where you can watch several short videos on the skills you are reading about, read the Advance Praise comments in full, order a signed copy of this book for yourself and others, and subscribe to our newsletter to continue the conversation. You can also learn more about the 2-day Conscious Choosing for Flow training and how to become a certified trainer to bring this valuable approach to your own clients or your own company by adding an additional 2-days certification to the training itself.

For additional information about keynotes and book signings, please send an email to Info@ConsciousChoosing.com.

I wish you all the best as you apply your new awareness and skills to transform conflict into creativity,

Hayden2

TABLE OF CONTENTS

Introduction—Winning Hearts and Minds · 1
   Under Stress, We Tend to Digress · 2
   Conflict Derails Us From Results We Seek · · · · · · · · · · · · · · · · · · 3
   Making a Difference · 5

Section I—Conscious Choosing · 7
Chapter 1—Looking For a Common Thread · · · · · · · · · · · · · · · · 9
   Compassionate Communication · 10
   Discovering the Power of Curiosity · 12
Chapter 2—Choosing Flow · 15
   Conflict and Strained Relationships Are Costly · · · · · · · · · · · · 17
   The Ability to Transform Conflict · 18
   What Creates Human Connection? · 19
   The Four Components of Our Human Connection · · · · · · · · · · 20
   Our Human Energy · 22
   Entering a State of Flow · 23
   This Works for Me! · 24
   What Is Your Experience of Flow? · 25
   The Power of Choice · 27
   Choosing to Create Flow · 30
   Your Response to the Stimulus · 31
Chapter 3—Cycles of Failure and Success · · · · · · · · · · · · · · · · · 33
   What Is the Cycle for Success? · 34
   What Is the Cycle of Failure? · 36
   Reptilian Reactions · 38
   Typical Flight Response · 39
   Your Default Mechanism · 41
   Curiosity Can Change Your Default Mechanism · · · · · · · · · · · 43
   Staying Curious Produces Different Results · · · · · · · · · · · · · · 45
   Take the Curious ABC Pause · 46

Chapter 4—Curiosity Is the Catalyst for Flow and Success · · · · · · · · · · 51
What Is Conscious Curiosity? · 53
Curiosity Is the Catalyst for Creativity · 53
Questions That Tap Into Wisdom · 55
Where Focus Goes, Energy Flows · 57
Chapter 5—What Is the Formula for Flow? · 59
Process #1 for Connection: The Skill for Connection · · · · · · · · · · · · · 60
Process #2 for Results: The STAR Process for Results · · · · · · · · · · · · · 60
Personal Application: Transform Conflict Into Creativity · · · · · · · · · · 62

Section II —The Skill for Connection · **65**
Chapter 6—What Is The Skill for Connection? · · · · · · · · · · · · · · · · · · 67
Connecting for Results · 70
Chapter 7—The Skill for Connection - Observations · · · · · · · · · · · · · 73
What Are Observations? · 73
Meaning-Making Creates Problems · 75
Observations Have Innate Power · 77
Ungrounded Meanings Create Conflict · 80
Your Perspectives Drive Your Meanings · 81
Perspectives Create Geniuses · 83
Perspectives Determine Feelings and Dictate Actions · · · · · · · · · · · · · 85
Fundamental Attribution Error Creates Disconnection · · · · · · · · · · · 86
Applying The Skill for Connection—Observations · · · · · · · · · · · · · · · · 88
Facts Before Meanings · 89
Personal Application: Observations · 91
Chapter 8—The Skill for Connection – Feelings · · · · · · · · · · · · · · · · · 93
What Are Feelings? · 93
Emotional Intelligence is an Ingredient of Life Success · · · · · · · · · · · · 94
Understanding Feelings Leads to Emotional Intelligence · · · · · · · · · · 95
No One Can Make You Feel Anything · 96
Why Do You Resist Expressing Your Feelings? · · · · · · · · · · · · · · · · · · 97
Use Your Feelings as GPS · 99
Feelings Tell You Whether Your Needs Are Satisfied, or Not · · · · · · · 102
Empathy Is Not... · 104

TABLE OF CONTENTS

    Honestly Express Your Feelings · *107*
    Applying The Skill for Connection—Feelings · *109*
    GPS Before GAS · *115*
    Personal Application: Feelings · *117*
Chapter 9—The Skill for Connection - Needs · 119
    Our Human Needs · *119*
    Needs Predict Behavior · *120*
    Needs Connect All Human Beings · *120*
    Feelings and Needs Are Inextricably Linked · *121*
    Fulfillment of Needs Determines Outcomes · *124*
    List of Needs · *126*
    The Difference Between Needs and Strategies · *128*
    Put Needs Before Strategies · *130*
    Our Worst Disagreements · *131*
    How to Diffuse Conflict · *133*
    Needs Hidden in Blames, Complaints, or Judgments · · · · · · · · · · · · · · *135*
    Revealing Needs Behind Meanings · *138*
    Curiously Investigating to Uncover Needs · *141*
    Applying The Skill for Connection—Needs · *143*
    Focus On Needs Instead of Reactions · *145*
    Personal Application: Needs · *147*

Section III —The STAR Process for Results · · · · · · · · · · · · · · · · **149**
Chapter 10—What Is the STAR Process for Results? · · · · · · · · · · · · · · · 151
Chapter 11—Step 1: Stop—Current Needs and Shared Goals · · · · · · · · 159
    A Common Destination Brings Everyone's Thinking Together · · · · · · *160*
    Handle One Topic at a Time for Clarity · *161*
    First Make a Request to Stop and Identify Needs · · · · · · · · · · · · · · · · · · *163*
    The Value of a Shared Goal · *165*
    Coaching Occurs in the Gap · *166*
    Listen to Understand and Not Just to Reply · *169*
    Clearing Up Misunderstandings Through the
    "What I Heard" Conversation · *170*
    Using the "What I Heard" Conversation · *174*

CONSCIOUS CHOOSING FOR FLOW

Restorative Dialogue Restores Justice · *177*
Restorative Dialogue Circle · *177*
Focus On Our Needs and Our Shared Goal · *181*
Personal Application: Shared Goal · *183*
Chapter 12—Step 2: Think—Brainstorm Strategies · · · · · · · · · · · · · · · 185
Choose Your Route · *186*
Brainstorming Basics · *186*
Brainstorming Occurs Within the Gap · *189*
What We Don't Know, We Don't Know · *190*
Strategies Often Vary, So Manage Your Expectations · · · · · · · · · · · · · *193*
Managing Expectations · *195*
Leaders Poison the Well · *195*
Make Requests to Brainstorm Strategies · *196*
Consensus Tool for Collaboration · *198*
Hand Notifications Measure Support · *200*
Respect Is a Core Human Need · *203*
Respect and Trust · *205*
Needs Before Strategies · *207*
Personal Application: Brainstorm Strategies · *209*
Chapter 13—Step 3: Act—Requests for Commitments · · · · · · · · · · · · 211
Assign Roles and Responsibilities · *212*
WALK the Talk to Build Accountability · *212*
Follow Up to Achieve Specific Results · *215*
Actions Close the Gap · *216*
Agreements Manage Expectations · *217*
Managing Expectations · *218*
The Difference Between Requests and Demands · · · · · · · · · · · · · · · · · *219*
Requests Are an Opportunity to Connect · *220*
Two Types of Requests · *221*
The Power of Positive Doable Requests (PDR) · · · · · · · · · · · · · · · · · · · *223*
Make Requests for Connection and Results · *227*
Make Requests Instead of Demands · *230*
Personal Application: Requests · *232*

Chapter 14—Step 4: Review—Stop, Modify, or Start 235
    The Importance of a Rest Stop 236
    Review to Fine-Tune Relationships and Results 236
    Review Often to Keep Space Clear 237
    Review to Affect the Future 239
    Have You Filled the Gap? 241
    We Are What We Repeatedly Do 242
    Review to Reach Shared Goals 244
    Personal Application: Review 245

Section IV—Putting It All Together With the STAR Process for Results 247
Chapter 15—Company Application 249
    Application: Software Company 249
Chapter 16—Coaching Application 259
Appendix I—Worksheet for Agendas and Decisions 265
Appendix II—Personal Challenge Worksheet 267
Bibliography 273
Endnotes 279

Introduction

WINNING HEARTS AND MINDS

"The deepest secret is that life is not a process of discovery, but a process of creation. You are not discovering yourself, but creating yourself anew. Seek therefore, not to find out who you are, but seek to determine who you want to be."

— Neale Donald Walsch[1]

Conflict and disconnection from those we care about is not something we enjoy or can completely avoid. It is a natural part of life, yet if we could minimize it or completely remove it from our lives altogether, I think we would all like to do so. Perhaps the biggest challenge of dealing with conflict, whether it is a small, recent irritant or a large, long-lasting dispute, is finding the key that can unlock its mysteries and shift it in real time into something positive. So what is this key? What would it take to win the hearts and minds of those we work or interact with each and every day, especially during conflict?

CONSCIOUS CHOOSING FOR FLOW

This question has perhaps stumped you, as it has me.

The answer, found in the pages of this book, involves the required awareness to consistently turn conflict and disconnection from others into creativity and connection in real time—not three hours after the conflict is over and has done its damage, but on the spot. I'm not talking about managing it, resolving it, or negotiating it, but transforming conflict when it is happening.

To do this, the concept of curiosity has been elevated to the level of a skill, so you can **Consciously Choose Curiosity** over your habitual reactions to conflict when an interaction isn't going well. Learning to use Curiosity is what this book is about.

UNDER STRESS, WE TEND TO DIGRESS

Many wonderful training tools provide insights and enhance interpersonal skills for improving communication and getting results, such as the following:

- Myers-Briggs Type Indicator
- Situational leadership
- Servant leadership
- The Seven Habits of Highly Effective People
- The Speed of Trust
- Crucial Conversations and Crucial Confrontations

But what usually happens to the insights and skills you have learned and tried to keep straight in your head in a moment of conflict?

Maybe you're thinking,

"They go right out the window."

"You revert back to old patterns, etc."

There is an old saying that "under stress, we tend to regress." But what if it didn't have to be that way?

When our knowledge and learning are head-based, and we're trying to keep it all straight in our heads, it's easy to forget our better selves during times of conflict and stress. Whatever situation we find ourselves in, we need to employ a type of human technology that lives at a level beneath all other interpersonal skills trainings. Addressing what is common to all humans at the core level of our needs—and the feelings attached to them that drive everything we do—supports the philosophies, skills, and processes we have learned, making them more understandable and easier to use. This type of learning is both heart-based and head-based.

During times of conflict and disconnection from others, using this human technology can affect both future outcomes and relationships. Let's start with a basic premise: When our needs as humans are not satisfied, we experience negative feelings; when they are satisfied, we experience positive feelings. This is true for both teams and organizations. We can use this aspect of our human technology to guide us to the needs that are most pressing in order to get the results we most often want and desire for our lives, our teams, and our companies.

CONFLICT DERAILS US FROM RESULTS WE SEEK

Think back to a time when something went wrong at home, work, or at play. Was it because of a technical problem? Or was it due to interpersonal challenges of conflict, disagreements, and lack of connection with others?

Almost always, conflict involves an issue with people, not with technical skills. It may begin with technical problems, but when it isn't handled properly, it quickly becomes a people problem.

Conflict is consistently the most dreaded aspect of work, the thing that derails us from much of the results that we could achieve. Here are some startling statistics about U.S. employees:

- 85% report experiencing conflict in the workplace.
- On average, 2.8 hours of each work week are devoted to dealing with conflict, leading to a significant loss of organizational productivity and resources. In 2008, these paid hours were calculated as costing businesses $359 billion.
- 31% of managers think they handle conflict effectively, but 78% of their employees disagree.
- 27% of employees have witnessed workplace conflicts that escalate into personal attacks.
- 25% report that they have missed work in order to avoid conflict.
- 75% of employees believe that going through a conflict resulted in positive outcomes that could not have come about otherwise.
- **95% of those who receive conflict management training say it is the biggest contributor to their professional success**—but nearly 60% of U.S. employees have never received such training.[2]

In June 2012, *Vanity Fair* published an article called "The Lost Decade of Microsoft."[3] The article stressed the fact that Microsoft certainly is one of the most technically talented organizations on the planet, and yet they lost billions of dollars in 10 years, as well as losing the race to bring several key products to market. Apple beat them to market even though Microsoft was years ahead of the company in the development of the technology those products were based upon.

The article went on to explain that Microsoft's issue wasn't about technical problems, but rather about interpersonal skills, or the lack thereof! When teams are not able to deal with conflict, instead struggling to work with each other, this causes the company to move slower or even get stuck, which will eventually affect the bottom line.

MAKING A DIFFERENCE

Conscious Choosing, LLC, is committed to changing the conversation about conflict and disconnection from others by bringing Conscious Choosing for Flow into companies. Taking feelings and needs seriously and being curious about the needs of the organization, teams, and individuals nurtures morale among employees and improves the bottom line. Abraham Maslow, Carl Rogers, and Marshall Rosenberg were all behavioral psychologists who used needs and feelings as a guiding force in the work they did around the world. Up to this point, the work of these giants in the field of social and individual behavior has not been widely utilized in corporations. Conscious Choosing for Flow seeks to bridge this gap by introducing applications of their work for businesses.

The distinctions and processes covered in this book include the Formula for Flow, the Skill for Connection, and the STAR Process for Results. These processes have proven beneficial for companies in the following fields: healthcare, manufacturing, software, construction, airlines, nuclear power and even in municipal and state governments.

SECTION I
CONSCIOUS CHOOSING

Chapter 1

LOOKING FOR A COMMON THREAD

As an entrepreneur, I've started, owned, operated, and sold more than a dozen businesses in my life and I've dealt with conflict and disconnection with others on a continual basis. When disagreements or even conflict showed up, I did my best to handle them. But having grown up in New York City, I'm afraid my early style was more about manipulation and control than diplomacy and collaboration. In fact, my favorite book during the '80s was the classic, *Winning Through Intimidation*.[4] Then if manipulation or control didn't work, I disengaged from the situation or from the very people I was supposed to care about. This worked to a point, but ultimately it really didn't work for those I interacted with or for me, for that matter. I was stuck in this default mechanism, so I started looking to find an alternate way of interacting that was more positive and effective.

After receiving my master's degree in human development and counseling and graduating from an executive coaching school, I thought I was getting close to understanding conflict between people, and yet I still knew I was far from proficient at making the difference I hoped to make. After some research in 1998, I found a company that appeared to have it figured out. VitalSmarts offered the training products *Crucial Conversations* and *Crucial Confrontations*.[5] I thought both of these could give me a handle on what conflict was and how I could consistently address it to make a positive difference in people's lives. Eventually, I became a master facilitator of both programs. I knew I was making headway in dealing with uncomfortable situations and personality differences, yet something was missing. I didn't have a consistent and effective way of dealing with conflict when it was actually happening. Yes, I had some very head-based skills that would help to control and even manipulate the emotions that arise and the resulting conflict that would ensue. Yet I knew deep down inside that there had to be an easier approach that identified and gave access to transform the destructive tension of conflict and disconnection into the dynamic energy of creativity and connection, when it was happening. Even all the education, training, and experience I had gathered over the years didn't give me the access I felt sure existed out there.

People would say to me, "Hayden, you're too much in your head." Now, I don't know if that was because of the plethora of books I read on a regular basis or because I delved into information and research so thoroughly, even creating grids and flow charts to make sense of it all. What I do know is that my heart was having trouble connecting with all the knowledge in my head. Something was missing, and I kept the hope alive that *it* was out there somewhere.

COMPASSIONATE COMMUNICATION

During 2009, a friend of mine, Pat Siebert, introduced me to the work of Marshall Rosenberg, who wrote the book *Nonviolent Communication*.[6] Since he had studied with Rosenberg, he suggested I read the book and let him know what I thought about it. At that point in my journey, I thought I had all the answers and the best handle anyone could have on dealing with conflict; it took me a year to finally read the book.

As a psychologist who had studied with Carl Rogers, Marshall Rosenberg addressed the very challenge I sought to access: dealing with conflict, small or large, and our disconnection from others. His approach helped me understand the value of emotions within all of us, and why we have negative and positive emotions. I no longer had to try to control or manipulate emotional people. I now knew what caused the negative emotion and how to deal with it respectfully and safely. My friend Pat later urged me to go to an international intensive program and study with Marshall Rosenberg in person. This time it didn't take a year to take action; I went as soon as a course was offered.

During an international conference in Albuquerque, New Mexico,[7] Marshall shared his experiences of working in some of the most troubled areas on our planet, in Rwanda with tribes that had been killing each other, in Palestine and Israel, and in Kosovo with the Serbs and Croatians. Where chaos and conflict existed, he was able to bring peace and harmony. His focus was on the needs of the people in conflict and whether or not they were being met. Once he identified their needs and they found they had needs in common, it was relatively easy to create agreements that stopped the bloodshed and let both parties live in peace with each other. Many have called his approach compassionate communication.

According to Rosenberg, if you want to win the hearts and minds of those you work and interact with on a daily basis, you must take their feelings and needs seriously. People don't leave their feelings and needs at home when they go to work or out with others. They accompany them wherever they go. It's what makes us human.

When we take people's feelings and needs seriously, identifying the needs we all have in common and the feelings attached to them that drive everything we do, we have truly found the thread that is common to all of us in times of peace and in conflict.

I finally had the key to dealing with conflict to create peace and harmony in any situation, as well as a new level of understanding about what makes each of us tick. Key to affecting how we tick is the power of curiosity.

The Key: Choose Curiosity

Choosing Curiosity is the key to unlocking the energy from the tension of conflict, and transforming it into dynamic energy of creativity, in any situation in your life.

DISCOVERING THE POWER OF CURIOSITY

I first learned about the power of curiosity and the profound effect it could have in my relationship with my wife at a retreat outside Austin.

Lani and I married on Valentine's Day 2004, on a beach in Hawaii, accompanied by friends and family. One year later, we decided to attend a retreat on Valentine's weekend put on by Gay and Katie Hendricks. Gay Hendricks is the author of *Conscious Loving*[8] and *Conscious Living*.[9]

Gay and Katie brought about 50 couples through many exercises designed to enhance each couple's relationship. In one exercise, each couple sat on cushions facing each other and held hands. We were instructed to look into our partner's eyes and say, "Mmmmm? I wonder . . . " as a response to the question of how could two people have the best relationship possible. Of course, we had to warm up to the idea by first saying, "Mmmmm?" to get our heads buzzing and invigorate our thinking, then we had to become truly curious by saying, "I wonder . . . " and think silently about what it would be like to create an even more wonderful relationship. This stimulated visions of what our life could be like and helped us envision the behaviors, actions, and commitments it would take to make them happen.

When we returned home, Lani and I sat down and wrote out what we were committed to as a couple and what we wanted our relationship to look like. That document, what we call our vows, has served us well over the years as we check in with each other to determine if there is anything we need to stop doing, modify, or start doing in order to have the most incredible relationship any two people can possibly have.

After that retreat, I saw the value of curiosity from a new light, one that could inspire greatness and new possibilities. "Mmmmm? I wonder . . . " became a consistent saying for Lani and me in our relationship. I began to use it in my consulting and executive coaching practice with profound results. It has finally come full circle in the development of Conscious Choosing for Flow trainings to help organizations and companies get the best results possible. Throughout this book, I will give you many more examples of how this approach has helped companies and individuals in discovering how to create what they truly want in life and in their relationships with each other.

We'll begin in the next chapter by exploring Conscious Choosing for Flow, which is both the name of Conscious Choosing's signature training and a mindset for attaining amazing personal and professional results.

Chapter 2

CHOOSING FLOW

> "You must learn a new way to think before you can master a new way to be."
>
> — Marianne Williamson, author and speaker[10]

We make millions of choices a day—some consciously and most unconsciously. How can we learn to connect the outcomes we most want with the actions required to produce those results? An old Chinese proverb says,

> "If you want to know your past, look into your present conditions. If you want to know your future, look into your present actions."

Conscious Choosing for Flow brings thought and contemplation to the decision-making process, helping us to produce results and connect with others. At its most literal interpretation, Conscious Choosing means intentionally making choices while keeping the consequences in mind. Taking this further, it is consciously connecting these possible outcomes or consequences with the choice itself. At a deeper level, Conscious Choosing is

CONSCIOUS CHOOSING FOR FLOW

a mind-set or awareness that for every action of ours, there is likely to be a reaction by others for which we are responsible. This means we are accountable for what we create in the world. Understanding Conscious Choosing for Flow is about discovering a new way of thinking and being so that we produce the results we really desire in our lives.

You can use Conscious Choosing for Flow in decisions such as the following:

- Will I talk with my spouse about this problem or not?
- What should I do to deal with this work situation?
- Is there *really* anything I can do?

You may be aware of the concept that, in our lives, we operate in four possible ways:

1. Unconsciously incompetent
2. Consciously incompetent
3. Consciously competent
4. Unconsciously competent

In this book, you will learn to shift your choices from unconscious to conscious so that you are competent to consistently make choices that produce the results and relationships you want.

For example, if someone is speaking to you in a rather straightforward and emphatic manner, you may immediately think that they're being aggressive and pushing their idea on you. If this is your immediate and only reaction, thinking there is only one way to look at this, then you are being unconsciously incompetent about other possibilities. You've locked yourself into one possible truth. If, at that point, you realize that you have latched on to one possibility, but don't know how to do anything about it, you're now consciously incompetent. You realize what you've done, yet you don't know what to do about it. If you pause and say, "I wonder what other ways I could take what they just said or did," and then explore other possibilities with others or yourself, and even go to that person and ask them how they meant it, then you're being consciously competent. If you automatically use this skill and consistently ask yourself, "I wonder what else might be true or what other perspectives there might be," then you're unconsciously competent because this way of thinking and being in the world has become consistent and automatic.

Conscious Choosing for Flow is first awareness and second an approach to creating respectful and safe interactions with others to put you into Flow with others. Flow is the positive, dynamic, creative, forward-moving energy between people. Most of us would agree that we have room for improvement in how we interact with others, especially in adversarial relationships. When our interactions with others are going well, we just Flow along and enjoy the process. However, when things aren't going well, it often turns into a big hairy deal about how to turn that destructive tension into something positive. When you are able to do this, you will get better results and enjoy life far more than if you simply struggle along in your tolerations and annoyance with others.

When you are in Flow with others, you use dynamic energy, skills, and awareness to shift from any negative or destructive mind-set and feelings you may have to more positive and supportive ones. You are able to see what is driving your habit of attacking, blaming, or judging others and then address those people in a way that will consistently help you get the collective results you truly want for your life. This is not as difficult as it might seem, but it might require you to change your default reactions to more conscious actions. After all, how many of us, from the time we were growing up to our adulthood in the professional realm, were ever trained how to do this? Adopting this skill requires a new awareness and a different approach than what you've perhaps been accustomed to thus far.

CONFLICT AND STRAINED RELATIONSHIPS ARE COSTLY

Research reveals that 60-80% of all difficulties in organizations come from strained relationships between employees, not from deficits in individual employee's skill or motivation.[11] Conflict and disconnection from others can also result in high turnover, which can be extraordinarily costly. Ernst and Young reported that the cost of losing and replacing an employee might be as high as 150% of the departing employee's annual salary.[12]

Relationships, both personal and professional, are the lifeblood of all organizations and all human endeavors. When relationships work, or go smoothly, nothing is more satisfying. They meet our needs and the needs of others simultaneously. However, when our relationships aren't working, nothing is more painful or frustrating.

Conflict management or resolution is certainly a step in the right direction. Conflict resolution skills are highly coveted in organizations because when relationships go south, the wrongful termination lawsuits, loss of company intelligence with the exiting employees, lost time from absenteeism, and inefficient operations that ensue waste significant time, financial resources, and energy. Therefore, the ability to transform this conflict into something that works for everyone will help companies spend their money on the things that will make the greatest difference for them, their customers, and their investors.

THE ABILITY TO TRANSFORM CONFLICT
Conscious Choosing for Flow ...

... is not conflict avoidance. Most of us have honed this skill quite well, but it hasn't led to deeper relationships.

... is not conflict management. We could manage conflict our entire life and still struggle with the best way to manage it in each situation.

... is not conflict resolution. Resolution and negotiation require compromise. We must give up something in order to get something else in return.

... **is conflict transformation**. Transformation turns conflict into creativity and disconnection into connection. This process works for everybody while helping you get the results you most want.

Conscious Choosing for Flow presents a profoundly different option from avoidance, management, or resolution of conflict and disconnection because it begins with an entirely different premise. Conflict, rather than a sign that something is wrong or amiss, often indicates that the wealth of insights, experiences, and strategies one person expresses in a given situation are in tension with another's thoughts and ideas. What this means practically is that challenges and crises, instead of being events you wish to avoid or simply manage, could possibly be catalytic moments. If properly understood and leveraged, you could transform this conflict into something cathartic and positive. When a couple, a team, or an organization leverages their diverse strengths through making Conscious Choices, they can create agile and sustainable outcomes. These results are not in spite of the conflict, but because of it.

If you have the awareness and understanding of what the state of conflict and disconnection is, as well as why you are in it and at odds with another person, you can address that disagreement in a new way that gets the results you truly want. You will have the ability to transform conflict in a way that is safe and respectful, no matter what the circumstances or situation might happen to be. When you have the required awareness about conflict, you are able to relate to it differently. Using this new paradigm, you will be able to deal with some of the most vexing problems you face, both personally and professionally, by taking feelings and needs seriously while addressing them with your co-workers.

You will hone skills and insights that can short-circuit the regressive spiral of conflict, allowing yourself and those involved to pull back from the brink before doing real damage to the relationship or to the business. This process—which is key to addressing conflict and disconnection from others and understanding human behavior and why we connect or disconnect from others—brings together insights from neurobiology, psychology, and the social sciences, as well as the lived wisdom of those who learned about conflict the hard way.

WHAT CREATES HUMAN CONNECTION?

> "To be free is not merely to cast off one's chains, but to live in a way that respects and enhances the freedom of others."
>
> — Nelson Mandela[13]

Human beings are hardwired to connect. Think of how social media has exploded onto our everyday landscape. We're connecting with friends from high school and even grade school. We're making business connections with our customers and colleagues through social media and networking events. Human connection is part of our DNA; it's what makes us tick as human beings. We all need human relationships, yet we sometimes struggle with what it really means to connect with others and how to do it.

Ronald Reagan said that he felt his greatest accomplishment during his presidency was sitting down with Mikhail Gorbachev, which allowed both of them to see each other not as evil enemies, but simply as human beings (human connection). This led to the nuclear arms treaty, which made our world a safer place. Some people think that Reagan's greatest accomplishment was the nuclear arms treaty; Reagan, however, was clear that this would not have happened if he and Gorbachev had not first taken the time to see each other as human beings. Their primary connection as humans allowed them to create powerful results as leaders of their nations.[14]

THE FOUR COMPONENTS OF OUR HUMAN CONNECTION

So what builds this human connection? Why do we connect with some people and not with others?

Some people connect through religion or common beliefs. Others connect through the college they attended or the city they live in. In his novel *Cat's Cradle*, Kurt Vonnegut called this type of connection a "granfalloon," meaning a connection formed because of some shared premise, whether it is membership in a political party or employment in a company.[15]

Connection occurs through sharing beliefs and values, a common perception of reality or life, or a common purpose. As we look for a pattern in all these different ways of connecting, we see four basic components to all of our connections:
1. Needs
2. Feelings
3. Meanings
4. Observations

Needs

The foundational building blocks on which all human behavior, motivations, and decisions are based are human needs. When you connect with others because of a common belief system or common associations, you are meeting your need for belonging and companionship with a group of people who have the same purpose or beliefs as you do. Learning to recognize, acknowledge, and honor your needs and those of others is the cornerstone of Conscious Choosing for Flow. Your needs drive your actions and motivate you, and are an integral part of your decision making. Consciously or unconsciously, you ask yourself, "What need do I have and what action will help me meet it?"

Feelings

Your feelings are indicators within your body that you have a need that is (or is not) being satisfied. Your human needs and your human feelings are inextricably linked. You feel happy when your needs are satisfied. You feel upset or annoyed when they are not. Human feelings are not just one of many internal guidance systems for determining if your needs are being satisfied. They are your *only* internal guidance system! So rather than labeling them as right or wrong, good or bad, let's use them as a guide for having a life that works for you and those around you. If you are conscious of your feelings and can receive the messages of whether or not your needs are being satisfied, you can use them to direct your attention to your needs and then refocus your energy on meeting those needs. If you ignore this message and simply express your feelings or emotions without considering your needs, you can cause problems and drama for others and yourself. We do this every day—consciously or unconsciously.

Meanings

Over time, human beings develop interpretations and evaluations to make sense of what happens in their lives. You have experiences and memories of those experiences, and you learn from them (or not). All of your life experiences create your meanings, and you use these meanings to *anticipate* what will happen in the future, as well as *interpret* what has happened to you in the past and present. There's an ancient Chinese saying that, "When we live in the past, it will determine our present condition and

CONSCIOUS CHOOSING FOR FLOW

predict our future." There is hope! You can shift your meanings by looking through different perspectives to change your present condition and generate a different future.

Observations

Your observations are as intricately linked to your meanings as feelings are to your needs. Observations are the external facts that you or others can see or hear, the facticity of life. When you observe a situation or interaction, unless you are very aware or conscious, you will begin, almost immediately and without thought, to assign a meaning to what you saw and heard. Then you begin to relate to your subjective meanings as if they were objective facts. This is when you get into real trouble! Author and Harvard professor Robert Kegan has said, "In the absence of facts, we make it up. We are meaning-making machines."[16] It is this unconscious *meaning-making* that disconnects us from others and causes conflict.

OUR HUMAN ENERGY

The dynamic interaction of your collective needs, feelings, meanings, and observations constitutes the foundation of all human connection, as depicted in this model that looks like an atom.

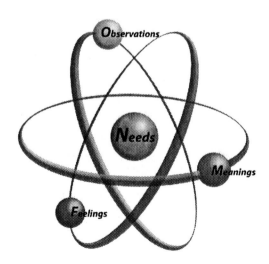

Observations, feelings, needs, and meanings are all inter-related. Yet when you identify and address needs, you affect all of the other components in the most profound way, since needs are the nucleus around which the other three revolve. When our needs are satisfied, we tend to have positive feelings and create positive meanings from what we observe around us. When our needs are not satisfied, we tend to have negative feelings and create negative meanings about what we are observing. This atom generates human energy, positive or negative, as feelings, meanings, and observations rotate around the central needs. This energy in turn promotes your behavior, motivation, and decisions as you work with and relate to others each day.

One of the unique contributions Conscious Choosing for Flow makes is distilling these basic components of connection into conscious skills and language that can be easily understood and readily applied in real time, during moments of conflict and disconnection from others.

ENTERING A STATE OF FLOW

The word *flow* has many connotations. The old expression "going with the flow" comes to mind. Over time, people have used this phrase to describe what it means to be easy-going, to not worry too much, and to enjoy the ride life presents to us.

In Robert Fritz's book on creativity, *The Path of Least Resistance*, he talks about Flow as following this path. "The water in a river flows along the path of least resistance. The wind blowing through the concrete canyons of Manhattan takes the path of least resistance. Electrical currents, whether in simple devices, such as light bulbs, or in the complex circuitry found in today's sophisticated computers, flow along the paths of least resistance."[17] We can certainly see the Flow he's talking about in nature and with people as they navigate congested city sidewalks. This path of least resistance happens naturally and appears effortless. In Conscious Choosing for Flow, Flow is the intentional creation of the path of least resistance with others, accomplished by removing any resistance to move through any project or interaction with new insights and ease.

CONSCIOUS CHOOSING FOR FLOW

The word *flow* has also often been used in connection with an individual's experience of being in the zone. In 1975, Mihaly Csikszentmihalyi interviewed and researched athletes who described their Flow experiences with the metaphor of water current carrying them along. Flow is used to describe the experience of athletes, artists, or musicians in moments when, through years of practice, they experience a high level of performance that feels almost effortless.[18] The work of Csikszentmihalyi's team was inspired by observations of artists who seemed to get lost in their work while finding a deep sense of fulfillment in what they were doing. At times, they even forgot their need for food, water, or sleep. It is thought that Michelangelo painted the ceiling of the Vatican's Sistine Chapel while in a state of Flow, since it was reported that he would paint for days, forgetting his need for food or sleep, until he passed out. Upon waking, he would feel refreshed and would begin painting again, entering into Flow once again.[19]

Csikszentmihalyi wrote, "Flow is the mental state of operation in which a person performing an activity is fully immersed in a feeling of energized focus, full involvement, and enjoyment in the process of activity. In essence, Flow is characterized by complete absorption in what one does."[20] His research showed that when a person's skill level is high and they can handle a challenge that has a high level of difficulty, then they can enter Flow. If not, other feelings arise, short of Flow, like anxiety or worry.[21]

As with Csikszentmihalyi's research, I've found that when the skill level of understanding and communicating is high, we can enter Flow when dealing with any conflict or disconnection from others. It's not hard. We must grasp hold of a few basic concepts to attain such a high level of awareness and skill. Csikszentmihalyi focused on the individual being in a state of Flow. Conscious Choosing for Flow focuses on the interaction between people that is required to enter this same state.

THIS WORKS FOR ME!

Conscious Choosing for Flow adds another layer of understanding or meaning to the word *Flow*. The Flow in this process is both an individual experience and the experiences of individuals in groups or organizations that occur between and among people. Flow is the state that highly functioning people enter as they work together in an atmosphere of mutual respect, safety, and trust where the needs of the organization, the team, and the individuals are considered and taken seriously.

When we're in Flow with each other, we have an internal conversation that sounds like "This works for me." Going back to Csikszentmihalyi's research, we are in a mental, physical, and emotional state of optimal experience. We are operating in way that enhances the quality of life and we are engaging every day so that it works not only for us but also for those we interact with. Said differently, Flow is the positive, dynamic, creative, forward-moving energy between people.

WHAT IS YOUR EXPERIENCE OF FLOW?

Most of us have experienced Flow in our lives at one time or other, and yet we don't often recognize it as such. So, let's do an exercise called the "Experience of Flow"[22] to get in touch with what I am talking about.

In this exercise, remember an optimal or peak experience, either professional or personal, in four categories:
1. Physical environment (What was the setting like?)
2. Social environment (What were the interactions like?)
3. Work (What were you trying to accomplish through the work itself?)
4. Payoff (What was the reward?)

Remarkably, when I've done this exercise over the last several years with hundreds of people, people continually describe an experience of group Flow. A constant theme in the descriptions of peak work experiences or Flow is that people experience mutual respect and that the work they did, as a result, was enjoyable and beneficial both to themselves and to those they served. The payoff was the human connection of service, empathy, enjoyment, happiness, and support. Monetary compensation is rarely, if ever, mentioned as the payoff. Rather, participants remember doing work that genuinely helped others—the human connection. Most of us have experienced this state of Flow in some areas of our lives, and it's possible to create it on a consistent basis, whether at work or at play.

CONSCIOUS CHOOSING FOR FLOW

Katrina Experiences Flow

Katrina Perryman, HR specialist at Jamail & Smith Construction in Houston, Texas, described her experience of Flow in training and later in an e-mail to me:

> I found my Flow in the strangest place—the cancer treatment center at M.D. Anderson in Houston, Texas.
>
> In 2006, I was diagnosed with a rare form of head and neck cancer. At that moment, I had no idea that what I now know to be Flow would manifest itself in every area of my life while undergoing treatment for the next nine months after diagnosis and beyond . . . now six years later.
>
> Within each of us lies the power of acceptance. It's difficult sometimes, but when we accept a situation that we are powerless to change, we can recognize that within the situation, we also have the power to choose how we respond to it (positively or negatively). The action of responding positively activates Flow.
>
> During my cancer ordeal, I could have disengaged, shut myself off, and isolated myself from everyone, family included. Instead, I chose to be a beacon of light to others in the cancer center and to my family. I chose to use my situation as a platform of awareness, to use my voice to speak about the general fears, emotions, and feelings as a fellow patient undergoing treatment. I became a Patient Advocate. I opened my home to those living outside of Houston who had challenges finding affordable lodging in the area. My family provided a carpooling service for those who needed transportation to and from the treatment center. During my treatment, I created effective interactions and better communications and decision-making in all

areas of my life—the textbook definition of Flow. Cancer changed my life, for the better. Because of it, my awareness is heightened, I have transitioned from a judgmental state of mind (pre-cancer) to the ability to empathize with those around me (post-cancer) and, most importantly, I understand and WALK the Talk with this concept of Flow daily.

THE POWER OF CHOICE

"The strongest principle of growth lies in human choice."

— Mordecai, in George Eliot's Victorian novel
Daniel Deronda[23]

As we see in Katrina's story, even in very challenging situations, we have the power to choose our response. Have you ever heard someone say, "We have no choice? We have to do it." What does this say about them? Should we take them literally? Do they really believe that choices don't exist and, therefore, the obvious solution is the only choice available? Perhaps they really aren't conscious of the power of choice in their life and business decisions to create Flow.

The mind-set and perspective of "I have to" or "we have to" is not that uncommon. Unfortunately, it usually produces a great deal of stress and conflict in our lives.

There are no "have tos." Consciously or unconsciously, people don't do things "just because," and they certainly don't do unpleasant, uncomfortable, or even painful things without a purpose. When is the last time you did something painful that didn't serve a greater need of yours? Ran a marathon? Attended a continuing education course on estate planning? Drove three hours in a storm to help your brother move? When we slow down and uncover the underlying need that is being met through our actions, it helps us to get in touch with a deeper purpose. When we give our personal power away to the feeling of "I have to," it creates an inner resistance and struggle in our own lives.

CONSCIOUS CHOOSING FOR FLOW

Of course, there are things we realize are very important for us to do, and yet it's ultimately all our choice to do those things. Otherwise, we wouldn't do them.

So, let's do an exercise to turn the thought of "have to" into "choose to." Please go ahead and do this with me. You may be surprised at what you discover about yourself.

Changing "Have To" Into "Choose To"

What do you do in your life that you do not experience as a source of fulfillment, playfulness, or enjoyment? List all of those things that you tell yourself you have to do, but would rather not, things in which you perceive that you have no choice.

<u>Example: File and pay taxes</u>

_____
_____
_____
_____

After completing the list, consider this: You are doing these things not because you must, but ultimately because you choose to do them. What are the underlying needs that you satisfy by doing these things? Write them on the following lines.

<u>Example: Taxes – freedom, contribution</u>

_____
_____
_____
_____

Next, given that you now acknowledge the need that doing these things satisfies for you, change the "I have to" thought to "I choose to." Now that you have chosen to do this activity, complete the statement "I choose to . . . because I want to . . ." as a means to get in touch with your intention behind your choice.

Example: I choose to pay taxes because I want to stay out of trouble and contribute to society.

_____
_____
_____
_____

Finally, as you consider the statements you have written here, you may discover important values behind the choices you have made. If we begin to see the need that is being served behind our actions and choices, we can begin to experience these choices as fulfilling or more playful, even when at times they involve hard work, challenge, or frustration. Next, write some of the values you got in touch with as a result of doing this exercise.

Example: Taxes – values = contribution, patriotism, free society

_____
_____
_____
_____

The value of this exercise is that when we shift our mind-set around the choices we make away from "have to," we are doing several things to enhance our lives and the results we get with others. First, when we realize that *it's all a choice* and that we have the power to choose our actions and our responses, we are taking back our personal power because there is freedom in having choice. Second, it removes us from viewing our interactions in terms of victim and villain to one of personal control over our actions. This shift puts us in the driver's seat of our lives. Finally, it removes procrastination from our lives because we're no longer putting anything off; we are simply making a decision to do it or not. It's our choice.

CHOOSING TO CREATE FLOW

With obesity an epidemic in the U.S., I consistently hear people say, "I have to lose weight," perhaps in order to feel better and look better. "I have to" statements don't make it happen, though, because they don't create a strategy for addressing the problem or plan the myriad of other decisions we must make in order to lose the weight. The only thing that will empower us to lose that weight is making a choice to do so. It's a choice, not an obligation. When we choose to lose weight, it will set in motion a whole cadre of choices. What food in my pantry should I throw out because it doesn't serve my goal to lose weight? What amount of food should I choose to consume each time I sit down to eat? What is the best time to eat in order to feel satisfied? What types of exercise will help me burn this fat off? Is there a weight-loss program that would be helpful? Choosing to do something taps into our commitment more than the rhetoric of "I have to" can, and it sets curiosity in motion around the best way to accomplish what we have committed to.

We can create Flow in any area of our lives that we *choose to* if we decide what it is that we truly want, as well as what it will take to accomplish that goal. For instance, my undergraduate degree is in music. To get my degree, I was required to have certain proficiencies on the piano. Yet, I'm not able to just sit down and play the piano without sheet music. I'd love to be able to improvise and play to my heart's content without reading the music. To do this, I would need to choose to take the time to play piano and practice improvisation; using my knowledge of music to play with chord progressions and perhaps trying to emulate songs I've heard on the radio. It won't happen unless I choose to take the time, choose to put in the effort, and choose to make it happen. I haven't made that choice yet.

Making a choice brings us to the point of understanding the underlying need we are going to satisfy. Perhaps other needs have higher priority for us. For me, writing this book, coaching, and consulting take a higher precedence than playing the piano. So I hold out for a future date and I don't put pressure on myself or make myself feel guilty for not being able to play the piano by ear. Ultimately, it is my choice and no one else's. If I were to run the "I have to" conversation in this area, it would be a victim-villain, push-pull struggle for me. In the end, I still wouldn't be able to play the piano and I would be putting stress into my life that doesn't need to be there.

YOUR RESPONSE TO THE STIMULUS

The power to choose was observed by psychologist Viktor E. Frankl while he was undergoing extreme circumstances as a prisoner of war in a Nazi concentration camp during World War II. He saw many situations firsthand in which he observed his fellow captives believe and act as if their choices were severely limited, and most people would agree that they were. Frankl also observed that others chose to exercise the only human freedom they had left, the freedom to choose their reaction to their unjust and horrifically cruel environment with a greater sense of purpose and hope. In his book *Man's Search for Meaning*, he wrote that "everything can be taken from a man but one thing: the last of the human freedoms—to choose one's attitude in any given set of circumstances, to choose one's own way."[24]

All who were interred in those awful camps were indeed victims in the truest and most painful sense of that word. As author Thomas Moore described in his book *Dark Nights of the Soul*, all were "victims in reality." However, many chose not to be "victims in character."[25]

What made the difference?

Frankl's observation and belief was that those who were able to survive in these worst of circumstances were those who believed they still had a purpose in their lives, that there was something yet for them to do. In response to what he was observing in the camps, he later wrote: "Between stimulus and response, there is a space. In that space is our power to choose. In our choice lies our growth and our freedom."[26]

Coming from a place of choice gives us the ability to take advantage of the space between the stimulus and the response that Frankl mentions. When I take a moment and identify the underlying need that will be met through my actions, I am now operating with autonomy and control over my own destiny. As Nelson Mandela said, "I am the master of my fate; the captain of my soul."[27] As we get clear on the needs that will be met, we will be able to tap into our own self-expression and creativity as the camp survivors were able to do—to live on our own terms to meet our need for autonomy, to have a say in our own lives.

The following chapter will help you gain more control over your choices by drawing attention to humanity's engrained, automatic reactions to stress. This understanding is key to moving from the cycle of failure to the cycle of success.

Chapter 3

CYCLES OF FAILURE AND SUCCESS

"We cannot sow thistles and reap clover. Nature simply does not run things that way. She goes by cause and effect."

— Napoleon Hill, author and speaker on personal success[28]

This chapter explores the effects of being (or not being) in Flow. In Conscious Choosing for Flow, we call these effects the Progressive and Regressive Cycles. One creates success, the other failure. In order to make conscious choices, we must have the required awareness of what those choices are and how to make them. Albert Einstein is famous for saying, "We can't solve problems by using the same kind of thinking we used when we created them."[29] In other words, if we do the same things we've always done, then we'll keep getting the same results we've always gotten. Daring to do something different—focusing on needs in order to create safety and respect—not only results in creativity and innovation, it feeds high morale. Considering cause and effect and seeking Flow consistently create exceptional results, growth, development, and positive forward momentum. It can work for any company, team, or relationship.

CONSCIOUS CHOOSING FOR FLOW

Let's begin by exploring the two cycles. When we are in Flow, enjoying the process and running the internal conversation of "This works for me," we're operating in the Progressive Cycle. When we're not enjoying the process, instead struggling with others and running the internal conversation of "This doesn't work for me," we self-protect, we don't take risks, and we live or work in the Regressive Cycle. Let's talk about what is inherent in both cycles.

WHAT IS THE CYCLE FOR SUCCESS?

You can see the evidence of the internal conversation of "It works for me" manifested externally through your interactions with others and the results you get. Consider for a moment what outcomes you'd see in relationships, teams, or organizations that would tell you that the members are experiencing a human connection and a state of Flow. Perhaps a high level of creativity emerges as people encourage one another to share their ideas and opinions. You may see consistent follow-through and follow-up with each commitment. When there's a problem or challenge, the members can work through it effectively and efficiently with each other. Here's a short list of outcomes with relationships or teams that signal, "It works for us."

- Exploring possibilities that create connection
- Expressing thoughts, feelings, and opinions
- Feeling safe to do so (explore and express) openly
- Leveraging difference in skills and insights, which increases creativity
- Following up and following through clearly on agreements
- Working through challenges together

The human connection creates Flow when people experience that their feelings and needs are being acknowledged and taken seriously. The feelings and needs of both the individuals and the team are taken into account, not ignored or discounted. When this occurs, a positive cascade effect results from Flow that we call the Progressive Cycle. It looks like this:

CYCLES OF FAILURE AND SUCCESS

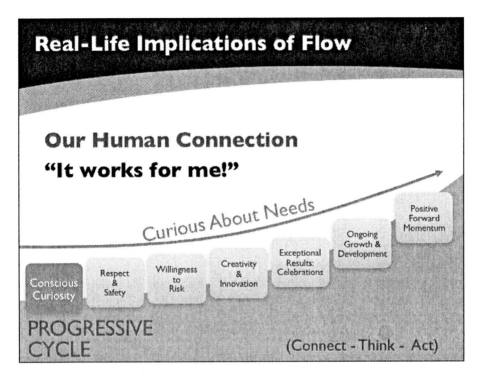

When you begin with Conscious Curiosity and stay curious about the needs of the organization, the team, and individuals, it sends a message that you care and are willing to talk about these needs. This is a different approach than most people have previously experienced. You could perhaps even call it Courageous Curiosity, which translates into respect and safety to anyone in the conversation. When you use it, you're consciously creating an environment where people are willing to take risks and say things that they might have left unsaid if they didn't feel safe or respected. The willingness to risk is what fuels creativity and innovation.

SAS Flourishes in the Progressive Cycle

One example of this is SAS, a company which specializes in creating business analytics software. In 2013, the North Carolina based company had worldwide revenue of $3.02 billion[30], which has kept its founder, Jim Goodnight, on Forbes list of the World's Billionaires. SAS treats its workers as its most valuable asset and focuses on providing for their needs through generous health benefits, a beautiful campus equipped with racquetball and volleyball courts, health-conscious cafeterias that serve wonderful, low-cost meals, an onsite clinic for medical and psychological services that are provided free of charge, and a day care center. Goodnight started SAS in the mid-1970s with the vision of addressing his employees' needs, and he developed a reputation of taking their feelings and needs seriously. The solutions the company has employed over the years have met the survival, safety, belonging and purpose needs of its workforce. When needs are taken seriously and met, profound results occur. For SAS, meeting needs resulted in creativity and innovation in their software systems that continue to this day.

WHAT IS THE CYCLE OF FAILURE?

So what happens when human connection and Flow aren't taking place? When people's feelings and needs aren't taken seriously? **Conflict and disconnection** from each other occurs. You can see it in the way people treat each other, how they interact with each other, and by the results they are able to achieve. If you were to think of any relationship, team, or organization that operates with conflict and disconnection among their employees, you would likely see something like this:

- ♦ Judgments of others that limit possibilities
- ♦ Knee-jerk reactions to others
- ♦ Perception of others' skills and insights as defective instead of just different
- ♦ Lack of clear agreements about follow-through and follow-up
- ♦ Inability to work through challenges

This happens when people experience that their feelings and needs are not being acknowledged or taken seriously. When this happens, people have a natural tendency to self-protect and disconnect from others. When this occurs, people experience a negative cascade effect that we call the Regressive Cycle. It looks like this:

CYCLES OF FAILURE AND SUCCESS

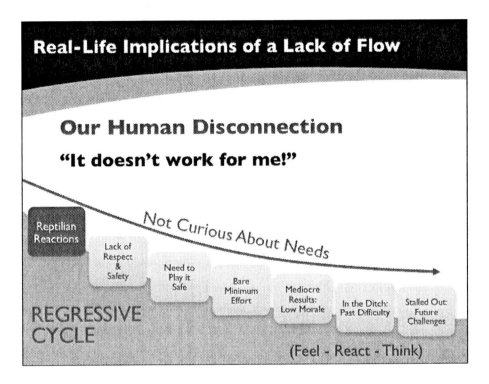

This Regressive Cycle of events occurs when people are not curious about the needs of both the individual and the organization. Employees then often disengage due to lack of safety or of respect. So, they play it safe and shut down. This leads to low morale accompanied by an inability to deal effectively with past difficulties or with future challenges. Ultimately, the bottom line of the business suffers because of this.

The 2013 Gallup report surveyed American employees and found that 70% are not engaged or are not actively engaged in their work.[31] This lack of engagement, from Conscious Choosing's perspective, is because employers are not curious enough about their employees' needs, or are not taking these needs seriously. Instead, employers are operating in the mode of "business as usual," shutting down emotionally to self-protect.

If you refer back to the graphics for the Progressive and Regressive Cycles, you will see a square at the beginning of each cycle, one for Conscious Curiosity and the other for Reptilian Reactions. We have default responses, developed over time, or situational responses triggered by certain people or events. These entrance points to the cycles are the responses to situations or triggers that directly and indirectly impact the results we obtain. Reptilian Reactions most often violate safety and respect, while Conscious Curiosity most often maintains them.

REPTILIAN REACTIONS

The Regressive Cycle begins with Reptilian Reactions which involve the fight, flight, or freeze responses. These are the natural reactions we all experience when we don't feel safe or don't think we're being respected. They are called Reptilian Reactions because they occur in our reptilian brain, the first part of our brain to develop at the brainstem and in the cerebellum. This part of our brain functions instinctually for our species survival, much in the same way that the brains of reptiles, fish, and birds do. The reptilian brain doesn't do much thinking, concerning itself instead with survival in the everyday business of gathering food, eating, drinking, sleeping, reproducing, and defending ourselves.[32]

The instinct to fight, flight, or freeze in response to perceived danger is important when our physical survival is at risk. When the message of fear is received by the brain, it immediately gives the reptilian brain the task to help us survive, giving us a shot of adrenalin to redirect the blood flow in our bodies to large muscle groups in our arms and legs so we can fight or run fast. Obviously, this is crucial when we are physically threatened. However, even though we've developed as a species, gaining the ability to feel and think differently than other animals, our reptilian brain still functions the same way as it always has. It kicks in when we feel our intellectual or emotional survival is being threatened, like when our ideas are criticized or our feelings are ignored. Our brain still receives the message that our survival is at risk, so we become aggressive, judge or blame others, get defensive, disengage, or simply identify our situation as helpless. These are the classic fight, flight, or freeze responses that we are all hardwired with for survival. Yet, responding in such a way when our lives are not truly threatened is like delivering a felony-level reaction to a misdemeanor behavior. It's overkill.

CYCLES OF FAILURE AND SUCCESS

A continuum of these responses looks like this:

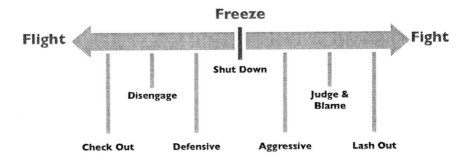

Opting for fight, flight, or freeze reactions to difficult situations puts the Regressive Cycle into motion. By responding negatively with Reptilian Reactions, we will shut down the very engagement we desire in our interactions, which generally doesn't help us to produce the results we would really like to achieve in our lives or in our business. As the journalist and satirist Ambrose Bierce (also known as "Bitter Bierce") wrote, "Speak when you are angry and you will make the best speech you will ever regret."[33]

TYPICAL FLIGHT RESPONSE

Allow me to share a personal story of reptilian flight response. I grew up 2 miles outside of New York City and my father was a Baptist minister. Imagine growing up as a preacher's kid, not to mention a Baptist preacher's kid in New York City! I often struggled with it. When I reached my teens, my father consistently told me:

I needed to stop hanging out with my friends.

I needed to go to church.

I needed to do better in school.

I needed to get along with my brothers and sisters.

Our family needed to set an example, and he wasn't going to look bad in front of the community and church.

He had a lot of needs. I simply needed (and wanted) him to leave me alone. (Actually, these are all strategies rather than needs, but I'll get to that later.)

CONSCIOUS CHOOSING FOR FLOW

At age 18, I'd had enough. I hopped onto my 650 Triumph motorcycle and drove it up to the back door, through the house, and out the front door. As I did, I waved good-bye to my angry father and upset mother. How's that for fight and flight?

At the time, I didn't know how to make a distinction between my needs and the various strategies I could employ to meet those needs. I thought I was fulfilling my needs by running away, but the thing that drove me—and my motorcycle, straight through the house—was just a strategy for achieving autonomy and personal freedom.

I could have used another strategy to fulfill my personal needs that would not have created such drama and would have kept my relationship with my parents intact. That strategy might have included an authentic and genuine conversation with my parents about my needs, as well as possible strategies for meeting them while accommodating their own needs. It would have included being more curious and less dogmatic.

In my past, the fight and flight reactions were ways that I dealt with relationships when things weren't going my way.

1. First, I would get aggressive and try to control the situation (fight mind-set).
2. Then if that didn't work, it went something like this:
   I'd tell myself, "I don't need this in my life. I'm out of here," and then I'd be gone (flight mind-set). I did this when I drove my motorcycle through the house and then didn't talk to my parents for a year in response to their demanding ways and judgments of my life.
3. As an adult, fight and flight reactions were my default mechanisms for how I ran my life and businesses, for far too long. I unconsciously chose aggression to interrupt other's ideas or control to force my way on the situation. I would disengage by checking out. I justified actions that were actually counterproductive to meeting my needs in a conscious and constructive way.

YOUR DEFAULT MECHANISM

While we're thinking about my default mechanisms for dealing with difficult situations, I'm wondering, do you know what yours are? Take a moment and examine your own life.

Likely, your reaction will change depending on who is involved and whether the situation is professional or personal. It will also generate the meanings you assign to your interactions and situations on a regular basis. Often, our default response is developed in our formative years when we develop what some call "our winning formula." This is the approach we've learned to use because it usually gets us the response from others we want. Maybe getting angry (fight) or playing nice (freeze) or leaving the situations (flight) allowed you to get what you wanted as a child. But does that same approach work for you as an adult?

Perhaps the best way to notice your default mechanisms is to first acknowledge your negative reactions to others. Once you have done that, take notice of what is happening to you physically, mentally, and emotionally in stressful situations.

- What are you experiencing physically?

    Take note of the physical sensations you experience in your body. For me, my stomach tightens up, almost as if I'm preparing to be punched. My breathing becomes more and more shallow. I sense my nerves revving up. Obviously, the meaning I'm creating at this moment is that I am under some sort of attack (physical, mental, emotional, or spiritual), so I'd better ready myself for battle! I've heard some say that their jaws begin to tighten or that their hands start sweating.

- What are you thinking?

    Notice what is running through your mind. Reflect on the mental chatter. For me, sometimes those old recordings still run: "I don't need this in my life." Perhaps you have similar internal chatter in preparation for separating yourself from the situation. You may get angry and either become more aggressive or leave. Something is going on in your head, whether it's conscious or unconscious. It's almost as if we have an internal audio tape that asks, "What is the worst or most personal way I can take what you just said or did?" Then we react based on this unconscious internal conversation. Unfortunately, these self-protective thoughts rarely improve relationships.

♦ What are you experiencing emotionally?

Notice what you're feeling and what your emotional state is. I usually feel nervous, anxious, and annoyed, wondering what will happen and how I will handle it. It's almost as if I'm reliving my childhood experiences of growing up on the streets of NYC. I'm going into reaction mode instead of choosing to use my new awareness and the skill sets that I've spent time and effort learning.

Maybe your emotions in difficult moments are typically anything but positive. When we're angry, upset, or frustrated, we trigger our meaning-making mind to generate negative meanings about the situation. This creates disconnection between others and us, since negative emotions have a way of moving us away from the situation in order to protect ourselves.

The author Ernest Hemingway said, "There is nothing noble in being superior to your fellow man; true nobility is being superior to your former self."[34] So, how do you become superior to your former self? You are the only one who can change yourself. No one else can. By becoming conscious of your instinctual responses and negative reactions to others during conflict, you can slow down your reaction time and self-monitor, rather than allowing your knee-jerk reactions to take over.

CURIOSITY CAN CHANGE YOUR DEFAULT MECHANISM

When we blame, complain about, or judge others, we are setting the Regressive Cycle in motion. These Reptilian approaches to meeting our needs disconnect us from others. To shift from the Regressive Cycle to the Progressive Cycle, we begin with Conscious Curiosity instead of making harmful statements. Curiosity sets the Progressive Cycle in motion because when we are genuinely curious about the thoughts, opinions, feelings, and needs of others, it sends a message that we care and that it's safe to share with us. It also says, "I respect you enough to ask you for your input and listen to it." By being curious and asking questions, we engage the higher reasoning centers of our brains, the neocortex.

Asking questions of ourselves and others invokes Conscious Curiosity. This opens up possibilities and draws us, and our relationships, toward what we really want. When we ask a question, we form a vacuum in the brain. Since our brain can't stand a vacuum, it goes to work to answer the question. When this happens, electrical impulses begin to fire. Now our higher reasoning center, the neocortex, is in the driver's seat, and the reptilian brain moves into the passenger seat. Our behavior shifts to a more reasonable and rational state and moves away from the aggressive or defensive way of operating. It takes time for the emotions to subside. If we keep being curious and asking questions, we can begin to engage those around us creatively rather than defensively.

What Makes Questions So Effective?

Questions invoke Curiosity.

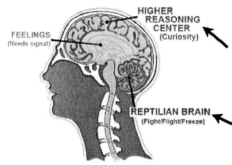

Curiosity activates electrical impulses in your brain turning on your higher reasoning center.

Without curiosity you "drive under the influence" of your fight, flight or freeze reptilian brain. (DUI)

When we self-monitor in this way, slowing down our responses enough to *Consciously Choose Curiosity rather than to unconsciously react,* the possible outcomes are far more positive. Remember, this is not about changing others, even though many of us probably have a long list of people we'd love to change. On the contrary, it's about being personally responsible so that we respond in such a way as to elicit reasonable and rational reactions from others. Remember, though, while we can certainly influence other people, the only person we can truly change is ourselves. As the director Rob Reiner has said, "Everybody talks about wanting to change things to help and fix, but ultimately all you can do is fix yourself. And that's a lot, because if you can fix yourself, it has a ripple effect."[35] When we change our reaction to others through *Consciously Choosing Curiosity,* something amazing happens. Our interaction with them also changes. We begin to operate in the Progressive Cycle, where safety and respect are present.

An orthopedic surgeon I was interviewing told me that unless both participants in a situation are willing to change, the interaction would not change. He was adamant that those around him had to change, even his wife. I asked him whether he thought that changing his tone of voice, facial expression, and choice of words might make it easier to work with these people. He wasn't quite sure. I told him I thought the interaction was like cooking. If we keep using the same recipe time and time again, we'll keep getting the same results. But what if we add a different ingredient, like cinnamon? The flavor and taste will automatically change. It's the same with our interactions. If we change ourselves and throw a different ingredient into the interaction, like curiosity, the interaction can't help but change. We are in charge of the ingredients we throw into our interactions with others.

STAYING CURIOUS PRODUCES DIFFERENT RESULTS

Note that being willing to Consciously Choose Curiosity about the opinions, ideas, feelings, and needs of others does not mean that you will remain in an open-ended posture forever, never pulling the trigger. Nor does it mean that you will give away your power to choose and decide. What is important here is the *sequence*—get curious about the ideas and positions of others *before* you advocate for your own position, not *instead of* advocating for your position.

If you find that you and your teams are embroiled in conflict after conflict (and this is not what you desire), then consider that you may have developed an unconscious habit of moving prematurely to advocating for your position before knowing the details about the position of others. So, instead of arguing and justifying your position, explore and discover what others are thinking prior to advocating your position.

In a similar vein, if you find that you are moving automatically toward diagnosing differences around the table as defective, you could very well be escalating the conflict by creating an atmosphere that communicates a lack of safety for new ideas and open discussion, as well as a disregard for the skills and insights of *all* the people around the table.

"The best way to break a bad habit is to drop it," says Leo Aikman, speaker, humorist, and past columnist for the *Atlanta Constitution*.[36] In other words, consciously choose to stop your default habit. Instead, use Conscious Curiosity.

TAKE THE CURIOUS ABC PAUSE

We often resort to blaming, complaining, or judging in an effort to self-protect whenever we are faced with conflict, stress, or confusion. When you are faced with such a dilemma, I encourage you to take the Curious ABC Pause. Hit the pause button on your personal meaning-making machine and choose to get curious.

Take the... Curious ABC Pause:

1. **A**cknowledge my reaction
2. **B**reathe deeply - 1, 2, 3
3. **C**hoose Curiosity *about* ...
   Observations, Feelings & Needs

'**A**' stands for acknowledge my own reaction. By self-monitoring, we switch from simply reacting to observing ourselves, helping us to connect with ourselves.

'**B**' stands for Breathe. Slow down. Quiet yourself and take a moment to breathe. Take a deep breathe in and let it out slowly. Do this two or three times. This will produce a calming effect on your own brain by changing the oxygen and carbon dioxide levels in your brain, sending a message to your reptilian brain that you are not going to get into a fight, allowing your higher reasoning center to turn back on.

'**C**' stands for Consciously Choose Curiosity about Observations, Feelings and Needs. What was observed that triggered your current state of mind? What unmet need triggered the feelings of upset or anger? What is the underlying need that is not being satisfied?

CYCLES OF FAILURE AND SUCCESS

Taking the **Curious ABC Pause** during these situations allows you the time to make a different choice about how to respond. Let's return to Viktor Frankl's quote, "Between stimulus and response is a space. In that space is our power to choose. In our response lies our growth and our freedom."[37] Visualize attacks, judgments, or statements of blame directed at you as a baseball that is heading straight for your head. If you allow the ball to hit you in the face, you will feel pain and will experience an immediate reaction. However, you could also catch that baseball. Mentally take the baseball in your hand and pause for a moment to look at it. Instead of reacting with your own attack, judgment, or statement of blame, you can respond with curiosity. Ask a question about the ball before deciding on the intent of the thrower. If you proceed with curiosity, the outcome is far more likely to serve your interaction with others than to break it down.

It's your choice. Will you begin your interactions with others by using Reptilian Reactions of fight, flight, or freeze, setting the Regressive Cycle in motion and creating disconnection? Or will you use Conscious Curiosity, asking questions to put the Progressive Cycle in motion and to create connection with others? As Ralph Waldo Emerson has said, "The only person you are destined to become is the person you decide to be."[38]

In summary, here are some attributes and consequences of Conscious Curiosity and Reptilian Reactions. Now that you are aware that you have a choice in the matter, you can have more control over which response you will employ in each interaction of your life from here on out to connect or disconnect from others. It's your choice!

Conscious Curiosity
- I am curious about others/myself
- I ask questions to explore & discover
- I create connection with others
- Safety and effectiveness follow

Reptilian Reactions
- I blame others/myself
- I make statements and argue
- I create disconnection with others
- Upsets & challenges follow

CONSCIOUS CHOOSING FOR FLOW

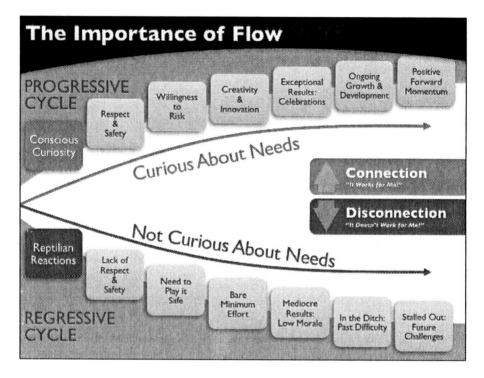

Father and Son Shift From the Regressive to the Progressive Cycle

I once worked with a father and son who owned a large company. For the last two months, they had refused to speak to each other. To get to the facts of the situation, I used Conscious Curiosity and simply asked what happened.

The father immediately started yelling and attacking his son, saying, "You don't respect me. You had no right to do what you did." Obviously, they had issues. Yet the father didn't say what had happened between them. Instead, he expressed the meaning he had created about the situation.

I asked again, "What happened?"

He replied, "We were playing handball together and I yelled at my partner to stay. When I did that, my son yelled at me that I'm not supposed to yell when he's going to take a shot. I took one look at the anger in his eyes and I left the court. I'm not going to put up with him yelling at me in front of others."

CYCLES OF FAILURE AND SUCCESS

They were obviously in the Regressive Cycle. On the court, the son had aggressively yelled at his dad, lashing out at his dad's impropriety. The father had gone into flight mode, leaving the court rather than resolving the conflict. It had been two months, and they were still angry at each other. Evidently, this type of thing had happened before.

I got curious and asked the son what happened. He explained about the rules of the game—what is acceptable and what isn't. He was tired of his dad breaking the rules each time they played. That day, he'd finally had it. We talked a bit about the rules, and then the father got curious about a look in his son's eyes.

He said, "I've never seen that look of resentment in your eyes before. Why?"

The son paused, looked at us, and then haltingly spoke. "Remember eight years ago when you made those business changes and never consulted me about it? I have never gotten over that. I never could understand it, and you sloughed it off like it was no big deal. Well, it was a big deal to me, and here's why... "

He shared information that the father hadn't been aware of and explained his frustration. The father asked questions and the son shared some more. They were finally making it safe for each other by asking genuine questions in order to learn more. After 10 minutes, the father apologized that he hadn't been more curious when he had made the business decision eight years earlier. Then, with tears in his eyes, the son apologized for what had happened on the handball court. They spent the next 15 minutes setting agreements around how they would handle such situations in the future.

They had shifted from their Reptilian Reactions and the Regressive Cycle to Conscious Curiosity and the Progressive Cycle. They became curious instead of making judgmental statements to each other. They asked questions to gather additional information instead of judging, blaming, or attacking each other. We'll continue to explore the role of curiosity to access Flow and wisdom in the following chapter.

Chapter 4

CURIOSITY IS THE CATALYST FOR FLOW AND SUCCESS

"Curiosity is lying in wait for every secret."

— Ralph Waldo Emerson, American essayist, lecturer, and poet[39]

History includes countless examples of **curiosity** as the engine that drives human progress. The old axiom that "necessity is the mother of invention" postulates the obvious; humans will generate new ideas, solutions to old problems, when there is a need. This held true with the early invention of the wheel and with automobiles, planes, and even the light bulb. Edison was so curious that he tried more than 1,000 times before perfecting the light bulb. He claimed that he did not fail 1,000 times, but rather that the light bulb's invention had 1,000 steps to complete.[40]

If human necessity has been the "why" behind our advancements, curiosity leading to decisive action has been the "how." Curiosity is the beginning means or strategy by which we solve problems and meet our collective human needs.

CONSCIOUS CHOOSING FOR FLOW

While many of us associate curiosity with *intellectual* curiosity, which is "interest leading to inquiry," the primary definition from the Merriam-Webster dictionary has to do with *human* curiosity, or an "inquisitive interest in others' concerns."[41] Curiosity that is motivated by a dual concern, a concern for meeting both your own needs and the needs of others, leads to safe, respectful, and effective outcomes, even in the midst of conflict.

You Never Help With the Housework

During one of the exercises in the Conscious Choosing for Flow workshop concerning identifying a need in the moment, a participant named Bill volunteered a conflict that he and his wife had on an almost daily basis. He said, "When I get home at night from work, my wife invariably says to me, 'You never help with the housework.'"

I asked, "How do you respond?"

"I tell her I'm at work all day. She stays at home and can take care of the housework whenever she chooses to do it."

"How does the rest of your evening go?"

"Not particularly well," he replied.

Then we identified her need for support and partnership with her husband and formulated what he could say the next time to be curious about what support and partnership she needed.

The following day, he returned to the training for trainer certification and announced to the class that his wife had confronted him with the same comment he had spoken about the previous day. When asked how he responded this time, he said, "I said, '**I'm curious**, do you need some support and help with the housework?'"

This may not sound like a big deal to us—to name the need in the moment—but listen to how he said his wife responded.

I asked, "What did your wife do?"

"She cried."

"Then what did you do?"

He said, "We sat down and talked about what help she needs and what support I could give her."

"How did the rest of your evening go?"

"Very, very well!"

WHAT IS CONSCIOUS CURIOSITY?

This example practically shows what it means to Consciously Choose Curiosity in a moment of conflict, in a way that restores safety and is respectful to all concerned. Consciously choosing curiosity by guessing at the underlying need that is driving the conflict, rather than unconsciously choosing aggression or defensiveness as Bill had previously done, changed the way Bill interacted with his wife, producing far greater collaboration and partnership between the two of them. When we are faced with conflict or disconnection from others, as Bill was, and we Consciously Choose Curiosity about the needs of others, new interaction and results become possible. Many of you may be saying, "Duh, it was so obvious that she needed help and support." I agree. It was the proverbial elephant in the room that was driving the conflict. And, until we specifically acknowledge and name the need, it will drive the conflict, and your interaction will be at the mercy of the unspoken elephant in the room while you continue serving the conflict.

CURIOSITY IS THE CATALYST FOR CREATIVITY

Elevating the concept of curiosity to the level of a skill involves:

- Learning how to be curious about the facts of the situation before we unconsciously assign meaning to those facts and to motives of the people involved
- Learning how to be curious about feelings (our own and those of others) that indicate whether a need has been satisfied or not
- Most importantly, learning how to be curious about the basic underlying needs of all stakeholders, which if acknowledged or satisfied can produce far more optimal outcomes in any situation

Being authentically and genuinely curious requires an open heart and empathetic mind. Closed and judgmental mind-sets keep us stuck in our Reptilian Reactions. Being curious and open to hearing what others have to say will put us in the Progressive Cycle. By asking questions instead of making judgmental statements, we are pulling information from the other person to understand more fully what triggered their thinking and established their current mind-set. Curiosity, authentic and genuine, is the catalyst for creativity. When expressing curiosity, it's helpful to start off with "I'm curious..." or "I'm wondering..." to reveal an open heart and mind-set. This is empathy in action.

"You're an Idiot and a Jerk!"

I applied the value of curiosity one evening when I ran into someone I hadn't seen in years. From the way he greeted me, it was clear he was relating to me based upon his experience with me many years earlier. Fortunately, I had learned the value of curiosity since then.

He said, "Hayden, you are the biggest idiot and jerk I have ever known." Obviously, there were issues.

In the past, I would have typically responded to a comment like this with my old New York, back-in-his-face style by saying, "Oh yeah! Well, you don't know me now. How dare you say that to me now after almost five years of not seeing each other? Who do you think you are?"

Thankfully, I didn't do that.

Instead, I decided to follow through on my personal commitment to make curiosity second nature for myself.

And so I said (curiosity to uncover facts), "I'm curious. What did I do or say to you that has you think I'm such an idiot and a jerk?"

At first I could tell by his troubled facial expressions that he wasn't quite sure how to respond. His puzzled look gradually gave way, and we had a conversation rather than a confrontation. I heard what he said and agreed with him. There was no pushing back or running away. I made the Conscious Choice that it was time I took responsibility for my part in what had happened between us. I embraced our meeting with curiosity and acknowledged his reasonable anger. The conversation then continued in a respectful tone, and we eventually went our separate ways. I would like to believe we did so as friends. At least, I think that he no longer considered me an enemy. Curiosity helped to create a connection where before only disconnection existed between us.

Curiosity—asking my confronter a question—provided the space we needed to open up dialogue. Even the simple question, "What did I do or say to you that makes you think I'm a jerk?" began to create Flow with this person as I focused on the observable facts and his meanings around them. I didn't discount him and tell him he was off his rocker. I took his comment seriously and got curious about what triggered his judgment of me. Memory exists in the higher reasoning center of the brain. When we ask a question, the brain can't help but search through our memory to find the answers to questions; the electric impulses firing in the brain causing us to act more rational. This allows us to deescalate conflict and it promotes creativity for problem solving.

A professional at a child learning and day care center shared with me the power of curiosity with children. She said, "Before working with kids, we're taught that if you are with children and one of them starts crying and becoming hysterical, ask them an unrelated question like, 'That's a pretty dress or those are really nice cowboy boots. Who gave them to you?' This takes their mind off of the upset and helps them calm down. Eventually you can then ask them about what happened and they'll be better able to tell you."

QUESTIONS THAT TAP INTO WISDOM

There are many ways to get curious in the Curious ABC Pause and many types of questions to ask yourself and others. I'd like to focus on an approach that will provide the quickest and most effective results that tap into your wisdom and the wisdom of the person or people you're interacting with.

Most of us were taught the six question words in grade school:

- Who?
- What?
- Where?
- When?
- Why?
- How?

All of them are looking for a particular answer that may be immediately accessible without much thinking, except for one. Here are the answers that five of them are looking for.

CONSCIOUS CHOOSING FOR FLOW

- ♦ People—Who?
- ♦ Location—Where?
- ♦ Time—When?
- ♦ Purpose or intention—Why?
- ♦ Process or structure—How?

The one question word that isn't looking for a particular answer is "what." Starting a question with the word *what* is a "wisdom access question" because it's not looking for a particular answer like people, time, location, or process. Finding the answer requires digging inside your memory and logic to tap into your wisdom, years of experience and insights.

For example, suppose I asked myself, "Why did I do that?" The answer might be readily available to me: "Because I'm an idiot and a jerk." (That guy sure had an effect on me, huh?) My answer did not require much thought because the answer to "why" came to me from what others had told me. However, if I were to ask myself, "What were you hoping to achieve by doing or saying that and what can you do differently next time to get a different response?" Mmmmmm? I'm going to have to dig deep to come up with that answer. The answer is not instinctual. It requires some thought. Asking ourselves questions to determine our pathway forward is one of the greatest self-managing tools we can learn as human beings. In fact, Conscious Choosing for Flow states:

The quality of our lives is directly proportional to the quality of questions we ask ourselves and others.

I heard someone say, "We live in a world we create with our own questions." In my executive coaching practice, I tell clients, "You get to say how your life goes. What are you saying?" It's the questions you ask yourself that determine what you say and how you interact with others. The deeds that you choose will then in turn determine who you are in the world. As George Eliot wrote in the novel *Adam Bede*, "Our deeds determine us, as much as we determine our deeds."[42]

It's important to note that not all wisdom access questions are created equally. Just putting "what" at the beginning of the question is not the point. The wisdom is achieved by focusing on connection instead of disconnection. For instance, you could ask yourself, "What is the worst and most personal way I could take what you just said or did?" This unconscious or conscious question will always elicit the Reptilian Reactions of fight, flight, or freeze because you are putting your focus on disconnecting from another.

A different question you could ask might be, "What happened that has prompted you to feel or think that way?" This is what I did with the guy who called me an idiot and a jerk. I said, "What did I do that has you think that I'm an idiot and a jerk?" By asking that question, I put his focus on what happened five years ago—observable facts. He had to dig into his memory and recall the actual event. This turned on his higher reasoning center, helping us to have a more rational and decent conversation. By asking this question, the focus was on making a connection and aligning on the facts, not about disconnecting and triggering our Reptilian Reactions.

WHERE FOCUS GOES, ENERGY FLOWS

I was coaching an executive who was having difficulty in some of his interactions with his direct reports. Specifically, he was moving too quickly into his fight reaction, and was not remaining curious long enough to keep safety and respect in the forefront of these conversations. I gave him a question to ask himself the next time one of these situations came up, as a way to slow down and turn his brain back on.

When the time came, however, he forgot the question but remembered that questions in general could help him. And so he asked himself, "What is 9,360 divided by 3?"

The effect of this unrelated question was that he did indeed slow down. He found that the internal switch for his fight mode had been flipped off, and he was able to stay curious in the situation, producing a much different outcome than he had before.

When our rational brain is back in the driver's seat, even if we are still shaky, the reactions of our reptilian brain modulate down, and we have a chance to make conscious decisions rather than to simply unconsciously react. Curiosity—asking questions of others and ourselves—is the skill that helps to make this happen.

Remember to be careful which wisdom access questions you ask yourself or others. They have the power to put focus on connection or disconnection. I like to say,

"Where focus goes, energy Flows."

Chapter 5

WHAT IS THE FORMULA FOR FLOW?

"Without conscious and deliberate effort, inertia always wins."

— Tony Hsieh, CEO of Zappos.com[43]

I've been talking about the common thread of human connection, our feelings and needs, as well as how to transform conflict into creativity by using Curiosity to create Flow with others. Now let's shift to the model and processes that provide the construct for gaining awareness and developing skills to do so.

The Formula for Flow integrates two tried and proven processes, one for connecting with others and the other for getting results. When these two processes are used consciously and deliberately in tandem with each other, Flow, connection, and results will follow. This can't help but happen! The results are built into the formula.

PROCESS #1 FOR CONNECTION: THE SKILL FOR CONNECTION

Marshall Rosenberg championed empathy as a way to connect with others 30 years ago. As a behavioral psychologist, Rosenberg studied with Carl Rogers, furthering the work of Abraham Maslow, and wrote the book *Nonviolent Communication*. He has worked in some of the most troubled areas on our planet with people who were literally killing each other, and was able to bring peace and harmony to their chaos and suffering by using empathy that incorporates observations, feelings, needs, and requests.[44] This is what we call the Skill for Connection. This skill addresses the components for human connection—observations, feelings, and needs—while making curious requests along the way. Conscious Choosing calls this the Heart of Flow because connecting with others at the heart level is the first priority in creating Flow to work and play successfully with each other.

PROCESS #2 FOR RESULTS: THE STAR PROCESS FOR RESULTS

The second part of the Formula for Flow is the STAR Process for Results. STAR stands for Stop, Think, Act and Review. This process is central to high-reliability organizations (HROs). HROs are distinctive because of their efforts to organize in ways that improve quality by enhancing people's alertness and awareness to details so that they can respond and make adjustments effectively (i.e., use collective mindfulness). Industries that are successfully implementing high-reliability practices include nuclear power plants, airlines, and health care organizations. Their success in improving safety for the environment, passengers, and patients reveals the power of this process. Conscious Choosing incorporates this process to create safety and optimal results in our interactions with others.

WHAT IS THE FORMULA FOR FLOW?

For a quick visual depiction of the Formula for Flow and the integration of the Skill for Connection and the STAR Process for Results, check out the four-minute video at: http://consciouschoosing.com/video-formula-for-flow/

PERSONAL APPLICATION: TRANSFORM CONFLICT INTO CREATIVITY

To apply the concepts in this book, I suggest that you come up with a challenge you are having with another person that you would like to resolve. It can be personal or professional. Choose someone you have access to talk to, preferably in person. At the end of each section of this book, I will refer back to this challenge and give you a chance to apply the skills you have learned. For now, in three sentences or less, simply name the person, who they are in relation to you or the position they hold in the company, and what the challenge is. You don't need to write a novel about this challenge. Just make it as factual as you can. Next, in one or two sentences, identify the results you would like to achieve in this situation. Finally, write down what you think is preventing you from getting the results you want. Please take the time to do this before reading the next section, "The Skill for Connection." You can write your answers down here or in the full personal challenge worksheet at the end of the book.

PERSONAL CHALLENGE: TRANSFORM CONFLICT INTO CREATIVITY

State a challenge you are having with someone that you would like to resolve. It can be personal or professional. Choose someone you have access to talk to, preferably in person.
- Name of person: _____
- Relationship/position: _____

WHAT IS THE FORMULA FOR FLOW?

- What is the challenge? Give the challenge a name and write 3 sentences about it.
  Name: _____
  Description: _____
  _____
  _____
  _____
  _____
  _____

- What results would you like? In 1 or 2 sentences, describe what you imagine the best outcome could be.
  _____
  _____
  _____
  _____

- What do you think is preventing you from getting those results?
  _____
  _____
  _____
  _____

SECTION II

THE SKILL FOR CONNECTION

The Skill for Connection

Consciously Choose Curiosity
about
**Observations
Feelings
Needs**
Curious Requests

Chapter 6

WHAT IS THE SKILL FOR CONNECTION?

> "If you want to awaken all of humanity, then awaken all of yourself. If you want to eliminate suffering in the world, then eliminate all that is dark and negative in yourself. Truly, the greatest gift you have to give is that of your own self-transformation."
>
> — Lao Tzu, sixth-century Chinese philosopher and author of the Tao Te Ching[45]

Most divorces, relationship breakups, and conflicts tear down and destroy what has taken years to build up. Without a clear and identifiable way to create healing and build upon what we've put our energy and time into, our lives, businesses, and relationships continually break down. However, there is hope.

The purpose of the Skill for Connection is to have an approach for connecting with others that works each and every time. As human beings, we live in relationship with others. It's what gives our lives purpose and meaning. An old Zulu proverb says, "I am a person through other people.

My humanity is tied to yours."⁴⁶ This connection defines who we are as human beings.

The Skill for Connection is the human part of the Formula for Flow. It is being Consciously Curious about observations, feelings, and needs. This is how we connect with others through the Heart of Flow—the observations, feelings, and needs that connect all human beings.

At its core, the Skill for Connection builds upon the established work of psychologists Abraham Maslow, Carl Rogers, and Marshall Rosenberg, who have applied this behavioral humanistic approach with their patients, define human behavior as how we relate to each other at the core level—focusing on whether our needs have been satisfied and on the power of empathy to affect our feelings as we relate to one another.

Abraham Maslow (1908-1970) was widely regarded as one of the founders of the humanistic approach to psychology. He was best known for his development of the hierarchy of needs, which addresses human psychological health in terms of the fulfillment of innate human needs as a predecessor to self-actualization. He stressed the importance of focusing on the positive qualities in people, as opposed to treating them as a "bag of symptoms."⁴⁷ We use his hierarchy of needs in the Skill for Connection.

Carl Rogers (1902-1987), one of the most eminent psychologists of the 20th century, was best known as another founder of the humanistic approach to psychology. The client-centered approach (or, as Rogers referred to it, "unconditional positive regard") involves basic acceptance and support of people regardless of what they say or do. Rogers believed this was essential for healthy development.⁴⁸ (Isn't this how we'd like people to treat us when we're having difficulties?) We build upon Carl Rogers' realization that extending respect to all people, simply because they are part of the human race, and acknowledging that each person has feelings and needs leads to the empathetic curiosity that would work for us all.

Marshall Rosenberg (b. 1934) studied with Carl Rogers as a doctoral student at the University of Wisconsin, learning the person-centered approach from him. Rosenberg later referred to this as *empathy*. He realized that empathy is best used in conjunction with the needs that Maslow identified in order to connect with others. He saw feelings as occurring in a direct relation to whether needs had been satisfied or not. Rosenberg is best known for founding the Center for Nonviolent Communication, an international non-profit organization, and for writing the book *Nonviolent Communication*.[49] We incorporate his empathetic approach of OFN (observations, feelings, and needs) in the Skill for Connection's Conscious Curiosity.

Nonviolent Communication (NVC), also called Compassionate Communication or Collaborative Communication, is based on the idea that all humans have the capacity for compassion. We resort to violence or behavior that harms others only when we don't recognize more effective strategies for meeting our needs.[50] NVC states that all human behavior stems from attempts to meet universal human needs and that these needs are never in conflict. Rather, conflict arises when strategies for meeting universal needs clash because people use different approaches in an attempt to meet their needs. NVC proposes that when people identify their needs, the needs of others, and the feelings that surround these needs, they can achieve harmony.[51]

Building on the ideas of Carl Rogers, Rosenberg made education reform of a student-centered learning a major component of his work. By focusing on childhood education, Rosenberg believed that he would better prepare children for the path before them. He was trying to apply the same principle, which he called life enrichment, with adults. Life-enriching organizations have the following characteristics:

1. The members are empathically connected to what each is feeling and needing—they do not blame themselves or let judgments implying wrongness obscure this connection to each other.
2. People are aware of the interdependent nature of their relationships, and they equally value their own fulfillment and that of others—they know that their needs cannot be met at someone else's expense.
3. The members take care of themselves and each other with the sole intention of enriching their lives—they are not motivated by (nor do they use coercion in the form of) guilt, shame, duty, obligation, fear of punishment, or hope for extrinsic rewards.[52]

CONSCIOUS CHOOSING FOR FLOW

Let's see how this humanistic behavioral approach plays out in real organizations.

CONNECTING FOR RESULTS

Chapter 3 talks about how the company SAS in North Carolina took their employees' feelings and needs seriously, which resulted in great success. This organization was Consciously Curious about the needs of their employees, which started the Progressive Cycle in motion. Employees became more engaged as they felt respected and safe within their organization, which led to greater creativity and innovation. This is a direct and natural response of connection to those with whom you work and live.

We can also look at other companies like Google, which was incorporated in September 1998. It experienced tremendous growth and, in 2012, surpassed $50 billion in annual revenue. As PhD students at Stanford, Larry Page and Sergey Brin identified a need for greater global communication and research. They came up with a strategy to use the World Wide Web for search engines for massive data gathering.[53] They worked on meeting that need and, in so doing, also paid attention to the feelings and needs of their employees by providing for them in much the same way Jim Goodnight did with his employees at SAS. Both companies connected with their employees' feelings and needs.

One additional need Google is famous for addressing is the creative and innovation power of their employees to self-actualize. They instituted a policy that if you had a good idea, you could take a day out of the week and work on it. Many of the company's innovations were initiated because their employees were given the opportunity to express their insights and ideas and to further connect with their customers worldwide. This is the Progressive Cycle in action, and we all experience its result in our everyday lives as we use Google to search for anything from recipes to white papers.

Success stories are not an aberration, but a predictable and sustainable result when companies connect with their employees and customers by paying attention to their feelings and needs. From this, we not only create better results, we also enjoy the process far more.

When we connect in this positive manner, we say, "This works for me," and we enter Flow so we can work more effectively and efficiently with each other instead of against each other. It's about shifting the "I versus you" conversation to the "we" conversation. I don't know about you, but when I'm connecting with others (and not butting heads), getting results is almost effortless. We are in Flow with each other, and we enjoy the work at hand far more than we would if there was conflict, stress, or confusion.

The Skill for Connection requires that we focus on three specific areas to connect effectively with each other. They are observations, feelings, and needs, or the Heart of Flow. When we take people's feelings and needs seriously and relate them to our observations, we are connecting the dots of all that is important to each of us. Author and psychotherapist Virginia Satir wrote, "I see communication as a huge umbrella that covers and affects all that goes on between human beings. Communication is the largest single factor determining what kinds of relationships we have with others and what happens to us in the world: how we manage survival, how we develop intimacy, how productive we are, how we make sense of the events in our life, how we connect . . . all depend largely on our communication skills."[54]

Chapter 7

THE SKILL FOR CONNECTION - OBSERVATIONS

WHAT ARE OBSERVATIONS?

In order to connect with others, it's important that we begin with the facts. Observations are the first external input we receive, from which we begin our process of connecting with others. This is a critical step in our connection with others because facts are objective and verifiable by others and are not subject to our own subjective interpretation or evaluation. Our observations are what we see and hear. They are the objective facts that are indisputable, that we can all agree upon.

If I asked you what your observations of this man in the picture are, what would you say?

CONSCIOUS CHOOSING FOR FLOW

When I've asked groups of people, almost immediately some will begin to say things such as:
- "He's drunk!"
- "He's mad at another driver!"
- "He's yelling at someone who's in front of him and not moving out of the way fast enough!"

After a short period of time, I ask if they would be surprised to learn that *none* of what they have shared are observations. Rather, these responses are all evaluations or meanings they created in their own head, which they have stated as facts.

This is typically an aha moment, especially for those whose work is grounded in the ability to observe and diagnose situations based upon the facts. At one workshop, with a group of physicians, of all the "observations" shared, only one was an actual observation.

One physician finally said, "He has brown hair and he is in a car."

This is an actual observation. Here are other examples of observations, or external facts:
- He has on a jacket with the number 4 on it.
- He is a wearing a wristwatch.

- He has his hand on the steering wheel.
- He is pointing.

This is not a trick I play on people to make them feel dumb. This exercise simply highlights an example of what we typically do as human beings. We make stuff up and relate to it as if it was a fact. As Robert Kegan, professor of adult learning and professional development and chair of the Institute for the Management of Lifelong Education at Harvard Graduate School of Education, wrote, "In the absence of facts, we make it up. We are meaning-making machines."[55]

MEANING-MAKING CREATES PROBLEMS

Facts come to you constantly, in real time. Observations are limited only by what your senses can take in and what your brain can hold in its memory. Because the human brain needs to make sense of all the data it is receiving, it goes about categorizing, filtering, and storing it for future use, thus creating meanings out of the facts.

When you do not make a clear distinction between meanings or interpretations and the observations or facts from which they are derived, you create problems for yourself. The problem lies in the alignment between our meanings and the meanings that others have created. By relating to these subjective meanings unconsciously as if they were objective facts, you find yourself at odds with others because you do not share the same external truth. Then it becomes your meaning against their meaning, the "I versus you" conversation, which creates arguments and defensiveness in your interactions with others. However if you connect first with what is outside of your heads and in the common reality of life, you have a common ground to build upon.

Remember the guy who called me an idiot and a jerk? That was his "meaning-making" (see chapter 4 for full anecdote). When I asked him what I had done that prompted him to think that way about me, I was attempting to get him back to the facts of what he had observed 5 years ago. When he described what happened, we were then looking at the same scenario, and I could go along with the meaning he made up about me.

CONSCIOUS CHOOSING FOR FLOW

The facts led me to the same conclusion as he had made—I had done some things back then that I needed to accept responsibility for. However, before we could discuss his anger in a productive way, we had to get back to the facts so we could find a common ground for our conversation.

So, let's get clear about what facts are. Observations and facts are equivalent; they are what we see and hear that trigger our response to a situation. Some ways to describe them are as follows:

- **External**—something that can be seen or heard by anyone
- **Verifiable**—something that can be checked or known by other people, like contracts, e-mails, or quotes from others
- **Not subject to personal interpretations**—they simply are what they are
- **Highly influential**—they are indisputable and therefore influence others because there is a common reference point

The tricky part is that we love to operate in our meanings in response to what we observe. We tend to express our reactions alone, leaving out the important facts that brought us to the meaning we created. Here are some examples of what I'm talking about:

- He's such an idiot and a jerk.
- She's the nicest person you will ever meet.
- That group is so boring.
- You are so disrespectful.
- I am so scattered.

The meanings you create are the culmination of your observations combined with your interpretations, evaluations, and judgments, and a whole lot of your past experiences and future fears thrown in for good measure. So, let me describe what meanings are:

- **Internal**—what I say to myself about what I saw or heard
- **Personal**—what I make up about the person or situation (i.e., my own story or interpretation)
- **Influenced by past experiences and future fears**—the layers added onto or filters applied to what actually happened

- **Least influential**—They can be disputed because the judgments and interpretations I made up may or may not be grounded in fact.

Here are some simple statements for comparing facts and meanings.

Facts	Meanings
My father slammed the door.	My father has anger issues.
I attended community college.	I did not have the opportunities others had.
Jane was 15 minutes late.	Jane is disrespectful of my time.

OBSERVATIONS HAVE INNATE POWER

Will Rogers, the actor and syndicated columnist, once wrote, "People's minds are changed through observation and not through argument."[56]

Will Rogers was on to something.

Imagine that you are meeting a co-worker for lunch, so you drop by his office to pick him up. Earlier on the phone, when you asked him how he was doing, he said, "Hey, I finally feel like I'm getting my act together. I'm better organized than ever before."

Yet, when you arrive at his office, you look around and are surprised to see pizza boxes on top of piles of papers and old magazines. There are several paper cups on the windowsills, some with coffee still in them.

When you ask to see the report he promised to give you, he picks up papers and puts them down, pulling out drawers while talking to himself. After a few minutes, he says, "I know it's here someplace, I just can't find it right now." Based upon what you are observing, you begin to doubt that he *really* is "getting his act together and being better organized."

Observable facts are the *most influential and least controversial* form of persuasion because they are not the products of our evaluations or interpretations. If you were to say to your co-worker that it appears that he is "somewhat disorganized," this would probably come across as an unwelcome judgment. If, on the other hand, you were to say, "It looks as if you are having difficulty locating the report," and point to the evidence, chances are that while he may not appreciate the observation, he would not be able to dispute it.

To put it most simply, making evaluations before stating your observations and then unconsciously relating to them as objective facts will most likely push any interaction into conflict. By contrast, sticking first to the facts and staying grounded in them will create a much stronger chance of staying connected while influencing the interaction. The drama and upset occurs around your meanings and not around facts. Facts are simply what happened. For instance, consider your reaction if someone said, "You are totally unreliable." There's a whole lot of drama and upset contained in that one little phrase. You are not quite sure what you did that has them calling you unreliable. Yet what if they said instead, "You texted me and said you'd pick me up at 1:00, and now it's 2:00. I'm curious, what happened?" This is common ground for beginning the discussion. Because the conversation begins by stating an observable fact instead of throwing out judgments like "unreliable," the space is open to find out what happened. This feels safer and far more respectful.

Whenever there is conflict, stress, or confusion,

Take the...
Curious ABC Pause:

1. **A**cknowledge my reaction
2. **B**reathe deeply - 1, 2, 3
3. **C**hoose Curiosity *about* ...

Observations

Consciously Choose Curiosity about observations by asking yourself, "What facts might I possibly be missing?" Or ask others, "What happened that has you feeling that way?"

By taking this curious pause, we stay open to new information that could possibly change our minds. This is the beginning of creating understanding. One missed fact, when revealed, can alter our perspective and the meaning we place on a person or situation.

How Facts Change Perspective

A few years ago, I purchased a new car, a Cadillac CTS. I'd had it for two weeks when I went to downtown Austin, Texas, for a lunch meeting at a restaurant. As I pulled in front of the restaurant to park on the street, I noticed an old, beat-up Toyota Corolla and decided to park in front of it so that if someone came along and sideswiped the parked cars, they would hit that old Corolla and not my car.

As I sat in my car, gathering my papers for my meeting, I noticed a lady come out of the restaurant and get into the old car behind me. I thought, "Well, there goes the protection for my car." As she pulled out of her spot, she sideswiped my car. I could hear the sound of scraping metal as she continued to crush the left side of my car. I looked to the left, and there she was, stopped alongside of me with her eyes open wide in shock. I motioned for her to pull back. As she did, I could hear the sound of metal scraping in reverse.

I thought, "What is wrong with this lady? Doesn't she know how to drive? What is her problem?" I had to climb over the middle console of my car to get out the passenger side door. By the time I got out, the old lady had gotten out of her car and was lying across the hood of her car and crying. I went over to her and she turned around. As I watched her crying, I thought, "She's upset about wrecking my car and what will probably happen to her insurance rates."

When she gathered her composure, she said to me, "I was here at the restaurant, picking up my husband's last check. He died of a heart attack last week."

That one additional fact changed my perspective and created a whole new meaning around whether this lady was present to drive. I went from judging her as incompetent to having compassion for her and her loss.

One additional fact can change our entire meaning if we only slow down and get curious of whether there might be information that we may not be aware of.

UNGROUNDED MEANINGS CREATE CONFLICT

Often, simple misunderstandings about observable facts are enough to drive relationships and business teams into conflict. A past business partner of mine once got angry with me about the way I handled our business development. He said, "You're doing what all CEOs do. It's all about you!" (There's a whole lot of meaning and no facts.)

I said, "What do you mean?"

He responded with, "You're not including me in your travel plans when you're going to meet with companies." (Now we're getting to some facts.)

I responded to his comment with, "Do you remember in our meeting with our partners last month that you said, 'I'm not able to travel during the week when my wife is at work and my daughter is out of school.' These are the summer months and your daughter is out of school."

He paused and looked at me, and I could tell he was recalling our meeting. His anger gave way to recollection and acknowledgment that he had said such a thing. The conflict was over before it built up steam, simply because we recalled facts.

The power and influence of meanings in our lives cannot be overstated or underestimated. The way in which you interpret events is a human filter we call perspective. This is the lens through which you view what is happening to you now, what has happened in the past, and what you think will happen in the future. Your perspectives generate the judgments, evaluations, and meanings that you will use to interpret your life and make up the psychological house in which you live.

You can choose to make your meanings conscious by being curious about them. You can reflect upon them, determining whether they seem to fit the facts or not. When you remain curious about the meanings you've created and ask questions instead of making statements, you tend to maintain connection with others as opposed to creating disconnection from them, as my past business partner was beginning to do with me.

Because our meanings can have such shaping power over our reality, real or perceived, and because we can choose them, slowing down and becoming curious about them is a make-or-break aspect of the Skill for Connection.

You Don't Appreciate Working Here
I met recently with the CEO of a large construction company. During our conversations, he said things to me such as, *"My employees don't have any respect for our company or appreciation for even having a job!"*

> **Observation or Meaning?** *Meaning—This is an evaluation of their motives or mind-sets.*

Trying to get to the facts, I then asked him how he knew that.
He said, "They consistently come in 15 to 30 minutes late and don't complete their projects on time."

> **Observation or Meaning?** *Observation—This is external evidence that he or others have seen.*

Next, I asked him if they ever stayed late or brought their projects home on the weekends. This was my attempt to add other facts to his judgment. He said *yes*.

> **Observation or Meaning?** *Observation—This is verifiable information that he or anyone else could confirm.*

I responded that, based upon these additional objective observations, I could just as easily make up a meaning that these people care very much for their jobs and appreciate the work. I then wondered aloud with him if he treated them differently because of what he had chosen to *"make up"* about them and asked if he believed they might feel judgment coming from him in his words, tone, or attitude? If so, how long could he expect them to remain with the company? He admitted the turnover rate was rather high.

YOUR PERSPECTIVES DRIVE YOUR MEANINGS

One perspective can drive a whole host of meanings. In other words, if I have the perspective that most people are disrespectful and self-absorbed,

CONSCIOUS CHOOSING FOR FLOW

then my meaning-making mind can come up with a plethora of meanings that will support some aspect of disrespect and self-absorption. The perspective I have chosen to latch on to taints all the meanings I create.

Have you ever talked with someone who has a negative perspective of someone? You know prior to talking with them that whatever they say about that person will also be negative. It's the starting point for all the meanings, interpretations, and evaluations they create about that one person. When you create enough meanings to support a perspective, you may lock into that perspective and perhaps make it the only one you'll consider looking through. It's like you've established automatic tapes that click on and run on their own of how your interaction will be with that person. You have solidified them over time, and so they have a quality of "already" or "always" to them, which leads to a self-fulfilling prophecy. The same pattern keeps repeating unconsciously. To short circuit this automatic way of responding, you must choose to make your responses conscious at first until you have successfully interrupted and altered your habitual response. This unconscious way of looking at and relating to others often says more about you than it does about the other person. It's what reputations are made of.

This is exactly what happened with the CEO of the construction company I mentioned earlier. His perspective was, "My employees don't have any respect for our company or appreciation for even having a job!" This meaning created negative feelings in him about his employees, and he then judged and treated them with some form of disrespect. When he shifted his perspective to, "My employees do respect the company and are doing their best to get work done by working late and taking work home," he then had more positive feelings about them and started treating them more respectfully in future interactions.

When Henry Ford, the founder of the Ford Motor Company and the inventor of the assembly-line technique for mass production of automobiles was creating this new technique, the negative rhetoric (perspective) was so fierce about the ability to create an assembly line to produce cars that he asked his staff to "go get [him] some 25-year-olds who don't know it can't be done." He realized that the negative attitude and lack of thinking about new possibilities would hold him and his company back from the results they wanted.[57] One of his more famous quotes is, "If you think you can or you think you can't, you're probably right."[58]

If you think about the perspective of "I can't" and the associated feelings attached to that perspective, you can easily imagine that a person may feel discouraged. They may have low energy and probably won't even take any action to try. On the other hand, if you think about the perspective of "I can" and the associated feelings attached to it, it would be easy to imagine that a person would feel empowered and hopeful, and would be more than likely to give it a try. At that point, new possibilities would be afforded this person.

Eclectic Magazine once wrote about the "three kinds of people in the world: the wills, the won'ts, and the can'ts. The first accomplish everything; the second oppose everything; the third fail in everything."[59] Perspectives are the way we see things, and they affect both the results we achieve in our lives and our relationships. Alan Kay, father of the personal computer, says that curiosity about different perspectives is worth 80 IQ points.[60]

Dr. Todd Sorensen is the CEO of Regional West Health Services in Nebraska, a company I've been working with that has been going through tremendous transition with respect to the changes happening in health care. He said, "Our perspective of the facts in relationship to health care change will determine our ultimate results. We can take the perspective of embracing change and participate in the creation of our own future. We can take the perspective of accepting change as developed by others and we will survive. Or we can take the perspective of fighting change, in which case those individuals will be happier and more successful pursuing an occupation in some other field."

PERSPECTIVES CREATE GENIUSES

A wonderful way for us to understand and get good at looking at different perspectives is the perspective game. Kids love to play it. Once adults get the hang of it, they see its value and can use it as they make decisions and view situations in their lives. An American expatriate poet, Ezra Pound, once said, "Genius is the capacity to see ten things where the ordinary man

CONSCIOUS CHOOSING FOR FLOW

sees one."[61] The perspective game will help people see at least 10 different perspectives.

On little Post-it notes, write down meanings you make up about the following scenario. Come up with as many as you can. Write one meaning on each Post-it note and see if you can come up with 20 or more meanings.

Scenario: You walk by someone in the hall. You say hi. The person doesn't acknowledge you or say hi back.

What are different meanings you can make up about what just happened? Ask yourself, "What else might be true?" Write them down.

Did you come up with meanings like these?

1. They were pre-occupied by a meeting they just came from or are going into.
2. They didn't hear me.
3. They're a snob.
4. They don't like me.
5. They're an introvert and like to keep to themselves.
6. They had a rough night.
7. They're worried about something at home.
8. Maybe I didn't say it loud enough.
9. Perhaps they have trouble hearing.
10. Did I mumble?
11. They're hung over from the night before.

How many did you come up with?

Now take your meanings and divide them up into two columns of two general perspectives—one column that left room for possibilities and showed a bit more curiosity, creating more positive feelings inside of you about the person, and the second column that was more judgmental and left you with more negative feelings about them.

What was your ratio of positive to negative meanings? Which ones left room for possibilities and which ones closed off possibilities? Did you get in touch with the feelings they produced inside of you when you read each meaning?

Dividing up your meanings into two perspectives in this manner will help you look at how the perspectives you choose will promote the Progressive Cycle (positive possibilities and connection) or the Regressive Cycle (negative conclusions and disconnection). The bottom-line question is, "Does the meaning you create promote the human connection or human disconnection?"

So, what determines which perspective you latch onto? It's your choice which perspective you take and what feelings you generate within yourself. You are responsible for how you view others, the feelings you create in yourself, and the actions you decide to take or not. Your perspectives make up your attitudes about yourself, other people and situations. The motivational speaker and author Earl Nightingale wrote, "A great attitude does much more than turn on the lights in our worlds; it seems to magically connect us to all sorts of serendipitous opportunities that were somehow absent before the change."[62]

Have you ever heard someone say, "There's only one way to look at that"? This person is short on perspectives, and is keeping themselves stuck on their viewpoint of life and others. Helen Keller, deaf-blind author and activist, wrote, "The most pathetic person in the world is someone who has sight, but has no vision."[63]

So, whenever you're faced with conflict, stress, or confusion, check out your perspectives and the meanings you are creating. Try to come up with a list of positive meanings that leave room for possibilities, neutral meanings that will involve mostly facts, and negative meanings that create disconnection from others. When you are able to look at a person or situation from different viewpoints and then pick the one that will benefit you and them the most, you now have the capacity to see 10 things where the ordinary man sees one.

PERSPECTIVES DETERMINE FEELINGS AND DICTATE ACTIONS

As I said earlier, your perspectives will determine your feelings and dictate your actions. You may be triggered by your observations, but it is the perspective you latch onto that will determine the meanings you create and the feelings you have, not what someone else did or said to you.

No one can make you angry. This is an impossibility. It is your perspective, your interpretation of that person's actions (the stimulus), and the meaning you place on them or the situation that creates that anger in yourself. You own your own anger. The other person doesn't own it or even generate it in you. Malachy McCourt, an Irish-American actor, writer, and politician, said that "resentment is like taking poison and waiting for the other person to die."[64]

To develop your perspective muscles, exercise them on a regular basis by playing the perspective game. The moment you latch on to a perspective, coach yourself by asking yourself a wisdom access question. Ask, "What else might possibly be true?" Then, come up with at least 5 (and as many as 10) more meanings that are positive, negative, and neutral. Choose the one that will benefit you and the relationship the most. This is not a delusional Pollyanna approach to relationships that ignores reality. It is an approach that will help you see more possibilities and gather more information before choosing your response.

FUNDAMENTAL ATTRIBUTION ERROR CREATES DISCONNECTION

The psychological term for attributing ill will to other people's motives and intentions is called the fundamental attributions error.[65] This is a meaning you create about others' intentions or motives that has the automatic result of creating disconnection from them. When you take the perspective that they mean you harm or are only out for their own interests, it creates a separation between them and you. After all, who would want to work with or interact with anyone who is only out for themselves? Don't we want to interact with those who have our best interest at heart? By creating this meaning in your own head and relating to it as if it's an objective fact, you are the one creating the problem in your interactions with them. So what can you do? Consciously Choose Curiosity and ask them what their motive or intention was for what they did or said. Gather different facts that may generate different meanings. If you don't ask, you will be the one generating the conflict and creating the disconnection. Perhaps they did operate out of a vindictive mind-set. By asking them and letting them tell you, at least you will know.

"You're Making a Sales Pitch."

I recently spoke with the executive team of a large company about the importance of growing and developing in several areas to better serve the company, each other, and their employees. I thought I was being passionate and clear on my message so there wouldn't be any misunderstanding. I spoke with conviction with a clear and passionate voice, speaking loud enough so everyone in the room could hear clearly. (Now, this is my perspective and the meaning I placed on my actions.)

When speaking with one of the senior VPs the following day, he informed me that the team met and all agreed that I was being aggressive with my "sales pitch." (This was their perspective and the meaning they created about my actions and message.)

They thought I was being aggressive. I thought I was being passionate and speaking with enthusiasm. They thought I was giving a sales pitch. I thought I was being clear of the steps and process that would be required for them to connect with each other and their employees. We had two different perspectives and meanings placed on the same situation. Both had some semblance of truth. One tended to be negative and the other more positive. One perspective contained the fundamental attribution error, creating disconnection between me and them, and the other, more positive perspective had the possibility to create connection.

My perspective is that everything in life is a learning opportunity, so my lesson from this was to prepare my audience for how I will speak and the message I will deliver. I wonder what would have happened if I had delivered a "pre-emptive strike" and had told them ahead of time, "I will be presenting something that is a bit different than you've probably thought about before, and I'll present it in a way that will be passionate with plenty of enthusiasm. This is because of my conviction to not only the material but also for the outcomes it delivers. My intentions are to create value and direction for this project." I wonder what their perspective would have been then.

CONSCIOUS CHOOSING FOR FLOW

So, you can see how perspectives shape your meanings and determine your feelings and actions. Let's use this in our speaking with each other in the Skill for Connection.

APPLYING THE SKILL FOR CONNECTION—OBSERVATIONS

There are two approaches in the Skill for Connection: to Honestly Express and to Curiously Investigate. Honestly Expressing involves sharing what's going on with yourself and doing so in a safe and respectful way, allowing others to listen and interact with you without tapping into their reptilian brain's instinct to self-protect. Curiously Investigating involves asking others what's going on with them for the same purpose—of keeping it safe and respectful throughout the entire interaction, no matter how stressful it might be. We will use the approaches in tandem with each other and will build upon them throughout this book.

Observations are the common ground we all can see or hear, the facts of the situation. The first step in the Skill for Connection is to share your observations and to make a curious request for others to share theirs.

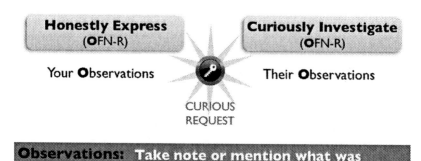

Let's see how this works.

THE SKILL FOR CONNECTION - OBSERVATIONS

HONESTLY EXPRESSING AND CURIOUSLY INVESTIGATING OBSERVATIONS:

OBSERVATIONS

Honestly Expressing: "When you came into the house just now, I saw that your face was red. You pushed the door closed with such force that the house shook."

Curiously Investigating: "I'm curious, is that what happened or did I miss something?"

FACTS BEFORE MEANINGS

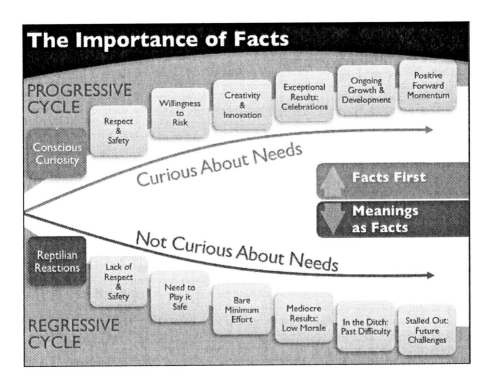

CONSCIOUS CHOOSING FOR FLOW

Progressive Cycle	**Regressive Cycle**
Facts First	Meanings as Facts
Verifiable, observable	Someone's opinion, surmised from partial data
Safe to share	Lack of safety to question it
Willing to take action	Need to play it safe and not speak up
Creative solutions considered	No one shares other ideas
Successful project completed	Project over budget and schedule
Look forward to the next job	Stuck dealing with fallout from project derailment
Company growth	Company stagnant

Whether you stay grounded in facts and observations or create meanings and relate to them as facts will determine the cycle you fall into. Meanings tend to create drama and upset, while facts are common ground where we can connect with each other. So, focus on **facts first** and don't rely on **meanings as facts**.

Focusing on Meanings Creates Problems

For a few years, I had a friendship with a co-worker I'll call John. Now I liked and respected John, and yet the relationship was often frustrating and aggravating to both of us. The frustrating part to me was that he seemed to have the perspective that everyone was out to get him whenever something happened that he didn't like or when things didn't go his way. He automatically applied this perspective and created a plethora of meanings based on it that he related to as if they were facts.

On several occasions, he said that I had ambushed him. When I pressed him to explain what he meant, he said that I hadn't given him fair warning that I was going to talk with him about a topic. He expressed the meaning he assigned to this with, "It's a fact. You ambushed me."

> For me, my meaning was that we had a challenge between us that we needed to talk about and my perspective was that that's what colleagues do to develop their relationship and understand each other.
>
> We had two different perspectives, two different meanings, and two different feelings on the same topic—neither was right or wrong, and both had some truth in them. The truth lies in the facts, not in the meanings we create about the facts. It's fairly easy to align on facts and often very difficult to align on meanings. How do you align "ambush" with "developing as friends?" You would really have to do some gymnastics around them to align them. This misalignment was putting us into the Regressive Cycle. Yet, we were both aligned on the facts that I had brought up a topic and I had not warned him that I was going to bring it up. Focusing on this fact, we could then talk about how and when to give "fair warning." From there, we moved into the Progressive Cycle.

PERSONAL APPLICATION: OBSERVATIONS

Now, refer back to your personal challenge and note all the facts and observations you have about the situation. Consider what observations or facts the person you are having a challenge with might be focusing on. Remember to state facts only, not your meanings. You can write either in the space here or in the full personal challenge worksheet at the end of the book.

Choosing curiosity is the key to unlocking the *facts* of a situation as opposed to staying stuck in each person's *meaning-making* thoughts.

PERSONAL CHALLENGE: TRANSFORM CONFLICT INTO CREATIVITY

The Skill for Connection	
Your observations:	**Their observations:**

Chapter 8

THE SKILL FOR CONNECTION – FEELINGS

WHAT ARE FEELINGS?

> "Our Feelings are the source of our energy; they provide the **horsepower** that makes it possible for us to accomplish the task of living. Since our Feelings **work for us**, we should treat them with respect."
>
> — Scott Peck[66]

If observations are the first **external** common ground to consider for connecting with others, then feelings are the first **internal** common ground to consider since we have all experienced similar feelings in different situations and can use these memories to connect with others. For instance, if I say, "I'm feeling angry and upset," others may not have the same feelings at that moment. Yet they have, at some time in their lives, felt angry and upset. Feelings connect us at the heart level, while observations connect us at the head level.

Feelings have gotten a bad rap. A lot of us grew up thinking that if we or someone else has positive feelings, it's good, and if we have negative feelings, it's bad. When someone is angry and yells at someone else, we associate the anger with yelling and our reaction to it. It simply doesn't feel comfortable to have someone yell at us. I think we can all agree on that. Yet it's not so much the emotion of anger that feels uncomfortable to us. We dislike the yelling, the behavioral expression of the feeling.

Our personal feelings help us understand whether or not something works for us. Physician and psychologist David Viscott, author of *Finding Your Strength in Difficult Times*, wrote, "Our feelings are our sixth sense. They are how we interpret, arrange, direct and summarize the other five . . . because so much of what we know depends on our feelings. Not to feel is not to be alive. More than anything else, feelings make us human."[67]

EMOTIONAL INTELLIGENCE IS AN INGREDIENT OF LIFE SUCCESS

The concept of emotional intelligence (EI) was popularized after the publication of Daniel Goleman's book *Emotional Intelligence: Why It Can Matter More Than IQ*, which he wrote in 1995 while he was a science reporter at *The New York Times*. He happened to find an article in a small academic journal by two psychologists, John Mayer and Peter Salovey, who offered the first formulation of a concept they called emotional intelligence. At that time, value had been placed on an Intelligence Quotient, or IQ, as the predictor of things like job performance and income. Daniel saw a new way of thinking about the ingredients of life success and thus came up with his title.

Salovey and Mayer's research defined EI as the ability to perceive emotions, integrate them to facilitate thought, understand them, and regulate them to promote personal growth. Their ability-based model views emotions as useful sources of information that helps us to make sense of and navigate the social environment.[68] Further, the model proposes that individuals vary in their ability to process information of an emotional nature and in their ability to relate emotional processing to a broader understanding. This ability is seen to manifest itself in certain adaptive behaviors. The model claims that EI includes four types of abilities:

1. **Perceiving emotions:** The ability to detect and decipher emotions in faces, pictures, voices, and cultural artifacts, including the

ability to identify one's own emotions. Perceiving emotions represents a basic aspect of emotional intelligence, as it makes all other processing of emotional information possible.
2. **Using emotions:** The ability to harness emotions to facilitate various cognitive activities, such as thinking and problem solving. Emotionally intelligent people can capitalize fully upon their changing moods in order to best fit the task at hand.
3. **Understanding emotions:** The ability to comprehend emotion language and to appreciate complicated relationships among emotions. For example, understanding emotions encompasses the ability to be sensitive to slight variations between emotions, and the ability to recognize and describe how emotions evolve over time.
4. **Managing emotions:** The ability to regulate emotions in both ourselves and in others. Therefore, the emotionally intelligent person can harness emotions, even negative ones, and manage them to achieve intended goals.[69]

In 1671, John Milton wrote in *Paradise Regained* (the sequel to *Paradise Lost*) that "he who reigns within himself, and rules passions, desires, and fears, is more than a king."[70] Perhaps he was referring to EI even then!

UNDERSTANDING FEELINGS LEADS TO EMOTIONAL INTELLIGENCE

We generally use the words *emotion* and *feelings* interchangeably. By definition, emotion is "the affective aspect of consciousness" or "a strong feeling," and our feelings are "an emotional state or reaction."[71] I like to think of the subtle distinction this way: Emotions are the internal state that all human beings have, while feelings are the specific, unique experiences each individual has in the moment. Feelings are a core component of what it means to be human. While feelings are common to the human experience, no two people will experience the same feelings from the same stimulus on a consistent basis.

The fact is that we all have feelings. You may have trained yourself to repress or ignore them, either in response to messages you received when you were growing up or the prevailing norms at your present workplace

CONSCIOUS CHOOSING FOR FLOW

or in your current significant relationship, but they still exist. So, we have to ask ourselves, "Will I use my feelings, or will they use me?" In other words, who's in charge here—my feelings or me? Is it really possible for others to *make us feel a certain way*, or do we choose to feel a certain way based on the meanings we've created and the judgments we make of others?

NO ONE CAN MAKE YOU FEEL ANYTHING

Several years ago, I conducted trainings at IBM on communication. I would often make the statement, "It is impossible for anyone to make you feel any particular way. What they say and do can trigger your own judgments and interpretations. Ultimately, though, you choose to feel a particular way or not." Often, this idea would trigger a healthy dialogue on the topic.

In one class, a man named Michael stood out as absolutely confident in his judgment. "Of course people can make you feel a certain way," he'd say. He was quite passionate about his judgment and sense of how right he was, so I thought it advisable to take a break.

During the break, a Chinese-American woman named Lin came up to talk with me. I had an idea. I asked her if she would be willing to conduct an experiment with me when the class resumed. She would come up to the front of the class with Michael and speak Chinese to him. She had a little trouble thinking of what to say to him. I asked her to call him every bad name she could think of in Chinese. She hesitated, but then agreed for the sake of the experiment.

When the class resumed, I asked Michael and Lin to come up to the front of the room. I said to Michael, "Lin is going to speak to you. Afterwards, I want you to tell me how you feel." He agreed.

For the next two minutes, Lin spoke to Michael in Chinese. Her face was calm, her voice was soft, and her hands were still.

When she was done, I said, "Michael, how do you feel about what she said to you?"

He looked at me with a puzzled look and said, "It was Greek—I mean, Chinese—to me. I have no idea what she said. I don't have any particular feelings about what she said to me, either positive or negative."

"So she didn't make you feel any particular way?" I responded.

"Heck, no!"

I continued, "What if I told you she was saying what a handsome and wonderful person you are?"

"That would make me feel pretty damn good."

"What if I told you she was calling you a horse's ass?" I continued.

"Well, that would make me really angry."

"So, unless you understand what she is saying and are able to process it to determine that it either works for you or doesn't, it doesn't make you feel any particular way. Is that right?"

He looked at me with a smile on his face. "Touché. I now get what you were saying about how nobody can make me feel any particular way. I have to understand what is being said in order to internalize it and make it mean something. Then I choose my emotions and how to express them."

Before he left the front of the room, Lin apologized to him, in English, for saying all the mean and nasty things to him.

He looked at her and started laughing. "You really were cussing me out? How interesting."

WHY DO YOU RESIST EXPRESSING YOUR FEELINGS?

In the trainings I've conducted, I've often heard people say that early in their lives, whether at home or in other settings, they were told either to not talk about their feelings or to not express negative feelings, like anger and annoyance. I remember hearing as a child (and my guess is that a great many of you do as well) the expression, "If you don't stop crying, I'll give you something to cry about." For some reason, my parents' thought that making this threat would be enough to cause me to put my feelings aside and "behave" in the way they expected or wanted!

However, I soon learned that just because you do not express feelings does not mean they are not there. Quite the contrary! Repressed or unexpressed feelings are like a beach ball that you shove underwater at the pool. The farther you push it down, the harder and higher it will explode out of the water when it is finally released! Remember my fight-and-flight exit from home on my motorcycle when I was 18?

Feelings, I learned, could cause me genuine embarrassment. They could even get me into real trouble. Try as I might to avoid them, in charged situations, I had feelings. Quite often, because I was not literate about what I was actually feeling or what those feelings meant to me in that situation, I found myself being propelled by them into saying and doing things that I later regretted. I had not yet benefitted from the wisdom of theologian and author Lyman Abbott, who said, "Do not teach your children never to be angry; teach them how to be angry."[72]

I must acknowledge that in some respects we are challenging our cultural norms when we talk about our human need to feel, understand, and appropriately express our human emotions. Fortunately, thought leaders like Dr. Brené Brown, who wrote *Daring Greatly: How the Courage to Be Vulnerable Transforms the Way We Live, Love, Parent and Lead*.[73] are making these discussions mainstream. But even though we've come so far in terms of self-expression, self-awareness, and what I see as a desire to develop stronger human connections, the culture of many organizations still leans toward not addressing feelings in the workplace, or even avoiding them completely. Yet, being vulnerable around what we are truly feeling and being willing to express it in a way that is respectful and maintains safety is key to entering Flow with others. We don't leave our feelings and needs at home when we go to work or out to play, so we'd better learn what value they have and what they can teach us.

Let's name some of the many assumptions and myths about feelings:
- Feelings are messy.
- Feelings are weak.
- We don't talk about feelings at work.
- Dealing with feelings and needs is time consuming and ineffective.
- Being able to deal with feelings and needs is a trait that some people have and some people don't.

All of these prevailing, largely unspoken opinions about human emotions are due almost exclusively to our lack of information and training in how to effectively use our feelings. As a result, feelings rarely get expressed until there is a huge blow-up or breakdown of some kind, which only serves to reinforce our negative feeling about feelings!

USE YOUR FEELINGS AS GPS

The key distinction in Conscious Choosing for Flow is that feelings, in addition to being the energy that fuels our ability to take decisive action, also serve as directional guides to our needs. In fact, they are the **only** internal directional guides that human beings have for their needs. We typically haven't learned how to use our feelings as a type of GPS that guides us to our needs. Consequently, our feelings then become the unconscious fuel that drives our outbursts, much to our regret, like GAS ignites in our car's engine. It really is very straightforward:

- When we experience feelings that we enjoy, our needs are being acknowledged or satisfied.
- When we experience feelings that we do *not* enjoy, our needs are not being acknowledged or satisfied. (We will talk more about needs in chapter 9.)

Feelings are the internal nudge we experience within our body and our minds that tells us that something important is happening. When you feel frustrated, angry or upset, this is an internal signal that something isn't right. Pay attention! Feelings are like the GPS, as in our cars, that tell us when we're off course or on the right path. Identify the feeling and let it guide you to the need that is not being acknowledged or satisfied. I've heard it said, "If you're feeling emotional pain, let that pain lead you to a better place."

Reactions to Being Stood Up

Let me give you an example. Imagine that I have an appointment with a business partner to meet for lunch and talk about a joint project. I sit in the restaurant waiting for him to show up.

- Five minutes pass.
- Ten minutes pass.

I begin to feel a knot growing in my stomach. My jaw muscles tighten. My head starts to hurt and I rub my eyes wearily.

I feel the nudge of my emotions in my body.

CONSCIOUS CHOOSING FOR FLOW

Anger and frustration begin creeping into my being.
- Fifteen minutes pass. I call and there's no answer.
- Twenty minutes pass, and I finally order my meal.
- Thirty minutes pass, and my meal arrives. I eat it in silence, feeling upset and angry that I've been stood up.

I now have a choice. I can Consciously Choose Curiosity or unconsciously react.

I can immediately express my irritation to this person when I see him (fight reaction). Or, I can avoid him because I've made the assumption (meaning) that he doesn't really care about following through on his agreements (flight reaction). Or I can wait for him to contact me (freeze reaction). These Reptilian Reactions are typical of the natural fight, flight, or freeze instincts.

There is another approach—to Consciously Choose Curiosity about my feelings and which needs are being satisfied or not.

By being curious, I can now address my frustration by letting the feeling point to a need that was not being satisfied. I have a need for communication, which would have been satisfied by a courtesy call from my business partner when he knew he wouldn't be able to make the appointment on time. I also have a need for my partners to honor their agreements. On this day, that need wasn't met. By getting in touch with my need, it's easier to understand why I'm feeling the way I am.

Now that I've gotten in touch with my own needs, I need to think about the person who triggered my response of anger or frustration. By being curious first about the facts of the situation, I may learn that the reason he missed the appointment was because his daughter was sick at school and he had to leave unexpectedly to pick her up and, unfortunately, his cell phone battery ran out of juice so he couldn't call. I might learn that his doctor kept him late, and he forgot to make the call because of some troubling news he had received. Or maybe some other plausible event occurred beyond his control!

Being curious about what facts I might not know can help me shift my feelings. Perhaps he had no intention to disrespect me in any way, only to deal with the need within his current situation, the need that drove his actions and dominated his focus. By first identifying my business partner's need and then talking to him about my need for respectful communication or for kept agreements, we can then come to a mutual agreement on how to handle these types of situations should something similar occur in the future. At this point, the relationship is still intact, and both of our needs have been expressed in order to create a greater connection between the two of us. This will shift our feelings from anger or frustration to hope and encouragement. If I don't express my feelings in this way, the relationship will probably languish. At the least, the feelings will continue to build up and create disconnection between the two of us over time.

When you understand that every human feeling is attached to a human need, you are taking the first step to becoming literate about your feelings and the feelings of others. Thus, whenever there is **conflict, stress, or confusion,**

Take the...
Curious ABC Pause:

1. **A**cknowledge my reaction
2. **B**reathe deeply - 1, 2, 3
3. **C**hoose Curiosity *about* ...

Observations & Feelings

Consciously Choose Curiosity about the facts of the situation (observations) and the feelings you or others are experiencing in the moment by asking yourself, "What are the feelings trying to tell me?"

As I said earlier, our feelings can serve as a GPS, pointing to whether or not our needs have been satisfied, rather than serving as GAS that makes the situation explode and erupt on others. The choice is ours.

FEELINGS TELL YOU WHETHER YOUR NEEDS ARE SATISFIED, OR NOT

Look at the following list of feelings and contemplate your association with the words. If you were feeling any of the feelings listed here, would you say that at some level your needs were being taken seriously and perhaps satisfied by those you were interacting with? Having feelings like these during interactions with others tend to build and reinforce connections.

FEELINGS PRESENT WHEN OUR NEEDS ARE SATISFIED

Confident	Inspired	Grateful	Peaceful
Open	Amazed	Appreciative	Calm
Proud	Awed	Thankful	Comfortable
Empowered	Excited	Moved	Centered
Curious	Astonished	Touched	Content
Concerned	Eager	Hopeful	Quiet
Engaged	Energetic	Encouraged	Relaxed
Alert	Enthusiastic	Delighted	Relieved
Fascinated	Exhilarated	Joyful	Satisfied
Interested	Surprised	Happy	Refreshed
Intrigued	Stimulated	Pleased	Rested
Involved	Thrilled	Glad	Restored

Adapted from the work of Marshall B. Rosenberg and the Center for Nonviolent Communication, www.cnvc.org.

Now look at the following list. Conversely, if you were feeling any of those feelings, would you say that at some level your needs were not being taken seriously or satisfied by those you were interacting with? Having feelings like these during interactions with co-workers, family members, or people in other relationships create disconnection.

THE SKILL FOR CONNECTION – FEELINGS

FEELINGS PRESENT WHEN OUR NEEDS ARE NOT SATISFIED

Apprehensive	Confused	Agitated	Painful
Suspicious	Ambivalent	Alarmed	Regretful
Worried	Baffled	Disturbed	Hurt
Annoyed	Puzzled	Shocked	Sad
Aggravated	Hesitant	Surprised	Discouraged
Displeased	Torn	Uncomfortable	Disappointed
Exasperated	Lost	Uneasy	Tense
Frustrated	Disconnected	Upset	Anxious
Angry	Bored	Embarrassed	Edgy
Furious	Distracted	Fatigued	Cranky
Irate	Indifferent	Worn out	Vulnerable
Outraged	Uninterested	Tired	Hopeless

Adapted from the work of Marshall B. Rosenberg and the Center for Nonviolent Communication, www.cnvc.org.

Most of us have not been trained to take other people's feelings and needs seriously. Realizing that all people experience similar feelings associated with needs that are satisfied or not increases our awareness and helps us better address conflict, stress, or confusion in our own lives.

Dumper and Dumpee

When I first moved to Austin, Texas, in 1994, I had been divorced for two years. I knew I needed to process my divorce and go through some healing, so I joined a divorce recovery group led by a psychologist. The group of 20 people met one evening a week for 10 weeks. We covered a different topic each week. One week, the topic was "Dumper and Dumpee."

When the group gathered that evening, the leader asked us to divide up into two groups. He said, "I want all of you who dumped your spouses to go into the room on the right. All of you who were dumped by your spouses, go into the room on the left. When you get to your areas, you will see a flip chart. There are two columns on the paper—feelings and needs. Come to a consensus in your group of the needs you had in your marriage that weren't satisfied, and then discuss what feelings you had about the unmet needs." He gave us an hour and then called us back into the main room. He then put the two flip charts side by side. To our amazement and surprise, they looked almost exactly the same.

He helped us to realize that we all have pretty much the same feelings and needs. The things we do to try to meet our needs cause the problem. The Dumpers tried to get their needs met by leaving their spouses, choosing to either go it alone or hook up with someone else in an attempt to find happiness. The Dumpees did not use that strategy, opting instead for other choices that didn't include leaving their spouses. Neither strategy kept the relationship intact. Dr. Willard F. Harley, Jr. wrote a book called *His Needs, Her Needs,* in which he chronicled his 30 years of marriage counseling. He says in the book that a successful partnership comes down to whether your needs are being met or not to affair-proof your marriage.[74]

When we realize that everyone has experienced these negative feelings when their needs are not satisfied, then we can begin to empathize with others who are in similar situations, no matter what side of the situation we find ourselves on. This doesn't mean that we like or appreciate these difficult feelings. It does mean that we are now using our emotional intelligence in the second step in the Skill of Connection to connect with others, to identify our feelings, and to let those feelings guide us to the needs that are (or are not) being satisfied.

EMPATHY IS NOT . . .

When we take other people's feelings and needs seriously by using conscious curiosity and asking questions to understand, we are being empathetic towards them. We may not be sympathetic (that is, feeling what they are feeling), but we are being empathetic by acknowledging that they are having certain feelings about having their needs satisfied or not and being curious about them. This empathetic curiosity will build connection in two ways. First, it helps to develop trust with others because we are taking their feelings and needs seriously and we're not making the fundamental attribution error. Second, it helps with engagement because giving people the opportunity to be heard about their feelings and needs helps generate greater understanding and engages those involved.

It might be helpful to identify what empathetic curiosity *is not*, since it is common practice to try the following actions and call it empathy when we want to connect with others. There is nothing wrong with doing these things. These actions we employ are just not empathy or curiosity.

Advising or fixing:	"I think you should." "Why didn't you do _____?"
One-upping:	"You think that's bad, wait till you hear what happened to me."
Educating:	"This could turn into a very positive thing for you if you just . . ."
Consoling:	"It wasn't your fault. You did the best you could."
Story-telling:	"That reminds me of a time."
Shutting down:	"Cheer up, things could be worse. Don't feel so bad."
Sympathizing:	"Oh, you poor thing."
Interrogating:	"When did this begin?"
Explaining:	"I would have called, but . . ."
Correcting:	"That's not how it happened." [75]

In her book *The Empathy Factor*, Marie Miyashiro identifies that workplace thinking and doing is a two-dimensional approach in a three-dimensional world. Therefore, it's important to "unearth and energize this most vital and often overlooked third dimension—the human dimension of connection. A connection based on empathy."[76]

She further explains:

> Our workplaces are two-dimensional because the process of empathic connection requires a literacy and comfort with two human qualities that have been systematically devalued and misinterpreted in the world around us. [feelings and needs] Our organizations are born out of this same consciousness and simply replicate this world condition in our workplaces. These two misunderstood qualities are:
> 1. Our ability to be fluently aware of our feelings without judgment of them

2. Our ability to then connect these feelings to related human needs that are being met or not met[77]

Most of us have never been trained to label and identify our feelings, much less our needs. In her book, Marie identifies the need for all of us to grow in this area of awareness, learning to self-monitor for our own emotional intelligence.

Using Empathic Curiosity

This last spring, my neighbor Lou and I decided we needed to deal with our front lawns so that they weren't an eyesore to our other neighbors and our homeowner association. Individually, we weren't quite sure what to do until we met and talked about it. We decided to remove the old grass, put in new topsoil, and plant a particular grass that is drought tolerant to suit our Texas climate. As part of this project, Lou said he'd ask the friends of one of his boys, twins with their own pick-up trucks, to haul dirt and mulch for us. He said he and his wife would compensate them financially for helping us.

This project took three weekends to complete. During the last weekend, while driving in one of the twin's trucks, I found myself wondering whether the twins thought they were being treated fairly. I felt uneasy because I noticed that they didn't seem engaged or very talkative, and I was concerned that something wasn't quite working for them. I thought that perhaps they weren't satisfied with the money they were getting, but I didn't want to ask them how much money they received. Wanting to make sure their needs were being met, I first asked them a question to gather some facts. I said, "Jack, has Lou taken care of you and your brother for helping us?"

"Yes."

Then I asked a question to gauge whether their needs were being satisfied, "How are you feeling about what Lou has given you for helping us?"

He said, "Oh, my brother and I feel great. We really appreciate it."

His positive affirmation told me that he and his brother's needs had been satisfied. It was my covert way of making sure the money they received acknowledged their contribution to the project and showed the gratitude Lou and I had for their work. I had no need to be concerned or worried based on what they had said, since they felt "great and appreciated it." Yet, I was still concerned about what was going on with them, so I pressed on. "I'm wondering if there's something about helping us that isn't quite working for you." (This was my approach of being Consciously Curious and giving empathy to Jack.) He said there was a picnic they'd like to go to that had started an hour ago. Now I understood the uneasy feeling I was sensing. We quickly wrapped up our work so they could get on with their day. By continuing to give him empathy through curiosity, I found out they had another need that had not been acknowledged or met.

If we are going to connect with others on this feeling level, we have to either check in with them by Curiously Investigating, as I did with Jack, or Honestly Expressing our feelings to share what is going on with us.

HONESTLY EXPRESS YOUR FEELINGS

It's a common tendency to state our thoughts as feelings. We often say, "I'm feeling . . ." followed by a judgment, interpretation, or meaning. Expressing our thoughts by saying, "I'm feeling that . . ." or "I'm feeling as if . . ." describes what we've created in our heads, not what we are feeling in our heart.

Using the words *like*, *that*, and *as if*, as well as pronouns, names, or nouns after "I feel" expresses metaphors or thoughts:
- "I feel **like** I'm useless."
- "I feel **that** you don't respect me."
- "I feel John doesn't like me."

So, how do you honestly express your feelings? Keep it simple by stating feelings as feelings. This requires stating what is genuinely felt. To do this, try using a feeling word after "I feel . . ." (look back at the lists) and make sure you connect the feeling to an observation (the things that triggered your feelings) and not to a meaning you created.
- "I feel **discouraged** that what I contributed wasn't used."
- "I feel **worried** that I will not have enough time to complete this task."

Using a feeling word after "I feel" helps others to identify with how you're feeling and connect with you, since they've probably felt that same feeling at some time in their lives. Attaching the feeling to an observation leads us to understand what triggered your feelings.

The challenge comes when people use feeling words and connect them to the meaning they created, thus you have no real idea what triggered the feeling in them. For example:
- "I feel **hurt** that you disrespected me in that way." (How did I disrespect you?)
- "I feel **alarmed** that you haven't made if safe for me at work." (How haven't I made it safe for you at work?)

Great! I now know how you're feeling, but I have no idea what led you to I "disrespected you in that way" or that I "haven't made it safe for you at work." I am clueless and need some observations (facts) to back up what triggered your meanings of "disrespected" or "not making it safe." What did you observe that triggered you to think that way? This is the very same question I asked of the guy who called me an idiot and a jerk. "I'm curious, what did I do or say that has you think I'm an idiot and a jerk?" I need to get past their meanings to the facts of what they observed that triggered their feelings.

Ruled Out for Lack of EI

While sitting in the American Airlines lounge waiting for my plane, I overheard a conversation the man next to me was having on his telephone with someone at his office. They were conferring about a proposal they had made to a company and were planning the follow-up meeting to start the project. I heard him say a name and then give an analysis of whether that person should be included. Each time he brought up a name, he would talk about the person's body language and how they handled their emotions. Then he said a name and laughed. "That guy is like a loose cannon. You are never quite sure if he's going to wow the client or piss them off. He seems to pride himself on wearing his emotions on his sleeves for everyone to see. I not only don't want him on the job, I'm thinking we should fire him. We don't need that sort of angry expression in our company."

Far too often, people are excluded from opportunities because they don't have the required emotional intelligence to use their feelings as a GPS to what their needs are and then to effectively address the need that is not being met. Instead, they use their feelings as GAS to explode on those they are interacting with. I wonder what would happen to their careers and their relationships if they *used their emotions* rather than *having their emotions use them*.

APPLYING THE SKILL FOR CONNECTION—FEELINGS

Feelings are the internal cues that tell us whether our needs are being met or not. The next step in the Skill for Connection is to share your feelings and then make a curious request for others to share theirs.

The Skill for Connection

Honestly Express (**OFN**-R)

Your **O**bservations
Your **F**eelings

Curiously Investigate (**OFN**-R)

Their **O**bservations
Their **F**eelings

CURIOUS REQUEST

Feelings: Tune into and acknowledge the feelings that are being felt or expressed.

CONSCIOUS CHOOSING FOR FLOW

HONESTLY EXPRESSING AND CURIOUSLY INVESTIGATING FEELINGS:

OBSERVATIONS

Honestly Expressing: "I heard you raise your voice and say, 'You're not including me in your travel plans when you visit our clients.'"

FEELINGS

Honestly Expressing: "I'm beginning to feel a bit angry and concerned when I hear you say that."

Curiously Investigating: "It appears to me that you are also angry and concerned. Would you like to talk about how you're feeling and align on the facts so we can deal with our conflict?"

Learning to Honestly Express and Curiously Investigate may take some practice if you're not used to it. The following exercise will help you practice this valuable approach for communicating with others in a way that is both safe and respectful.

Try doing this exercise, by first Honestly Expressing and then Curiously Investigating.

Look at the list of five statements. Decide if the statement is clearly stating a feeling. If it is not, restate it so it does clearly name a feeling. Be careful not to judge, blame, or complain about anyone else creating the feeling in you. Own your own feelings by stating what you are feeling in relationship to what you've observed (facts), not to what you made up about it (the meanings you created). List additional information to Honestly Express your feelings in each situation. For example:

Original statement: "I feel like I'm useless."

Honestly Expressing: "I feel hurt that I wasn't acknowledged for the work I've done."

THE SKILL FOR CONNECTION – FEELINGS

Then assume that someone else has made the statement and Curiously Investigate what is going on with them. Try to uncover what feelings the other person may own by identifying what they observed instead of what they made up about it, their meaning. Be curious by asking or guessing what they are feeling about what happened or didn't happen (facts). You may need to translate their thoughts into feelings. List additional information needed to Curiously Investigate. For example:

Original statement: "I feel like I'm useless."

Curiously Investigating: Simply asking: "I'm curious. What has you feeling useless?" Guessing: "Are you upset that your graphs weren't included in the final report package?"

1. **"I feel you don't love me."**

   Honestly Expressing:

   _____

   Curiously Investigating:

   _____

2. **"I feel as if I'm living in a bubble."**

   Honestly Expressing:

   _____

   Curiously Investigating:

   _____

3. **"When you don't call me, I feel like you've forgotten me."**

   Honestly Expressing:

   _____

   Curiously Investigating:

   _____

4. **"Your comments are abusive."**

   Honestly Expressing:

   _____

   Curiously Investigating:

   _____

5. **"When you look at me that way, it makes me feel awkward."**

   Honestly Expressing:

   _____

   Curiously Investigating:

   _____

Here are some possible answers:
1. **"I feel you don't love me."**

   Honestly Expressing: "I feel sad when you don't say you love me during the day." OR
   "I feel (feeling word) when you don't (observation)."

   Curiously Investigating: *Ask*: "I'm curious. What happened that has you feel like I don't love you?"

   Guess: "Are you feeling sad because I didn't call you yesterday on Valentine's day?" OR "I'm wondering if you are feeling (feeling word) when (observation)."

2. **"I feel as if I'm living in a bubble."**

   Honestly Expressing: "I feel lonely and isolated when no one stops by my cubicle during the day to talk or say hi." OR "I feel (feeling word) when (observation/facts)."

   Curiously Investigating: *Ask*: "I'm curious. What happened that has you feel as if you're living in a bubble?"

   Guess: "Are you feeling hurt when no one stops by to say hello?" OR "I'm wondering if you are feeling (feeling word) when (observations/facts)."

3. **"When you don't call me, I feel like you've forgotten me."**

   Honestly Expressing: "When you don't call me (observation), I feel worried." OR "When (observation/fact), I feel (feeling word)."

Curiously Investigating: "I'm wondering, when I didn't call you yesterday, were you feeling angry or upset with me?" OR "I'm wondering if you are feeling (feeling word) when (observations/facts)."

4. **"Your comments are abusive."**

   Honestly Expressing: "I feel furious and aggravated when you make comments like that." OR "I feel (feeling word) when (observation/facts)."

   Curiously Investigating: *Ask*: "I'm curious, what did I say that you thought was abusive?" OR "How are you feeling about the comments I just made?"

   Guess: "I'm wondering if you are feeling (feeling word) when (observations/facts)."

5. **"When you look at me that way, it makes me feel awkward."** (No one can make you feel. You own your own feelings.)

   Honestly Expressing: "I feel awkward when you stare at me that way." OR "I feel (feeling word) when (observation/facts)."

   Curiously Investigating: *Ask*: "I'm wondering what I am doing that has you feeling awkward."

   Guess: "I'm wondering if you are feeling (feeling word) when (observations/facts)."

GPS BEFORE GAS

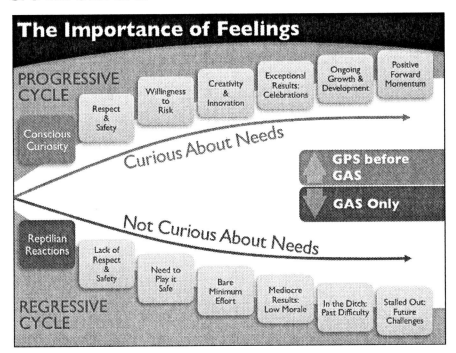

Progressive Cycle	Regressive Cycle
GPS before GAS	GAS Only
Feelings as GPS	Feelings as GAS
Identify needs	Spark drama
Safe to contribute	Fear of additional upset
Willing to take action	Need to play it safe and not speak up
Creative solutions considered	No one shares other ideas
New technology developed	Use last year's technology
New platform to build on	Lose market share

Anger as GAS at Work

Jim Jamail, the CEO of Jamail & Smith Construction Company in Texas, asked me to work with one of his directors managing their Dallas office. He informed me that the director had "anger issues," and was yelling at clients and employees. This was a detriment to their business since the clients he yelled at were refusing to work with him any longer. Rather than fire him, the company decided to give him a second chance to seek outside help.

Joe (not his real name) acknowledged that he had issues with anger and that it was causing both personal and professional problems in his life. When I asked him what challenges his anger had caused him, he said that it was the cause of his divorce, his two young sons were afraid to talk with him about their challenges, and his career was suffering. This final chance the company was giving him was critical to turning his career and life around.

We agreed that he wasn't pausing long enough to search for a more reasonable and rational response to stress and frustration. He reacted so quickly to stress that it was as though his emotions exploded on others, like GAS explodes in a car's engine to propel the vehicle forward. His intensity surprised people, and they withdrew for self-protection. This pattern affected all his relationships.

We talked about Viktor Frankl's quote, "Between stimulus and response there is a space. In that space is our power to choose our response. In our response lies our growth and our freedom."[78] We talked about creating a greater space between the stimulus and the response by simply taking the Curious ABC Pause—to slow down and Acknowledge his reaction of anger within himself, pause to Breathe deeply, and then start with Curiosity by saying, "I'm curious" before saying anything else. He said he would try to take a pause before reacting to anyone, either in his interactions or e-mails, and would commit to saying, "I'm curious" when his emotions got the best of him. He agreed to keep a journal of times during his day or week when he became angry.

The following week, he sent me his journal. He told me during our call, "You would have been proud of me since I started 90% of my anger challenges with 'I'm curious.'" He said it did help him slow down, yet he also acknowledged that he needed to work on his tone of voice and facial expressions because he found himself saying "I'm curious" through gritted teeth. After a month of applying this skill, his employees, clients, ex-wife, and children had commented that it had been much easier to talk with him since they didn't fear for their safety. They felt he was showing them a whole new level of respect by saying "I'm curious" prior to reacting to any of their comments or judgments.

"An interesting thing has happened," he informed me, "because now I'm seeing how other people's needs are driving their interactions with me. I'm now able to address those needs, to their relief. This whole thing of using other's feelings as a type of GPS, like in cars, to identify their needs is a pretty powerful tool. It causes me to think about others and not just about myself."

PERSONAL APPLICATION: FEELINGS

Now, refer back to your personal challenge and tune into the feelings you have about the situation. Consider what the person you are having a challenge with might be feeling. You can write in the space here or in the full personal challenge worksheet at the end of the book.

CONSCIOUS CHOOSING FOR FLOW

The Key: Choose Curiosity

Choosing Curiosity about yours and other people's feelings is key to creating connection because people have all experienced similar feelings. By using feelings as a GPS, it's also the key to uncovering unmet needs.

PERSONAL CHALLENGE: TRANSFORM CONFLICT INTO CREATIVITY

The Skill for Connection	
Your feelings:	**Their feelings:**

Chapter 9

THE SKILL FOR CONNECTION - NEEDS

OUR HUMAN NEEDS

> "Blessed is the person who sees the need, recognizes the responsibility, and actively becomes the answer."
>
> — William Arthur Ward[79]

While I was working with a hospital's executive team in 2012, the CEO got a scathing letter from a recent retiree. It troubled him so much that he held a meeting with all of the staff members who had retired over the previous year. When listening to their complaints, he said, "It seems like after working here for years, you weren't acknowledged for all of your hard work and support of the hospital." They affirmed this observation.

Then one spoke up and said, "All that we really wanted was a letter of appreciation from you, and we never received one."

The CEO now sends a letter of appreciation to each and every retiree. The retirees had needs for acknowledgment and gratitude. We all have this same desire—to have our needs satisfied.

Let me ask you a universal question: What do all human beings share—regardless of gender, race, socio-economic background, and religious and political preferences—that plays a central, shaping role in all the choices we make, whether in moments of relative calm or in moments of stress, conflict, and crisis? The common thread is **human needs.**

NEEDS PREDICT BEHAVIOR

In 1943, after observing the behavior of thousands of people from around the globe, the social psychologist Abraham Maslow released the results of years of research and study. Based upon his observations, he constructed a hierarchy of needs that was relevant to all human beings. These common human needs play a profoundly helpful and predictive role concerning human decisions, motivation, and behavior. Here they are, in order of importance:

1. **Survival:** the most fundamental physiological need
2. **Safety:** not having threats to our well-being
3. **Belonging and love:** interpersonal connection with others
4. **Self-esteem:** acknowledgement of our worth in terms of our contribution to the family, tribe, and larger social and work networks
5. **Self-actualization:** exercising our natural gifts and skills to the realization of our full potential[80]

NEEDS CONNECT ALL HUMAN BEINGS

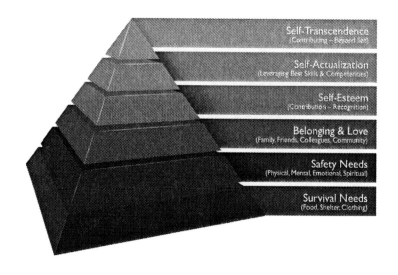

Maslow's theory was that this is **a hierarchy of needs**, meaning that we must first meet the basic needs of survival before we can effectively turn our attention and energies to meet the next need, and so on. By meeting each successive need, we can successfully move toward living into the values at the top of the hierarchy, for a life of both success and purpose.

Some years later, Victor Frankl added the need of self-transcendence to Maslow's hierarchy. Frankl defined self-transcendence as the need to contribute to something larger than oneself. In the dismal camps of the Nazi Holocaust, the ability some had to rise above their surroundings and to seek to care for the needs of others in addition to their own is possibly one of the most poignant historical examples of self-transcendence.[81]

FEELINGS AND NEEDS ARE INEXTRICABLY LINKED

How can we know what our own needs (much less the needs of others) are in the moment, especially in moments of conflict or disconnection? The answer lies in understanding that human needs and *the feelings* attached to them drive everything we do as human beings.

Like human feelings, human needs are ubiquitous—they are everywhere, all the time. Whether or not our needs have been satisfied is the determining factor for the feelings we have and, ultimately, the attitudes we form and the actions we take. Emotional intelligence is really all about this understanding of how needs and feelings are inextricably linked. We can use this understanding to connect with others and to deal with conflict in our lives. Consequently, needs and feelings form our psychological and emotional DNA.

CONSCIOUS CHOOSING FOR FLOW

We all have a myriad of feelings and needs,

swirling around inside us.

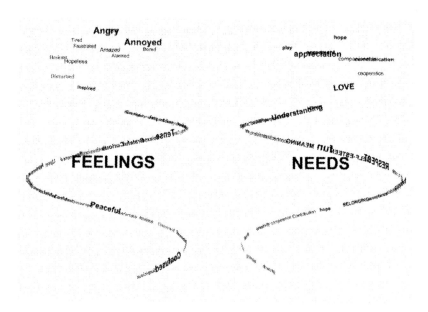

Our feelings express whether our needs have been satisfied or not and our needs determine our feelings.

THE SKILL FOR CONNECTION - NEEDS

They are inextricably linked, acting as our only internal guide to whether our needs have been satisfied or not, and sending us a message that we need to pay attention when they aren't.

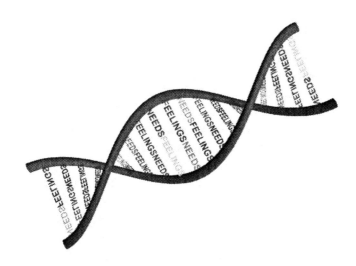

FULFILLMENT OF NEEDS DETERMINES OUTCOMES

Organizations must learn to address human needs and feelings in a conscious and healthy way in order to succeed. Here is a practical application for business drawn from events that happen thousands of times each day. Imagine a new employee arriving at work for his first day on the job. He goes to the lobby of the company headquarters, where the receptionist directs him to an HR orientation session in a large conference room. When he arrives, he receives his compensation and benefits package and a policy and procedures manual.

After orientation is over, he is shown to his office or workspace. After a "reasonable" period of adjustment, defined by the organization, this person is expected to be working for the company at his highest level of functioning—the level of self-actualization and self transcendence. As far as the organization is concerned, this requires the new employee to use his best skills and gifts to solve the most challenging problems facing the organization and to be willing to make sacrifices for something bigger than himself. In this case, that bigger value is the goals of the organization, so the new employee will be expected to stay late or take work home when needed. But there is a dilemma here. In this scenario, leaders in organizations often leapfrog over basic human needs, a course of action that could ultimately prove disastrous for the bottom-line business goals of the organization and their employees.

For starters, a compensation package will only meet a human being's basic survival needs. Expecting a new hire to then perform at the levels of self-actualization and self-transcendence without first meeting his needs for safety, belonging, and self-esteem is like trying to drive a car over a drawbridge when it is in the UP position!

Not a good idea!

Company Fails to Address Employees' Needs

While conducting a training of Conscious Choosing for Flow for a software company, I talked with company executives about the importance of addressing the needs and feelings of their employees (see chapter 15 for a full case study on this organization that uses the STAR Process for Results). They had recently gone through a company reorganization in order to deal with the financial considerations and productivity of their work force. We made a list of all the positive things being said about the change:

- "This is going to help us be financially responsible."
- "This is going to reduce the workload for all employees."
- "This is going to help us be more productive and get the work done faster and more efficiently."

They were able to come up with a lot of positive comments, made mostly by those who had made the decision to go ahead with the reorganization. Their rationale and logic spoke for itself, or so they thought. Then we identified what the employees had said about the reorganization. Here are a few of their comments:

- "You've got to be kidding me. You're taking me away from a team I've worked with for years."
- "I no longer know what my career path is. I now do only a quarter of what I did before—I just repeat the same few tasks time and time again."
- "You made this change, but didn't even have the courage to ask me what I thought about it. Give me a break!"

What these executives realized was that they had violated the values of safety and respect by not allowing the employees to have a say in the reorganization. They had taken away their employees' need for belonging by taking them out of their teams. Finally, they had challenged their employees' self-esteem by taking away responsibilities from their job descriptions, which confused career paths for their staff. Addressing these needs would have helped their employees cross the needs bridge to operate from a state of self-actualization. This is what the bridge would have looked like had they addressed the needs of their employees.

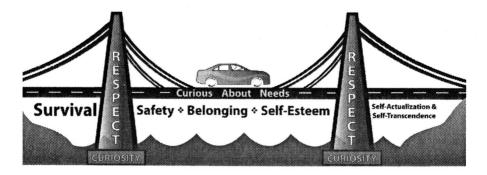

LIST OF NEEDS

Let's take Maslow's hierarchy of needs and expand upon it, adding additional sub-needs in each of the major categories. This is not an exhaustive list. You could add many more, should you choose to do so.

NEEDS LIST

Self-Transcendence Needs—A Cause Beyond Self		
celebration of life	inspiration	awareness
clarity	participation	contribution
commitment	joy	efficacy
Self-Actualization Needs—Fulfilling Personal Potential		
play	discovery	joy
autonomy	competence	humor
effectiveness	inspiration	clarity

THE SKILL FOR CONNECTION - NEEDS

commitment	contribution	growth
agreement	creativity	self-expression
Self-Esteem Needs—Recognition and Achievement		
humor	efficacy	fun
meaning	awareness	intimacy
challenge	discovery	mourning
clarity	understanding	participation
competence	effectiveness	purpose
consciousness	growth	self-expression
contribution	hope	stimulation
creativity	learning	to matter
play	respect	trust
Needs for Belonging and Love—Family, Friends, and Groups		
equality	contribution	fun
connection	closeness	empathy
acceptance	community	inclusion
affection	companionship	intimacy
appreciation	harmony	love
authenticity	consideration	mutuality
cooperation	to know and be known	nurturing
play	mourning	respect
communication	to see and be seen	to understand and be understood
Safety Needs—Security, Law, and Order		
trust	stability	support
security	order	consistency
respect	peace	structure
Survival Needs—Food, Shelter, and Clothing		
air	food	movement/exercise
shelter	rest/sleep	clothing

Adapted from the work of Marshall B. Rosenberg and the Center for Nonviolent Communication, www.cnvc.org.

CONSCIOUS CHOOSING FOR FLOW

THE DIFFERENCE BETWEEN NEEDS AND STRATEGIES

Consciously or unconsciously, we all do something before getting into our cars to drive somewhere. We ask ourselves, *"Where* do I want to go and *why?"* In other words, "What need of mine am I going to take care of now?" We may decide to go to the grocery store to meet our need for sustenance by buying food. We may decide to go to work to meet our need for survival by making enough money to pay our bills and provide for a roof over our heads and clothes on our backs. We may decide to go for a nice, relaxing joyride to meet our need for relaxation and enjoyment. Wherever we decide to go, a need is driving our decision. As Marshall Rosenberg has said, "Everything we do is in service of our needs."[82]

The challenge in transforming conflict into creativity in the moment is identifying the needs that are driving our actions because we are so focused on solutions. In other words, we tend to immediately think about strategies of what we're going to do to fix a challenge rather than pause to identify what is driving the challenge (an unmet need). Let's get clear on the distinction between the two.

Needs are the *why* of what we do.

Strategies are *how* we try to meet our needs.

Typically, if you were to ask people what they need, you might hear the following things:
- "I need more money."
- "I just need to be left alone."
- "I need more resources."
- "I need for you to give me a raise."

While these things may all be true, they are not needs. They are strategies. They are *how* we are going to meet our need for survival, peace and harmony, results, or support.

If you respond to the question, "What do you need?" with *strategy answers*, you will be unconsciously limiting your options. Confusing strategies or solutions with your underlying needs—mistaking the idea of how you are going to do something with the reason why you need to do it—creates confusion, stress, and conflict. (Remember the story about Dumpers and Dumpees from chapter 8?) However, when you learn how to focus on needs before attempting to come up with strategies or solutions to meet them, new possibilities arise that you may not have thought of before. There are endless *hows* to resolve the *why*.

Endless Strategies to Meet a Need

When I first moved to Austin, Texas, I had the need for survival—to make a living and provide shelter over my head, food in my stomach, and clothes on my back. Being a serial entrepreneur, I decided to start an advertising company that used a very different approach from those of other advertising companies in Austin. I started a company called Writings on the Wall, which used indoor billboards for advertising in the bathrooms of restaurants and gyms, above mailboxes in apartment communities, in public areas of meeting places, and as illuminated signs on top of taxicabs.

It took me several years to develop the contracts for board placement, get clients, and make money, yet I still needed to survive while developing a clientele. By staying focused on survival and not just on the strategy of making money, I was able to consider many other strategies. New possibilities became available to meet my needs.

To survive, I needed a place to live. So, I traded advertising for a beautiful new apartment at one of the nicest apartment communities in Austin. I needed to eat, so I traded advertising for accounts at restaurants. I wanted to work out, so I traded advertising for a gym membership. I needed transportation, so I traded advertising for a deal on a car at a car dealership. I wanted entertainment and something to do, so I traded advertisement for an all-expense-paid membership at a skydiving club, which included all my jumps and equipment. I think you get the idea.

When we make a distinction between needs and strategies and focus first on the need, new ideas for strategies become possible. The following list shows distinctions between needs and strategies that are often confused.

CONSCIOUS CHOOSING FOR FLOW

Needs	Strategies
Results	Control, manipulation, coercion, intimidation
Respect	Ultimatums, demands, sanctions
Safety	Rules, standards, processes
Trust	Keeping agreements, following through

Another way to look at the distinction between needs and strategies is that needs are the **why** (or intangible aspect) of our lives, including survival, respect, safety, belonging, and self-esteem. Strategies are the **how**, or actions we take to get something tangible (like money, clothing, and food) to fulfill our intangible *why*.

Needs (intangible concept)	Strategies (action to get something tangible)
Communication	Communicating
Collaboration	Collaborating
Partnership	Partnering

PUT NEEDS BEFORE STRATEGIES

It's easy to jump into strategies to meet our needs without first clearly identifying the need that must be met. For example, imagine you get a job doing data entry in the accounting department at a large company. The salary is high enough to pay your bills and provide for your basic necessities. However, you're miserable because you also have a strong need for creativity, and the repetitive nature of the data entry job doesn't satisfy that need.

By first focusing on your needs, including creativity, you expand your thinking to consider other possibilities and strategies for meeting those needs. Perhaps a job in the printing department would be a better fit—doing graphic design and newsletter editing could meet your needs for both survival and self-esteem. When you understand *why* you're doing something, you can easily formulate all kinds of ways *how* to accomplish meeting the *why*, your needs.

OUR WORST DISAGREEMENTS

Often, the worst disagreements occur when both parties believe they are right.

Why is that?

Because both parties have legitimate needs that have not been acknowledged or addressed. In other words, they very well may both be right!

The problem may be that the two parties are using very different strategies to meet their needs. In the moment when both parties have legitimate needs that at first appear to be mutually exclusive, the curiosity that leads to Flow can spur very different outcomes.

When we fight over strategies and try to push our own solution to a problem, we are focusing on the conflict. However, if we stop and get clear on our underlying needs, then new solutions to the problem become available. When we do this, we serve the need instead of the conflict. Remember the example from chapter 4 about the wife who complained to her husband that he didn't help with the housework? This went on for years until he stopped and said, "It seems like you need some help and support with the housework." When you read that story, you may have been thinking, "Of course that's what the conflict was about. Her husband hadn't been paying attention." This elephant in the room had been driving the conflict. Until it was consciously recognized and verbally acknowledged, the conflict remained. By stopping and acknowledging the need (for help and support), the couple became able to come up with solutions to address their regular conflict about the housework. They learned to serve the underlying need in their relationship.

When we confuse needs with strategies, our relationships (whether personal or professional) become complicated in a hurry, and the conflict continues. Separating the two and focusing on the needs first will transform the conflict into creativity, allowing you to find the right solutions.

Separating Needs From Strategies Helped Two Brothers

While working with two brothers, the CEO and CMO of a company, who were in conflict with each other, I mentioned that "the worst disagreements occur when both parties believe they are right." I asked if that was the case with them. They agreed.

I asked them to share a recent conflict they'd had. They shared a consistent conflict they experienced when holding meetings together. Each would bring up topics or suggestions that the other brother disagreed with, so they came across as opponents rather than as a united executive team. Sometimes they even got into arguments with each other during meetings when other company executives were present. They agreed that this way of operating needed to stop, and yet they didn't know what to do about it.

One brother thought that the other intentionally brought up topics or made comments to get him angry and upset so that he would react negatively and then look bad in front of others. He agreed that he was easily triggered by his brother's "off-the-wall" comments.

We explored each of their needs. They both wanted harmony, alignment, and effectiveness in the way they operated with each other, including being a model for the other company leaders. We also agreed that the comments they made in meetings weren't serving the company, the other leaders, and themselves. They agreed to stop this destructive dance they had created with each other and to find a new way to lead together.

We talked about strategies that would help them show unity during meetings and conduct them in a way that was not disruptive. They ultimately agreed to come together before any meeting they held together to plan the subject matter and what they would each say about the topics. They agreed not to surprise each other with differing viewpoints during the meetings. They also agreed that if they had a different thought about the direction of the meeting, they would hold off and check in with one another afterwards. They wrote this agreement out and signed it.

Once we mutually agreed on this strategy, the brothers looked at each other and smiled. I took note of the difference in energy between them, and they shook hands. What a win they experienced once they separated needs from strategies and then talked about strategies that would work for both of them.

HOW TO DIFFUSE CONFLICT

People express their needs every day when they speak and act. Our needs are right out there, in plain view, in our language and in our behavior. The problem is that many of us haven't been trained in how to hear and read these needs for what they are. Even worse, we might ignore the needs of others because we are so busy championing our own need or position. However, once we learn how to become curious about the needs of others and to acknowledge them, a strange thing begins to happen, almost immediately—**the conflict loses its charge.** We can now talk about meeting the need.

The primary question to ask yourself in order to create Flow and the Progressive Cycle is,

"What needs of mine, and yours, are not being satisfied?"

This question, and the behaviors it fosters, signals to others that you are serious about taking concrete action to meet the psychological, physical, and emotional needs of all concerned. Our words, attitude, and tone of voice open up the conversation to one of exploration and discovery rather than argument, defensiveness, or judgment. By being Consciously Curious about needs, we provide the empathetic connection we require for entering Flow and the Progressive Cycle.

When we are really listening to another, not just waiting for others to take a breath so we can jump in and give them our two cents worth, we can begin to focus our attention on the clues and cues being given off in body language, tone of voice, and other subtle tips about the need of the other person that either is or is not being satisfied.

The best clues come in the expression of feelings, which point to underlying needs:

- ♦ Positive feelings indicate a need has been satisfied.
- ♦ Negative feelings indicate a need has not been satisfied.

It's as simple as that.

We often have a tendency to take things personally by asking ourselves an unconscious question, "What's the worst and most personal way I can take what you just said or did?" We focus on the meanings (created by ourselves or others) rather than on the underlying needs being expressed. Taking the Curious ABC Pause will give us the greatest possible chance to turn the conflict into creativity. So hit the pause button on your personal meaning-making machine and choose to get curious whenever there is conflict, stress or confusion.

Take the...
Curious ABC Pause: ⏸

1. **A**cknowledge my reaction
2. **B**reathe deeply - 1, 2, 3
3. **C**hoose Curiosity *about* ...

Observations, Feelings & Needs

Consciously Choose Curiosity about the underlying needs that are not being met by asking yourself, "What needs of mine, and yours, are not being satisfied?"

Father Hears Son's Need

In a recent workshop, someone mentioned a comment his son had made a week earlier: "You just wasted two hours of my time." We can hear this statement and identify the negative feelings in the word *wasted*. Most likely, the son's tone of voice provided additional, useful information of the negative mind-set he currently had about this wasted time.

When we identify the concern about "wasted time," we can begin to guess at the underlying needs that are not being satisfied. Perhaps the son has a need to be effective in his contribution to the project or a need for a more organized workflow so he and his father don't experience inefficiency.

From there, we can ask clarifying questions. "Do you need greater effectiveness when we work together so that we don't waste time?" Or, "I'm sensing that the frustration you're experiencing right now is from a need to be efficient in your collaboration with me, and so perhaps we need a different process for how we work together."

If the response to either of these questions is yes, you have created a safe and respectful connection to the other person by acknowledging their need. Once you have acknowledged their need, you can now strategize, with their help, on how to address and meet that need.

After doing this exercise, the father acknowledged that, after 31 years of interacting with his son, he now understood him differently, realizing what was important to his son rather than just reacting to his complaints about wasted time. By separating the meaning ("wasted time") from the need ("effectiveness and efficiency"), the father de-escalated the conflict, and quite possibly removed it altogether. Instead, he put in place creative collaboration for mutually determining the best way forward. This human connection leads to interactions with others that are profoundly more enjoyable and business results that are profoundly more effective.

NEEDS HIDDEN IN BLAMES, COMPLAINTS, OR JUDGMENTS

To become skilled in actively listening in order to identify the need contained in a statement, simply begin with the complaint, blame, or judgment you are hearing. Focus on the topic in the statement. The underlying need that is not being met will become more obvious when you identify the negative reference to the topic. In the previous example of wasted time, *wasted* is the negative reference and *time* is the topic.

Let's do an exercise that will help you identify a need in a statement so that you can begin to see the value and effectiveness of hearing a blame, complaint, or judgment as an expression of an unmet need.

Take the following Reptilian Reaction statements of blames, complaints, or judgments and formulate a question to identify the underlying need that isn't being met. When you name the need, the conflict will lose its charge as you shift from serving the conflict to serving the need.

CONSCIOUS CHOOSING FOR FLOW

BLAMES

Peer: "If you knew how to do your job, we wouldn't be in this predicament."

Need: The needs might be competency or effectiveness.

Possible response questions:
- "Do you need a different level of competency from me?"
- "Would you like to talk about our work flow so we don't get in this predicament in the future?"

Roommate: "Can't you see how disgusting this kitchen is?"

Need: The needs might be order or mutuality.

Possible response questions:
- "It seems like you have a need for cleanliness or order and that I'm not cleaning to your standards. Want to talk about it?"
- "Would you like me to contribute more to the household chores?"

COMPLAINTS

Direct report: "I guess this will be another long night trying to figure out what you've done."

Need: The needs might be clarity and understanding.

Possible response questions:
- "Would you like me to walk through my process so you can understand my rationale?"
- "Do you need greater clarity and understanding around the project assumptions?"

Significant other: "The laundry doesn't wash itself, you know."

Need: The needs might be support and appreciation.

Possible response questions:
- "Would you like some help with the laundry?"
- "I appreciate the time and effort you take to do the laundry. Are you OK with doing it?"

JUDGMENTS

Boss: "That team is so dysfunctional, it's amazing this company is still in business."

Need: The needs might be harmony and commitment.

Possible response questions:
- "Would you like to talk about how we handle conflict or our commitment to the team?"
- "I wonder what isn't working for you about this team. Could we talk about this?"

Friend: "I guess you think my money grows on trees."

Need: The needs might be consideration or consistency.

Possible response questions:
- "Would you like some help with the finances?"
- "I'm wondering if you are upset by this unexpected expense. Would you like to know ahead of time how much it costs?"

Marshall Rosenberg describes blame, complaints, or judgment as "tragic expressions of unmet needs."[83] This is because when we blame, complain about, or judge others, we are actually preventing the very thing

CONSCIOUS CHOOSING FOR FLOW

we most want—to meet our needs. Instead, our negative behavior actually creates disconnection and resistance from others, which places us even farther away from our needs. **This is tragic.**

We can go ahead and make the fundamental attribution error to blame, complain, or judge others' actions and their motives, but it doesn't help us to get our own needs met a bit. Just like the caveman in this cartoon, we can make others wrong by saying they are disrespecting us. When we get that others are simply doing what they are doing (strategies) to meet their own needs (like the dinosaur chasing the caveman for food), we can now name the need they are trying to meet through these strategies. Or, we can turn our blame, complaint, or judgment into a request to meet our need. Either way, we will be far better off than if we had just blamed or complained about others.

REVEALING NEEDS BEHIND MEANINGS

Another way we unconsciously express our needs is by hiding behind the meanings we have created and using them to either defend ourselves or attack someone. The meanings we often create are the judgments, complaints, or blames addressed earlier. Buried beneath the meanings are the observations that led us to certain feelings because our needs were not being met.

Following is a list of meanings words, accompanied by some possible feelings and needs.

FEELINGS AND NEEDS BEHIND THE MEANINGS

MEANINGS	FEELINGS	NEEDS
Of what happened	From needs not satisfied	Possible unmet needs
Abandoned	Terrified, lonely, frightened	Nurturing, connection, support
Abused	Angry, frustrated, sad	Emotional/physical well-being
Attacked	Scared, defiant, hostile	Safety, consideration
Betrayed	Disappointed, enraged	Trust, respect
Blamed	Confused, hostile, bewildered	Accountability, fairness, justice
Bullied	Pressured, angry, scared	Autonomy, choice, safety
Cheated	Resentful, hurt, angry	Honesty, fairness
Coerced	Frustrated, angry	Honesty, freedom, choice
Criticized	Anxious, embarrassed	Acknowledgment, appreciation
Disconnected	Lonely, hurt, sad	Collaboration, friendship
Disliked	Sad, lonely, hurt	Connection, friendship
Disrespected	Irritated, angry, hurt	Respect, acknowledgment
Dumped on	Aggravated, suspicious, hurt	Respect, collaboration
Hassled	Irritated, distressed	Serenity, autonomy
Intimidated	Scared, anxious	Safety, equality, empowerment
Isolated	Lonely, afraid	Community, inclusion
Manipulated	Powerless, frustrated	Trust, equality, respect
Mistrusted	Angry, sad	Trust
Misunderstood	Upset, frustrated	To be heard, understanding
Neglected	Lonely, scared	Inclusion, participation
Threatened	Scared, alarmed	Safety, autonomy
Used	Sad, angry	Consideration, mutuality

Adapted from the work of Marshall B. Rosenberg and the Center for Nonviolent Communication, www.cnvc.org.

CONSCIOUS CHOOSING FOR FLOW

Imagine that someone is saying one of the meanings words to you. Then look at the feelings words and imagine them having those emotions. Finally, look at the needs and consider how they could drive that person's feelings, resulting in the meanings used to express what isn't working for them.

Imagine someone is using a meaning word with you, such as *attacked* ("I feel attacked!" or "You just attacked me."):

- ♦ How do you feel? Would you be inclined to help that person or distance yourself from them? This tragic expression of an unmet need creates disconnection from others because the statement places a meaning on whatever the speaker observed, instead of expressing a true feeling. This choice of words generates negative feelings and has a tendency to come across as a blame, complaint, or judgment.

When we use meaning words, our statements have a way of becoming "you" statements ("You attacked me." Or "You abandoned me." Or "You neglected me."). These statements come across that way even when we frame them as an "I" statement ("I feel attacked/abandoned/neglected (by you).") because when people hear this, they tend to take it personally and hear that they are the source of the condition. The person on the receiving end will then normally feel defensive, kicking into the gear of Reptilian Reactions and the Regressive Cycle.

- ♦ If that person shared their actual feelings and unmet needs with you ("I'm feeling pretty angry at what I just heard and what I really need right now is a little consideration and safety."), would you be more inclined to listen and possibly address their needs? Sharing our personal experience of feelings and needs, which others can empathize with, helps to create connection with others.

Feeling words lead to true "I" statements, such as "When you said that to me, I felt angry and frustrated, because I need for us to be able to work together in an atmosphere of trust." These "I" statements that accompany our feelings and our needs may cause us to feel vulnerable to further attack, at least at first. But in my experience, when one person stops blaming and attacking another person and then extends himself to the other with authenticity, this invites a similar response in return. Owning your feelings and needs in a heated moment of conflict takes consciousness, curiosity, and a measure of courage.

As Aristotle once said, "Courage is the virtue that makes all the other virtues possible."[84]

CURIOUSLY INVESTIGATING TO UNCOVER NEEDS

Let's experiment with how to Curiously Investigate to uncover the needs behind meanings.

> **Someone** says to you: "I feel you (insert any meanings word from the preceding list) me."
>
> **You** respond: **"So, when you say** (insert the meanings word they used), **are you feeling** (guess at possible feelings) **because what you need is** (guess at possible needs)?" (You can use the list on the previous page to fill in the blanks.)

The other person replies with yes or no. If yes, you can then talk about helping them meet their need. If no, ask or continue to guess until they say yes. From there, the conversation can switch to collaboration about meeting their needs.

For example:

> **Amy says to you:** "I feel you used me."
>
> **You respond:** "So, when I hear you say *used*, I wonder if you're feeling angry because what you need is mutuality in our interaction with each other—is that right?"
>
> **Amy replies:** "No. I feel sad because I need consideration. I would have liked to have known ahead of time how you were going to use that information I gave you."

The point of this exercise is to get to the underlying need that is driving the upset or conflict. The upset and drama are in the meanings created, not in the need or the related facts. The meaning we create usually has some sort of judgment, blame, or complaint in it, while needs and facts simply are what they are. When we are finally able to get to the underlying need, we can then make a difference that would not have been possible if we had stayed with the meaning the other person created. In that case, all we would have done was rev up the drama and upset.

CMO Shifts from Meanings to Needs

While coaching Oscar, the chief marketing officer of a large health care organization, I asked him to talk with the CEO about the problem we were discussing.

He said, "No way. All the CEO is interested in doing is castrating me." (I noted his interesting use of this term. I realized I had to explore his meaning if we were going to get any results on our call.)

I responded with, "When you say *castrated*, are you feeling discouraged and annoyed by the way he treats you when you meet?"

"Absolutely!"

I continued, "So, what I'm guessing you're wanting from the CEO is support and respect in your interactions with each other."

"Yes."

I responded, "Let's talk about how you can attain a different level of support and respect from the CEO than what you have experienced to date. Would that be all right with you?"

He questioned, "How?"

We then talked about how the interactions between them have typically gone in the past and what he could do differently this time to request the support and respect he most wanted. By filtering through his meaning, using his feelings to get to the needs, we were able to focus on what would make a difference in his interaction with the CEO and what would improve their relationship. We shifted from serving the meaning (What can you really do with the word *castrated* to effect positive change?) to serving the needs of support and respect.

The following week, Oscar reported that the different approach had worked remarkably well with the CEO. They had agreed to give each other a different level of respect and safety in order to talk about their challenges. The CEO actually apologized to Oscar because he hadn't realized that Oscar wasn't experiencing the safety and respect he really wanted.

APPLYING THE SKILL FOR CONNECTION—NEEDS

Needs are the common ground on which we all connect. The next step in the Skill for Connection is to share your needs and then make a curious request for others to share theirs.

The Skill for Connection

Honestly Express (OFN-R)
Your **O**bservations
Your **F**eelings
Your **N**eeds

CURIOUS REQUEST

Curiously Investigate (OFN-R)
Their **O**bservations
Their **F**eelings
Their **N**eeds

Needs: Guess or Ask about the underlying need that is driving the Feelings.

HONESTLY EXPRESSING AND CURIOUSLY INVESTIGATING NEEDS:

When honestly expressing and curiously investigating, you can do one before the other or combine them as you go through observations, feelings or needs. In this example, we first honestly express and then curiously investigate. Do what feels natural for the conversation.

OBSERVATIONS

Honestly Expressing: "When I hear you say, 'You don't know what you're talking about, ...'"

FEELINGS

Honestly Expressing: "I have to admit, I feel a bit annoyed and frustrated by that statement."

NEEDS

Honestly Expressing: "What I would really appreciate from you is a willingness to hear what I have to say. Then, I'd like for us to talk about it openly to explore and discover an approach that would work for both of us."

OBSERVATIONS

Curiously Investigating: "I'm wondering if you really think that I don't know what I'm talking about..."

FEELINGS

Curiously Investigating: ". . . and you're feeling angry and upset with me because . . ."

NEEDS

Curiously Investigating: ". . . you need a different level of competency from me or a different level of communication and understanding?"

When you address needs, it will affect all of the other components of what makes us human—observations (what we see or hear), feelings (how we honestly feel about whether or not our needs are being satisfied), and meanings (what we make it all mean). This atom of observations, feelings, and meanings rotating around our needs (whether or not they are met) is what creates energy in our lives. This energy will be either positive or negative depending on whether or not our needs have been satisfied, and will promote our behavior, motivation and decisions as we work and relate to others each day. Curiosity is the catalyst for creating an empathetic connection with our fellow human beings.

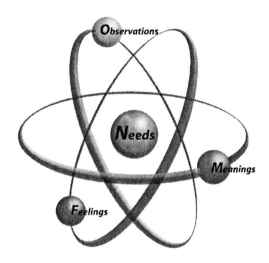

FOCUS ON NEEDS INSTEAD OF REACTIONS

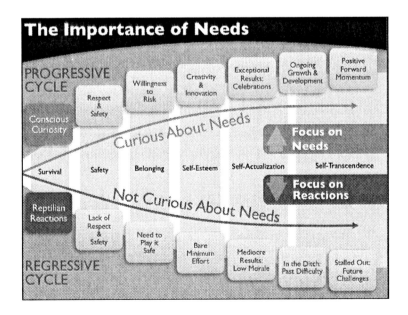

CONSCIOUS CHOOSING FOR FLOW

Progressive Cycle	Regressive Cycle
Focus on needs	Focus on reactions
All needs considered	Meanings assigned
Feeling acknowledged	Feeling upset
Willing to contribute	Individuals keep to themselves
Effective and efficient teamwork	Inability to work together
Rock-star team	Dysfunctional teams
Awards and acknowledgment	Pink slips looming
Team on to next hot deal	Layoffs

Orthopedic Group Gets Curious

In my work with the orthopedic group of a hospital, the CEO confessed that they had been having trouble with this group for the last 30 years. The surgeons were yelling at the nurses during surgery and at the administrators during rounds. The surgeons and members of their operating-room teams were refusing to talk with other support personnel. Surgeons were making demands for greater compensation and resigning if they didn't get it. Something had to be done.

In the ensuing workshop with all 36 members of the orthopedic group, we took time to stop and get clear on the needs of the surgeons, the nurses, the administration, and the executive team of the hospital. We wrote the needs of each group on paper and then put the lists side by side, circling the needs they had in common. To their surprise and amazement, they all had the same needs of support, respect, trust, and clear structure and process in order to do their jobs and enjoy their work. (Sounds like the chapter 8 example about Dumpers and Dumpees, doesn't it?)

They came to realize that the yelling, the refusal to speak to each other, and the demands and resignations of the staff were all strategies they used for meeting their individual needs. They had focused on the reactions of others rather than on their own needs that weren't being satisfied. With this new focus, new possibilities

> became available for new strategies that would work for everyone, not just a few. We came up with a charter, or set of collective agreements, on how they would treat each other in the future, how they would handle conflict, and what they would do to make sure an accountability structure was in place that was fair and reasonable for everyone, including the surgeons. They walked away from the workshop with a new sense of hope and encouragement.
>
> During the following months, they met as a group for one hour each week to read their charter and address any challenges they were having as they moved forward with a more respectful and safe work environment.
>
> The feedback I've heard from the office manager and executives is, "It's a miracle that after 30 years, we finally got to a place where no one is threatening to leave. What a different environment we now have to work within." All that it really took was getting clear on needs and the strategies they could agree on that would work for everyone.
>
> The next section covers the process we used to work through their challenges and create their charter, the STAR Process for Results.

PERSONAL APPLICATION: NEEDS

Now, refer back to your personal challenge and guess at the underlying needs that you and the person you are having a challenge with have. Remember to focus on needs, not on the strategies being used to meet the needs. You can write in the space here or in the full personal challenge worksheet at the end of the book.

CONSCIOUS CHOOSING FOR FLOW

The Key: Choose Curiosity

Consciously choosing curiosity about whether needs have been satisfied or not is the key to shifting focus from the conflict to the underlying needs.

PERSONAL CHALLENGE: TRANSFORM CONFLICT INTO CREATIVITY

The Skill for Connection	
Your needs:	**Their needs:**

SECTION III

THE STAR PROCESS FOR RESULTS

Chapter 10

WHAT IS THE STAR PROCESS FOR RESULTS?

"Efforts and courage are not enough without purpose and direction."

— John F. Kennedy, 35th President of the United States[85]

On January 15, 2009, Captain Chesley "Sully" Sullenberger landed US Airways flight 1549[86] on the Hudson River after the plane's engines hit a flock of birds and ceased to function. All 155 people aboard (passengers and crew) escaped without harm.[87] Captain Sully was a high-reliability officer who had trained for such emergencies using the core process of the STAR Process for Results (Stop, Think, Act, and Review).

Shortly after takeoff from LaGuardia field outside New York City, he noticed that the plane didn't have power. He *stopped* to gather facts and realized the engines were down. In his brief radio conversation with the control tower, he identified his needs and *thought* about his options, knowing that he wouldn't be able to make it back to the airfield. He chose his only viable option, landing on the Hudson River. He *acted* on this strategy,

CONSCIOUS CHOOSING FOR FLOW

doing what he knew he needed to do in order to save the lives of everyone on board. He landed the plane, got everyone out onto the wings during the chill of the New York winter, and then *reviewed* by personally running through the aircraft to make sure everyone was out of the plane and no one was left behind.[88]

> "If you can't describe what you are doing as a process, you don't know what you're doing."
>
> — W. Edward Deming, quality manufacturing guru[89]

The second part of the Formula for Flow is the STAR Process for Results. Section II focused on the Skill for Connection, how we are able to affect our human connection through observations, feelings, and needs. Now that we're able to connect with each other, what will we accomplish together?

The STAR Process for Results is a construct for decision-making, problem solving, and project management. It can be used in a full spectrum of challenges, from simple household projects to complex business projects. Since its structure is built around the core process that high-reliability organizations (HROs) utilize to keep their environment, passengers, and patients safe, then certainly partners, teams, and organizations can use it to create safety in their daily interactions with each other.

HROs are distinctive because they make an effort to organize in ways that increase the quality of attention across the organization, thereby enhancing people's alertness and awareness to details so that they can detect subtle ways in which contexts vary and call for contingent responding (i.e., collective mindfulness). Weick and Sutcliffe's book *Managing the Unexpected* elaborates on and refines this construct as "mindful organizing." Mindful organizing allows individuals to interact continuously as they develop, refine, and update a shared understanding of the situation they face and their capabilities to act on that understanding. This process proactively triggers actions that forestall and contain errors in crises. Further, it requires leaders and organizational members to pay close attention to shaping the social and relational infrastructure of the organization

WHAT IS THE STAR PROCESS FOR RESULTS?

as well as to establishing a set of interrelated organizing processes and practices that jointly contribute to the system's (e.g., team, unit, organization) overall culture of safety.[90]

The STAR Process for Results is a decision-making process that expressly organizes our thinking in order to make effective decisions. The human connection developed through the Skill for Connection makes the STAR Process work effectively. It follows the reasoning that if we take away our unconscious way of operating and mindfully organize our thinking in a particular way, then our results will be consistent and effective in most anything we choose to do.

Let's follow up on a simple example from chapter 9, the process we go through each time we get into our car. First, the underlying question we all address (whether consciously or not) is, "Where would I like to go and why?" ("Why" is always about meeting a need of ours.) Obviously, some of our decisions are pre-set by the regularly occurring strategies we've put in place, like going to work to meet our need for survival and safety. We wake up at a prescribed hour, get dressed, and drive to work. No problem. We do it every day. We do it when we need food for sustenance. We jump in our car, drive to the grocery store, pick up our food, and return home. No big deal. We do it regularly. So let's slow down a little and examine what we instinctively do.

> We **Stop** to get clear about a need (go to work, get food, seek entertainment, etc.).
>
> We gather **facts** (I have to be there at 8:00, there's nothing in the fridge for dinner, I want to see that movie that just came out, etc.).
>
> We create a **shared goal** with our family, friends, or team (to go to work each day, have dinner, go to a movie, etc.), completing the **Stop** part of the process.
>
> Next, we move to the **Think** part of the process to determine the best way of accomplishing our shared goal.

We determine when we need to get it done by or when we have to leave. We decide what food to buy to prepare for dinner or what movie we want to go to and whether we need to buy tickets ahead of time.

Once we **Think** of the best path forward, we **Act** to take decisive measures to reach our shared goal. We drive to work, we go to the store, or we buy the tickets to the movie.

At some point, we **Review** to see how we're doing. Is this the right job for me, or do I need to make a transfer request? Was this a good dinner and should we repeat it or not? Did we like the movie and will we go to that director's movies again?

Review takes into account the necessity of fine-tuning our relationships and results. In the **Review** process, we Stop, Modify, or Start in order to make sure we will continue to reach our shared goal as we progress through life and business.

When we follow the process, first identifying a clear destination or purpose for our endeavor or project, we can then be specific and clear about the action required. It all depends on the direction, the shared goal or final outcome we're seeking. Staying connected through the process is the thread that will make the journey more enjoyable, effective, and successful.

Behlen Manufacturing Clears Up a Long-Standing Problem

On July 18, 2013, I received an interesting e-mail from the chairman of the board of an international manufacturing company, Behlen Manufacturing. The subject line of the e-mail said, "Your friends at XYZ Company recommended you." I quickly opened it. The body of the letter explained:

WHAT IS THE STAR PROCESS FOR RESULTS?

"Our mutual friend, the CEO at XYZ Company, gave me a positive recommendation on the importance of working with you. I'm the chairman of the board of our company, one of my sons is the CEO, and my other son is the president. We are performing reasonably well and yet we have challenges with strong communication and the need for teamwork. We are a $185-million-dollar company with 900+ employees and are continuing to grow. It would be delightful if the three of us could have a little more fun as we carry out our responsibilities and no one threatened to leave the company."

Through further communication, we agreed that the three of them would meet with me for two hours. Two weeks later, they sent the company plane to pick me up and fly me to their headquarters. The four of us met at one of their homes, and I got the sense that they were expecting a miracle during our time together. It soon became clear to me from their facial expressions (especially their failure to smile), their body language, and the intentional lack of eye contact that there was consistent tension and upset among them.

We spoke for a while and then I shared my observations around their interactions with each other, which they confirmed.

I said, "Often the worst disagreements occur when both parties think they're right, and I'm assuming you all think you're right. Is that so?" They all nodded their heads in agreement. I continued, "You know why that is? Because you all have legitimate needs that have not been acknowledged or addressed. Would you say that's a possibility?" They agreed.

I then pulled out a booklet, our Quick Reference Guide, which includes a list of 48 feelings you have when your needs are satisfied and another with 48 feelings you have when your needs are not satisfied (see chapter 8 for both lists). I asked them to look at the two lists and tell me what feelings they were having. They identified several feelings from the second list, of feelings experienced when needs are **not** satisfied. They agreed that they had common feelings.

"You all have legitimate needs that have not been acknowledged or satisfied in those areas where you have such feelings. So, let's take one of your challenges. You tell me what the issue is, and I'll identify each of your

CONSCIOUS CHOOSING FOR FLOW

needs. Then we'll follow this process here." I held up a one-page sheet with the STAR Process on it. "We'll Stop first and get clear on each of your needs and the related facts, and then we'll come up with a shared goal we'll all work on before moving into the Think part, where we'll think of strategies to meet your shared goal. After that, we'll pick the strategy that you all like, and we'll move to Act by making agreements on what to do moving forward. Sound good?" They agreed to try this little experiment.

Facts: When there is a corporate issue and Phil, the CEO, wants input from the senior leadership team, he calls an emergency meeting. His brother, Tony, the president of the AG Division, thinks this grinds the other leaders to a halt on their own projects because they have to cancel and reschedule their meetings in order to attend the CEO's emergency meetings. It drives him crazy because he has other work to do. He often writes e-mails and does other work during these meetings, since he has no idea how long the meeting will take, and he's concerned about failing to complete his own work. Many of these emergency meetings have lasted well over an hour. He said, "It disrupts workflow."

Stop: They expressed their individual needs, and I identified them as follows:

- Phil (CEO) needs inclusion of senior leadership for important company decisions, flexibility to call meetings, and agility to lead.
- Tony (President of AG) needs consistency of workflow, clarity and understanding of schedules, and stability in planning meetings for all leaders.

Shared goal: They then created a shared goal to eliminate upset around meetings and to have a dependable and consistent process that will meet all of their needs.

Think: Then we brainstormed strategies. Some were a bit off the wall, and some even evoked some smiles. After a few minutes of discussion, they came up with a strategy that worked for all of them, meeting their needs for flexibility, agility, consistency, and stability. They agreed to tell all the leaders in the company not to schedule any meetings between 1 and 2 p.m.

each day. If the CEO wanted to call a meeting, he would call it at 1:00 and make sure to complete it by 2:00.

They looked at each other and smiled. This seemingly simple yet frustrating conflict had been going on for years, and they had just solved it in 15 minutes. We gave each other high fives all the way around the table.

Act: They agreed to put the strategy into action the moment they got back into the office.

We agreed to work together and meet a month later for two days in order to learn the process and skills I've talked about in this book and to put together a charter of how they will all interact with each other moving forward.

The following week after our two days together, I received an e-mail from TR, the chairman of the board. He wrote that during all the work they've done together over the last 20 years, they thought they had been operating at a level 5 on a 10-point scale of working and communicating effectively with each other. After our time together, they said they had advanced to a level 7 or 8, and the future looks hopeful. They reported that the leaders within the company are taking notice, saying, "What happened? This sure is different, seeing you guys acting and speaking with unity." My work with this company continues to yield positive results.

Chapter 11

STEP 1: STOP—CURRENT NEEDS AND SHARED GOALS

Common Destination

CONSCIOUS CHOOSING FOR FLOW

"Things which matter most must never be at the mercy of things which matter least."

— Johann Wolfgang von Goethe[91]

A COMMON DESTINATION BRINGS EVERYONE'S THINKING TOGETHER

The first step in the STAR Process for Results, Stop, is establishing a common destination. This common destination is determined based upon two components: current needs and a shared goal. Stopping and agreeing on a common destination builds the confidence and commitment necessary to work toward a common goal. Remember Marshall Rosenberg's saying, "Everything we do is in the service of our needs."[92] Our current needs are what matters most to each and every one of us. They are also what matters to all organizations as well. If the needs of the organization aren't being met, the organization will have difficulty meeting the needs of its customers and employees.

Current need: When you **Stop** and get clear on individual, team, and organizational needs, you are focusing on and paying attention to what motivates every human being and what drives organizations. I've already talked about the importance of needs for building connections and transforming conflict into creativity between individuals. This concept is even more important with group interactions. Unless you align on your needs as a group, hidden agendas or mismatched strategies, struggles, and challenges inherent in teams and organizations tend to crop up. When you **Stop** to get clear on the various needs of stakeholders, it sends a message that you care and that you are taking the needs of all seriously.

Shared goal: Shared goals are the common destination of all stakeholders. We arrive at these goals by considering the needs that have been identified and creating a common objective that the group is committed to reaching. While the shared goal of any endeavor may be focused on meeting the specific needs of some stakeholders more than those of others, at a core level, it must meet the needs of all involved. Taking the time to Stop

STEP 1: STOP—CURRENT NEEDS AND SHARED GOALS

and develop the shared goal will pay off later because of the clarity, focus, transparency, and commitment established up front.

HANDLE ONE TOPIC AT A TIME FOR CLARITY

When using the STAR Process for Results, identifying needs, and creating a shared goal, it's important to stay focused on one topic at a time. When you try to handle lots of topics all at once, you create confusion because each topic has so many moving parts and needs. This is the first step in a process that will entail brainstorming, taking action, and reviewing. So, to avoid confusing and overwhelming the participants in a discussion, limit its scope to one topic or agenda item at a time.

For example, in meetings when there are several decisions to be made, make sure that you cover one topic or agenda item at a time. Seton Family of Hospitals in Austin, Texas, told me that they manage this by appointing one person to be "conscious of the meeting," focusing on keeping order, safety, and respect in the room. This person also makes sure that the group stays on one topic at a time, placing any new topic that shows up in a "parking lot" on a flipchart to address later.

Company Meetings With Too Many Topics

While working with a large construction company in Texas, I had the opportunity to observe one of their executive meetings. I was told that they have long meetings and that afterwards, each person wonders what had been achieved during the meeting. I sat against the wall, rather than at the conference table, to observe.

As I listened and took notes on what I was observing, I realized that I had a list of 14 topics that had already come up in their meeting, and only 30 minutes had passed. There was no resolution or action item agreed to by the group on any of the topics. The COO, Jim, turned and said to me in a whisper, "See! There are so many topics that show up in our meetings, it's like shooting ducks. I don't know which one to aim for."

When this team learned to stay with one topic at a time, putting new topics that emerged in a "parking lot" to cover later, and to follow the topic from beginning to end, including action items and who was going to do

CONSCIOUS CHOOSING FOR FLOW

what by when, everyone walked out of the meeting with a sense of accomplishment and satisfaction that they had truly accomplished something during their time together.

Let's see what identifying one topic and then getting clear on the current needs and shared goal would look like:

Topic: Complaints about departmental silo thinking and cliques
Needs:
1. Collaboration between departments (team needs belonging)
2. Financial success (organization needs security)
3. Improved employee morale (individuals need self-esteem)

Shared goal: All departments will communicate with each other effectively in order to collaborate and make decisions that are financially sound. We will also make sure we address the individual needs of our employees to increase the morale and enthusiasm within our company.

NFL Identifies Current Needs and Creates a Shared Goal

On July 25th, 2011, after fourteen and a half months of public nastiness, private negotiations, and court filings and rulings between the players and owners of the National Football League, who were squabbling over more than $9 billion per year, the fans finally saw the handshake and heard the words they awaited: "Football is back."[93] NFL commissioner Roger Goodell and the NFL Players Association executive director DeMaurice Smith both used that phrase while standing shoulder to shoulder, announcing their agreement on a 10-year deal that ended the lockout that began in March. During the announcement on national TV, the center for the Indianapolis Colts, Jeff Saturday, wrapped one of his big burly arms around New England Patriot's owner Robert Kraft and enveloped him in a hug while saying, "Without this man, this deal would have never happened."

At the end of the season, during the preliminary TV coverage of Super Bowl XLVI, Bob Costas interviewed Robert Kraft, the owner of the New

STEP 1: STOP—CURRENT NEEDS AND SHARED GOALS

England Patriots, one of the teams in the Super Bowl. Bob Costas commented on Mrs. Kraft's struggle with cancer and how Mr. Kraft had stayed by her side until she said to him, "Robert, you need to save football." With that, she gave him permission to go to the negotiating table. He did.

Mr. Kraft reported that he thought about the stalled negotiations and the rumors of the players saying that the owners' current deal was "probably the worst deal in sports history." He realized that the negotiations had to get past the name-calling and negative rhetoric.

When he walked into the room, to the surprise of everyone who knew of Mrs. Kraft's struggle, Mr. Kraft reported that he said to those assembled in the room, "Gentlemen. There are only three questions we need to answer: 1: What do the players **need** from the owners? 2: What do the owners **need** from the players? 3: What do the fans **need** from the NFL?"

A few months later, both sides agreed that they had a "fair and balanced deal" in the 10-year deal, the longest deal in NFL history.

Mrs. Myra Kraft died of cancer one week before the July 25 announcement of the deal. During the announcement, Robert Kraft thanked his wife for encouraging him to participate in the negotiations and then took a verbal jab at the nearby White House and Congress, saying, "I hope we gave a little lesson to the people in Washington, because this debt crisis is a lot easier to fix than this deal was."

Throughout the entire 2011 season, the New England Patriots wore the initials MK on their helmets in memory of Myra Kraft.

Focusing on needs prior to any negotiation and creating a shared goal helps everyone involved in the interaction to get into Flow and work together. What seems like an obvious beginning step towards making a decision or engaging a new project is often passed over as those involved jump into generating strategies for solutions or even taking actions around an idea. This is a classic case of putting the cart before the horse.

FIRST MAKE A REQUEST TO STOP AND IDENTIFY NEEDS

Since it's a common tendency to jump right to solutions, it's important for someone to make a request to first Stop to get clear on the needs that are going to be addressed and create a shared goal that all will align on before talking strategies for solutions. This is a shift from *how* we're going to solve our problem with the various strategies or solutions suggested to *why* there is a problem in the first place, the needs that must be addressed if we are going to be successful with our strategies. This is what Robert Kraft did in the NFL negotiations. It's crucial that someone slows down the process to address these two critical aspects to bring the thinking of the group together. A request is rather simple, and it shows respect to the group or other individuals. It starts with, **"Would you be willing to . . . ?"**

In the previous example about the NFL lockout, Mr. Kraft identified the core components of the negotiations—what the fans needed, what the players needed, and what the owners needed. His request would sound like, **"Would you all be willing to** stop and get clear on what those needs are for each of the groups before we talk about how to address them?" Obviously, Mr. Kraft, owner of the New England Patriots, had a lot of clout, as well as respect from everyone in the negotiations, because his reputation as a fair and reasonable man preceded him. Yet without someone making a request, the negotiations would have continued to languish as they had before, with no agreement on strategies for solution. Stopping and getting clear on needs before identifying a shared goal brings everyone's thinking together.

The Skill for Connection

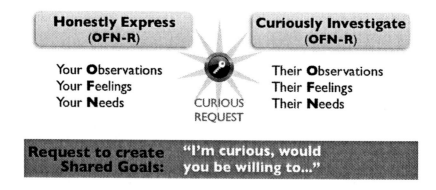

STEP 1: STOP—CURRENT NEEDS AND SHARED GOALS

HONESTLY EXPRESSING AND CURIOUSLY INVESTIGATING USING MR. KRAFT'S EXAMPLE:

OBSERVATIONS

Honestly Expressing: "I've kept tabs on the negotiations and comments have been made by the players that the current deal is the worst agreement in sports history."

Curiously Investigating: "I'm curious—what have you heard or seen?"

FEELINGS

Honestly Expressing: "I'm feeling frustrated that we haven't been able to work out anything that is mutually agreeable by all."

Curiously Investigating: "Are you feeling the same way?"

NEEDS

Honestly Expressing: "I have a real need for fairness, to know that we as owners have come to a deal that all sides are enthusiastic about."

Curiously Investigating: "I'm curious if you have the same need?"

Make a Curious Request: "Would you all be willing to pause for a moment to get really clear on what the players need from us, what we need from the players, and what the fans need from us before trying to create an agreement?"

THE VALUE OF A SHARED GOAL

The shared goal brings the thinking of all those involved to bear on the challenge at hand. The challenge most individuals and teams have is

CONSCIOUS CHOOSING FOR FLOW

jumping to solutions or strategies before clearly identifying the needs and what their shared goal will be. From there, it's easy for one person or a fraction of the group to push for their agenda or form silo thinking, which create individual actions that are not coordinated to produce effective results for the entire group or organization. Completing this first step brings everyone's thinking together to solve the most troublesome problems of any relationship, team, or organization, as Robert Kraft did.

Unless we have created and written down a conscious and clear shared goal, we won't have the certainty that the team is moving toward the same end goal. Therefore, to save time, energy, and focus of the group, never start a project unless you have determined and agreed upon your shared goal. To determine whether everyone is on board, ask how each person feels about it. Remember the feelings lists and the difference between needs that are satisfied or not? Getting in touch with each person's passion and enthusiasm to go for the shared goal will pay off in spades later on down the road through creativity and innovation. For example, if someone says, "Yeah, sure. I'm good with it," and their tone sounds submissive rather than upbeat, stop and talk with them about what they really think to confirm whether they are really onboard or just giving lip service. (Once you learn about the hand signals of the consensus tool, you will be able to get a good read on everyone's commitment, simply by using a hand signal. More on this in the **Think** section.)

COACHING OCCURS IN THE GAP

In coaching an individual, a group or organization the first step is always assessing where they are currently. In other words, what are the facts and what are the current needs. The second step in coaching is where do they want to go? In other words, what's the shared goal? This establishes the gap from where they are to where they want to go. Coaching always occurs within this gap and it looks like this for the first step in the STAR Process of Results, Stop:

STEP 1: STOP—CURRENT NEEDS AND SHARED GOALS

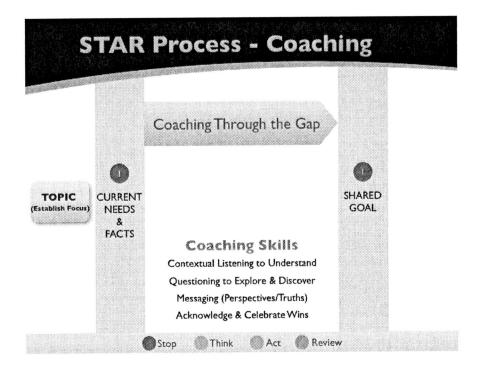

Two Midwestern Insurance Companies Create a Shared Goal

Back in 2009, two large, related Midwestern health care insurance companies in two different states got together and talked about the impending changes in health insurance, especially due to the implementation of the Affordable Care Act. They expressed their concern about how it would affect their profits as well as customer service. They identified a need to serve their customers better for enrollment and claims processing in order to maintain financial solvency and cut costs for both organizations. The strategy to make this happen would require a new technology.

They negotiated with several vendors and realized it would cost them $400 million and take up to 10 years to meet their needs, with no guarantee that the system would work as advertised once completed. So, instead they created a shared goal to keep the control in house and establish their own software development company to meet their needs.

CONSCIOUS CHOOSING FOR FLOW

One company put in $15 million and the other provided the software license, the people, and the building to create a company called Data Tech Services (name changed for confidentiality). It took them four years to complete the new software platform to meet their needs and a total cost of $175 million to:
1. Develop the Data Tech software functionality to accept and service their members
2. Cover the duplicate costs incurred in having two systems operating for almost four years
3. Disconnect the 80+ other systems internal to the companies and reconnect them to Data Tech.

Approximately half of the $175 million was paid to Data Tech; the other half was incurred internally for the duplication and reconnection work. The two insurance companies confirmed that Data Tech worked prior to converting business. Ultimately, they were able to turn off their old mainframe in late 2013, which was a big side benefit to meeting their shared goal to meet their objectives of lowing costs, establishing the required technology, and improving customer service.

Along the way, there were challenges between the two companies, and they committed to staying connected and working through them. Otherwise, Data Tech would never have become a reality.

Data Tech established a new way to handle claims and serve the clients of both companies at a considerably reduced cost. It took forward thinking and insight from the leaders of both companies to come up with such a plan. They were able to collaborate with each other, working through their challenges to address the structural needs that the entire insurance industry faced in order to stay competitive.

By using creativity and coming together to create a shared goal, they were able to implement a strategy and take actions to manage client administrative costs that hadn't happened before. This positive, dynamic, creative, forward-moving energy between the two companies created Flow, resulting in creativity and innovation.

STEP 1: STOP—CURRENT NEEDS AND SHARED GOALS

The overall need of the two companies was to self-actualize in an industry that was being challenged with the new health care laws. In order to do so, they needed to get into Flow with each other to create something new in Data Tech. The ability to identify a **need**, gather **facts,** and create a **shared goal** helped put them into Flow with each other and the entire health care insurance industry.

LISTEN TO UNDERSTAND AND NOT JUST TO REPLY

> "Most people listen to respond rather than listening to understand."
>
> — Stephen Covey, author of *The Seven Habits of Highly Effective People*[94]

You may be thinking that creating a shared goal sounds easier than it really is. How can you really get to a common objective that meets everyone's needs when sometimes you haven't a clue what *they* mean when they're waxing eloquently? What the heck does "create a supportive culture" mean? Or, you thought you understand the directive, but now you've found yourself in hot water because you misunderstood the nuances of the instructions and took action beyond your authority. Most upsets and misunderstandings happen when there is not mutual understanding.

Have you ever noticed those people (not us, of course) who listen to respond as opposed to listening to understand? Human tendency is to listen to others while formulating our response in our head, preparing to prove the other person wrong or give our rebuttal for or against what they are saying the moment they take a breath so we can squeeze our comments into their tirade. We've all been guilty of it at one time or another in our lives. While growing up, my mother used to say an interesting little phrase to my father, when it appeared to her they were not communicating or when she didn't understand what he was saying.

She would say, "You talk to me when you think you do, but you don't."

What my mother meant by this was that my father would say things to her, assuming that she understood, but often she didn't really get the message, and she wanted him to know that. To her, he was speaking at or around her, but not to her. The exchange was not working for her because little effort was being made by my father to confirm that she understood what he actually meant. He just assumed my mother understood and correctly received the message he was sending. Disconnect?

CLEARING UP MISUNDERSTANDINGS THROUGH THE "WHAT I HEARD" CONVERSATION

One solution for making sure that there is mutual understanding is the **"What I Heard" Conversation.** The purpose of this particular tool is to confirm the understanding of the message between two people. It can be used any time you find yourself feeling disconnected or in conflict with someone. When there isn't clarity of understanding and agreement on the meaning, the facts, and how they are being interpreted, arguments and upsets often ensue. Truly listening to another human being to the point of mutual understanding is an act of compassion, and therefore helps to create connection with them.

There is a simple structure to the **"What I Heard" Conversation.**
1. You begin with authentically acknowledging what the other person said by saying,

"What I heard you say was . . . Was that it?"

(Note: Pay particular attention to your tone of voice and body language to convey respect and safety during the entire conversation.)

If they say no, have them continue to explain and clarify what they're trying to convey.

After they clarify, continue to use ***"What I heard you say was . . . Was that it?"***

STEP 1: STOP—CURRENT NEEDS AND SHARED GOALS

   If they say yes, you have mutual understanding. This is not just about facts, but also about the meaning they are trying to convey to you. You may even want to throw in some of your own meanings to confirm you are really getting what they are saying.

2. Continue by asking questions, such as…

   "I'm wondering if what you're meaning is … ?"

   Again, if they say no, ask them to clarify further.

3. When the other person agrees with your understanding of what they said and meant, then **ask permission** to share your ideas and thoughts. The purpose for asking permission is to make sure they will listen to you with an open mind to understand. Without it, you may be speaking to a metaphorically closed door, throwing your words at it and never reaching the inhabitant of the house.

4. If the person does not acknowledge what you said or starts arguing with you, slow down and ask them to acknowledge what you just said by saying,

   "Would you please tell me what you just heard me say?"

   (This helps to create clarity and understanding with them, as well as slowing down their response before it turns into an argument. Often others are so focused on their rebuttal in their own thinking that they don't really hear or understand what you just said. When asking others to tell me what I just said, I often hear, "Would you say it again, please?")

5. If the misunderstanding persists, re-clarify with something such as,

CONSCIOUS CHOOSING FOR FLOW

"Sorry, I don't appear to be making myself clear. Let me try to explain this differently." Then after you clarify further, ask, "Can you share with me what you heard me say this time?"

Remember how annoying you find people who are just waiting to add their 2 cents worth rather than being present to what is being said to them? Stay focused on what the person is saying. Stay in their satchel, and don't jump in with what you want to say concerning your satchel or your 2 cents. You'll have time to share your thoughts after there is complete understanding around what they are trying to convey. At this point, you may even find that you aren't in disagreement; you just had different meanings or perspectives.

The purpose of the "What I Heard" Conversation is to create mutual understanding, not to convince or sway others from their viewpoint. This is about gaining understanding about the topic. That's it—nothing more or less. After you gain mutual understanding, you will have a common ground to talk about the merits and benefits of each from your viewpoints.

Using the "What I Heard" conversation will assist you in bringing absolute clarity that what was said has been understood. Without mutual understanding, you may each be reading off a different sheet of paper in your own minds. When you read off the same page in your individual minds, solutions tend to find themselves.

Lack of Mutual Understanding Creates Problems

I heard a joke that demonstrated the need for mutual understanding that went like this. A man was watching his wife look at herself in the mirror. Since her birthday was not far off, he asked what she'd like to have for her birthday. "I'd like to be six again," she replied, still looking in the mirror.

On the morning of her birthday, he arose early, made her a nice big bowl of Lucky Charms, and then took her to Six Flags theme park. What a day!

STEP 1: STOP—CURRENT NEEDS AND SHARED GOALS

He put her on every ride in the park—the Death Slide, the Wall of Fear, the Screaming Roller Coaster, everything there was. Five hours later, they staggered out of the theme park. Her head was reeling, and her stomach felt upside down.

He then took her to a McDonald's, where he ordered her a Happy Meal with extra fries and a chocolate shake. Then it was off to a movie, with popcorn, a soda, and her favorite candy, M&M's. What a fabulous adventure!

Finally, she wobbled home with her husband and collapsed into bed exhausted. He leaned over his wife with a big smile and lovingly asked, "Well, Dear, what was it like being six again?"

Her eyes slowly opened and her expression suddenly changed. "I meant my dress size, you f&%$ing idiot!"

The moral of the story—Even when a man is listening, he may still get it wrong. Perhaps if he had used the "What I Heard" conversation, he would have saved himself and his wife a lot of trouble and exhaustion.

Rosenberg Uses the "What I Heard" Conversation

I studied with Marshall Rosenberg at an International Intensive for nine days, along with 50 people from around the world. There were people from Australia, Africa, India, Italy, Netherlands, Germany, Israel, and many other countries. English was not the primary language for many of the people in attendance.

Marshall Rosenberg would sit in front of the entire group each morning and afternoon for about two hours, before the group broke into various learning modules, to talk about a particular topic or concept. The interaction between Marshall and the group was often lively and animated, with many misunderstandings being expressed from individuals about what the Master was saying. When this occurred, Marshall would ask the group to pause, and he would say to the individual, "Would you please tell me what you heard me say?" The individual would express what they understood, to which Marshall would often say, "Not quite. Let me take another stab at it." He would explain it again and then ask that same individual, "Now what did you hear me say?" He would continue this process until what the person repeated back to him was in alignment with what he actually meant. Sometimes the interaction went on so long that when mutual understanding was finally reached, the group would break into applause to celebrate the mutual understanding.

I am confident that I probably heard Marshal say, "What did you hear me say?" about 300 times or more during the nine days. For me, this attests to Marshall's unwavering commitment to making sure there is absolute understanding of what he was saying, even with those whose native language was not English.

USING THE "WHAT I HEARD" CONVERSATION

So let's work through a scenario using the **"What I Heard" Conversation:**

> **Scenario:** You are having a disagreement with your boss about which consultants to use to solve an issue with a project. They want to work with a friend of theirs and you want to make sure you bring in someone that has the expertise needed. Your boss begins the conversation with, "We can bring in Sally to help since we already know her and like working with her, and she's really good at doing research."
>
> **You** respond with, "What I heard you say was that we already know Sally better than some of the other consultants and everyone likes working with her. You also think she can do the needed research so that we're successful with our project. Is that about right?"
>
> **Your boss** says, "Absolutely! It's not like it takes a rocket scientist to come up with the data we need."
>
> **You** respond with, "So, are you saying that we really don't need an expert consultant who has significant experience with this sort of project? We simply need to have someone who can do research?"

STEP 1: STOP—CURRENT NEEDS AND SHARED GOALS

Your boss says, "Yes."

You ask, "May I share my thoughts?"

Your boss says, "Sure."

You share, "It's my understanding that we want the very best solution to this issue, and I'm not confident that someone who doesn't have the experience would be as effective in troubleshooting the problem. There are technical issues that require some depth of knowledge. Would you please tell me what you heard me say?"

Your boss says, "I hear that you think it's really important that we get someone with the expertise to guide us through this rather than simply working with someone we already know. Did I hear you correctly?"

You respond with, "Yes."

The value of the **"What I Heard" Conversation** is that it is safe and respectful. There is no judgment of what the other person is saying only confirmation of what they actually said. When clarifying, you can add your thinking of what they are perhaps saying to make sure your thinking and their thinking is in alignment. If it isn't, then you will know, and you can adjust your interpretation to confirm what they are actually trying to get across to you. With this understanding, you are far more likely to create a solution together since there is a basic, common platform from which you can build upon together.

For me, this is absolutely critical when interacting with my wife, because, like the man in the joke, I'm not always sure about the context and thought process she has. We are quite different in our personality styles and ways of operating in life. She's a CPA, and is very detail-oriented, factual, and task-oriented. I'm a big picture kind of a guy and the visionary, looking at possibilities and potential. Using the "What I Heard" Conversation helps to keep us in the Progressive Cycle in our daily interactions with each other as we express our needs to create shared goals with each other. Now instead of saying what my mother used to say to my father, "You talk to me when you think you do, but you don't," Lani can say to me, "Thanks. I get what you're saying."

The "What I Heard" Conversation Reforms the Prison System in Brazil

In October of 2010, I had the opportunity to study briefly with a man who has helped reform the prison system in Brazil over the last 15 years. In fact, his approach was included in the platform of the elections of both candidates during their last elections. His name is Dominic Barter, and he was a student and prodigy of Marshall Rosenberg.

Dominic shared a story when we first met that made me stand up and listen. He shared that, at the very beginning of his work, he was faced with a choice. He was standing on the street facing one of the many *favelas,* or shanty towns, in Brazil. Now these favelas have their own culture of governance and a sense of justice that is different from that of the nearby cities. They have high rates of crime, suicide, drug use, and disease. They have a higher maximum density of population per square mile than any city, and are built on the sides of hills without street grids or street names. It's a world unto itself. Dominic was deciding if he would enter these favelas to introduce a new sense of justice based upon Restorative Justice for healing.

He described his internal conversation saying, "I thought that those who make a significant difference in life tend to walk toward a challenge and not away from it. So I decided to walk toward this imposing favela and see what happened." That was 15 years ago, and he now has a reputation in the favelas he entered as a man who helps to restore justice in their system. He did the same thing with prisons, and his reputation is growing to the point of his approach being talked about in the previous election.

Dominic is not from Brazil. He is from England, and he has used this Restorative Justice with projects supported by the UN. His approach uses what we call, the "What I Heard" conversation.

STEP 1: STOP—CURRENT NEEDS AND SHARED GOALS

RESTORATIVE DIALOGUE RESTORES JUSTICE

First, there's an event that happens that violates someone's rights—someone is killed, or someone steals something, beats someone up, or causes harm to someone else. You now have the event, the author of the event, the receiver of the event, and the community affected by the event (which might be the family or friends).

The first step in Restorative Justice is to meet with the author, receiver, and the community members individually about the event and get agreement for them to all meet in person. Once you have made it safe for them to do so, you meet. What follows is the process I was taught by Dominic. I have had consistent results whenever I have chosen to use it. I call it the Restorative Dialogue Circle.

RESTORATIVE DIALOGUE CIRCLE

(based on the work of Dominic Barter called Restorative Circles)

Purpose: to express and to <u>be heard</u> about an event in a way that is respectful, responsible, and result-oriented.

THE THREE COMPONENTS OF THE CIRCLE:

1. The author of the event, the one who was responsible for the event.
2. The receiver of the event, the one who had the event happen to them.
3. The community affected by the event, the ones who felt grief or upset and had a relationship with the receiver.

RESTORATIVE DIALOGUE PROCESS USED IN THE CIRCLE:

(for mutual comprehension/understanding, self-responsibility and results)

1. One person addresses another.
2. The person addressed reflects back their understanding of the meaning of what was said.
3. The original speaker confirms or corrects. (Repeat the process with each and every speaker until the speaker confirms they have been heard.)

FACILITATED BY A PERSON ASKING THE FOLLOWING QUESTIONS:

- "What would you like known, and by whom, about how you are right now in relation to the act and its consequences?" (This is spoken to the Speaker.)
- "What did you hear her/him say?" (This is spoken to the Listener.)
- "Is that it?" And then, "What else would you like heard?" (This is spoken to the Speaker.)

THE FIVE STEPS IN THE FACILITATED TEAM DIALOGUE CIRCLE:

1. **The Act/Event.** Identify one act or event and agree upon the <u>facts</u> surrounding it. Address one act or event at a time by working through this entire process, and then pick a new act or event to work through.

2. **Mutual comprehension or understanding.** "What would you like known, and by whom, about how you are right now in relation to the act and its consequences?" (Any of the people making up the three components of the circle who wish to speak about the event will have an opportunity to do so. Normally, the Author or Receiver would speak first.)

3. **Self-responsibility or accountability.** "What would you like known, and by whom, about what you were looking for at the moment you chose to act?" (Any of the people making up the three components of the circle who wish to speak about the event will have an opportunity to do so.)

4. **Agreed-upon action.** "What would you like to see happen next?" ("What would you like to offer?" Or "What would you like to request?") (Any of the people making up the three components of the circle who wish to speak about the event will have an opportunity to do so.)

5. **Agreements put into place with timeframes by the team.** A follow-up date is set for all team members in order to confirm agreements have been kept or to readdress agreements to further clarify

STEP 1: STOP—CURRENT NEEDS AND SHARED GOALS

agreed-upon actions and make sure the team moves forward with their desired results.

Restorative Dialogue Circle Unites a Team

I used this process in "Fleet Services," a department in a municipality that was struggling with an event where one of the executives recorded a meeting without telling the others and leaked that recording to the local paper. An investigation ensued. The man was put on paid leave during the investigation while a lawsuit was pending. We now have the event, the author of the event (a manager of "Fleet Services"), the receiver (the director of "Fleet Services"), and the community affected by the event (the entire executive team of "Fleet Services").

I met with all of them, showed them the one sheet I just shared with you, told them how I planned to facilitate the circle, and created the safety they were looking for. I said the way I would facilitate the meeting was to first get clear on ground rules. They would be:

- One person would identify whom they were speaking to. After they were done, that person would say what they heard. We would continue until there was agreement on what had been said.
- Everyone in the circle would give me, the facilitator, the authority to manage this process.
- Each person would speak from an "I" position, and would not attack, blame, or judge others from the "you" position. The moment anyone shifted to the "you" position, I would stop them and ask them to speak from the "I" position.
- Agreement would be required on the ground rules before the process would begin.

The author of the event first spoke to the director. The paper he was holding shook, his voice cracked, and his knee had a nervous twitch while he spoke. The director said what he heard, to which the author clarified. After he clarified, the director responded with his understanding and comprehension. We continued this process until everyone in the circle who wanted to speak spoke. We achieved mutual comprehension and

CONSCIOUS CHOOSING FOR FLOW

understanding about the event and how the consequences affected each person. We had moved from step 1 through step 2 and into step 3 naturally, without anyone else or me forcing it. Tears were shed and anger was expressed. Members acknowledged their role in creating such a situation in the first place where the author felt alone and acted out of desperation. Although his actions were unacceptable to the team, they saw how they helped to create the person's feeling of exclusion and aloneness. Each person owned up to the part they played in the event.

At step 3 (about self-responsibility and accountability), one of the executives in the community addressed me. She said, "Hayden, I think we need to have a recommitment ceremony." I inquired what that would look like. She said, "I think if each of us would be willing to recommit to the team, doing it one at a time around the circle, it might help with healing and moving forward." I asked the group, and they said that all would be willing to do this after we had moved through step 4 and established agreements of what they were actually committing to.

In step 4, we agreed on the actions each member of the team would abide by, including the agreement that no recordings would be made without the explicit agreement from 100% of those in attendance. We wrote out all the agreements, and each person signed them. Copies were made for each member prior to having a recommitment ceremony. At the end of the ceremony, we moved to step 5 and agreed to meet in two weeks to make sure everyone was following through on the agreements they had signed.

This approach yields such powerful results time and time again when I've used it that I thought it would help the city deal with the plethora of grievances filed each year by employees that costs the city hundreds of thousands of dollars. Grievances can be filed without those in conflict ever getting together. Without getting them together, the city has to investigate and conduct interviews, often while the focus of the investigation is put on paid leave. What would happen if they got together, used this approach, and worked it out right there and then? Think of the savings this city and every other city would gain. They could then spend that money on projects that could make a real difference for the welfare and benefit of the inhabitants of their cities.

STEP 1: STOP—CURRENT NEEDS AND SHARED GOALS

FOCUS ON OUR NEEDS AND OUR SHARED GOAL

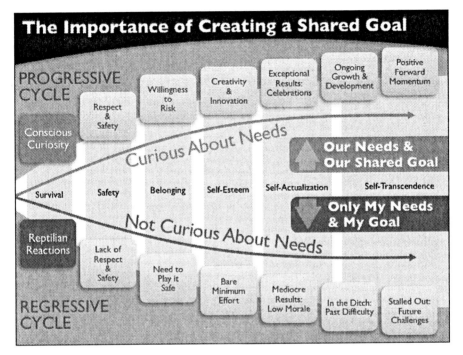

Progressive Cycle	Regressive Cycle
Our needs & our shared goal	Only my needs & my goal
All people considered	Individual agendas
Feeling acknowledged	Feeling alone
Willing to collaborate	Move into silos
Common vision	Independent objectives
Clear direction	Disjointed projects
Accomplishment	Confusion
Accolades for everyone	Finger pointing and justification

> *Seton Hospital Uses the STAR Process to Solve an Old Problem*
> The Seton Family of Hospitals in Austin, Texas, uses the STAR Process for Results in their high-reliability organization. Using this process in an area of the hospital other than for patient safety, one of

their directors in the food service department reduced the employee turnover ratio from 95% to 5% per year by identifying the current needs of employees and the organization concerning this problem. He then created a strategy that would address those needs. This is how he did it.

The food service department was in disarray, so the hospital brought in a new director. He looked at the situation and thought, "We need to do something about this high turnover." So he **Stopped** and surveyed the entire staff of the department, hoping to find out what was causing the revolving-door syndrome. In the past, this department had conducted business as usual without stopping to find out what exactly the problem was or which needs weren't being met. He found two major challenges that almost all of the staff encountered during their day. Most had children. When their kids were out of school on vacation or sick, they missed work to take care of them. The other challenge was that most staff members did not have their own transportation. They had to rely on the bus system, and sometimes they missed the bus and couldn't get to work. Having identified their most pressing needs, for dependable child care and reliable and consistent transportation, he then created a **shared goal** to address these needs. If he had not stopped to get clear on the department's current needs, any strategies to solve the 95% staff turnover would have been working toward an ill-advised solution. He successfully shifted the food service operation from the Regressive Cycle to the Progressive Cycle by stopping to identify the current needs and creating a shared goal.

In the **Think** part of the STAR Process, he brainstormed with staff strategies to address the challenges. They came up with ideas to create a child care center and a transportation system that involved carpooling and their own bus to drop off and pick up staff. They **Acted** on that strategy and put the strategies into action. The turnover ratio plummeted to 5% the following year. He addressed the needs of the staff; in doing so, he showed respect for them and made it safe for them to come to work. Finally, he **Reviews** their progress each year to make sure the department continue to address employee needs.

STEP 1: STOP—CURRENT NEEDS AND SHARED GOALS

PERSONAL APPLICATION: SHARED GOAL

Now, refer back to your personal challenge and create a shared goal that you think you and the person you are having a challenge with could both agree on and feel enthusiastic about, one that addresses both of your needs. You can write in the space here or in the full personal challenge worksheet at the end of the book.

The STAR Process for Results is meant to be interactive. Therefore, when you are finished filling out the STAR Process, you will need to interact with the person you are having the difficulty with, preferably meeting in person. Walk through the Process with them in the order that you have filled it out to make sure that you have correctly identified the needs and chosen a shared goal that works for both of you.

The Key: Choose Curiosity

Consciously choosing curiosity about the current needs of the group is the key to developing a shared goal.

PERSONAL CHALLENGE: TRANSFORM CONFLICT INTO CREATIVITY

STAR Process for Results
STOP ♦ THINK ♦ ACT ♦ REVIEW

1. **STOP: Current Needs and Shared Goal**
   Facts: Refer to the observations you listed in the Skill for Connection and feel free to add more.

CONSCIOUS CHOOSING FOR FLOW

Needs: Refer to the needs you listed in the Skill for Connection and feel free to add more.

Shared Goal: Create a shared goal that you think you and the person you are having a challenge with could both agree on and feel enthusiastic about. Choose one that addresses both of your needs.

_____
_____
_____
_____

Chapter 12

STEP 2: THINK—BRAINSTORM STRATEGIES

Choose Your Route!

"Your imagination is your preview of life's coming attractions."

— Albert Einstein[95]

CHOOSE YOUR ROUTE

The second step in the STAR Process for Results, Think, involves brainstorming strategies and choosing the best route to take for meeting your shared goals. The shared goal incorporates needs, the *why* we do something, while strategies represent the *how* we meet our needs. If your imagination is your preview of life's coming attractions, your route is limited only by the multitude of ideas that you can generate and the choices you can make along your journey.

BRAINSTORMING BASICS

I would imagine that most of us have a pretty good idea of what brainstorming is. Doing it effectively or consciously, though, is another matter. Do we really stretch ourselves to think outside the box, using our imaginations to come up with the best possible ideas we can and then putting them into action to reach our shared goal? Or do we think through a problem just enough to find a strategy that will get the job done? For brainstorming strategies effectively, some generally recognized components should be present:

- Operate with respect and curiosity.
- Look at different options and possibilities.
- Make it safe for everyone to contribute.
- No idea is a stupid idea.
- Think outside of the box.
- Use your imagination.
- Use "Yes and…"

Most obviously, the environment must be safe and respectful for all those participating in a brainstorming session. People need to feel safe enough to throw out ideas that may sound outlandish at first blush.

STEP 2: THINK—BRAINSTORM STRATEGIES

These off-the-cuff or out-in-left-field ideas can spark innovative and new approaches to old problems. We also need to respect that people have different personality styles, and we need to provide everyone with the space and time to contribute. Some people think aloud, enjoying the process of bouncing their ideas off of each other, while others think through things internally, even somewhat subconsciously, before they contribute to the group. Simple curiosity and wisdom access questions can spawn new lines of thinking that branch off the beaten route. "I wonder what would happen if..." Or you could make this request of someone who is quiet: "(Person's name), I'm curious...would you be willing to share your thoughts and ideas?"

In my experience and from what others have shared with me concerning business meetings, brainstorming strategies rarely happens. What does happen is a filtering or self-negation of ideas before they are ever expressed. Ideas that might sound stupid or off the wall or not plausible are suppressed before they are spoken. It is those ideas that often spark new ideas in others and have the opportunity to take the company to new and greater heights of productivity, products and relations.

I learned an exercise in an improvisation class that I find an effective way to get people to truly brainstorm. It's simple. First start any response to someone else's statement with, "Yes but . . ." Taking a playful example, if someone says, "Let's throw a party" and the continual responses are, "Yes but . . .", the party ideas fizzle. "But" is an eraser word, canceling out what the other person says in favor of something different, making it difficult to reach agreement. Alternatively, when a, "Yes and . . ." response is used, it has the effect of building onto what others have said, creating momentum and enthusiasm. The resulting party in this example would be inclusive of everyone's fun ideas that were not canceled out during the brainstorming session. Another benefit "Yes and . . ." has in brainstorming is the power to shift everyone's perspective in the moment to one of possibilities and innovation accompanied by the energy and feeling of empowerment and encouragement. "Yes but . . ." feelings are often discouraging and have low energy. Think about your own life. How does it feel to throw out an idea and the response is "Yes but . . .?"

Awesome Brainstorming Session

For three years, I was part of a mastermind group of six professionals in the consulting and coaching world who met on the phone once a month to talk and share best-case practices. My friend Bud Roth and I started the group, inviting others we thought would make the sum of the parts greater than our individual efforts. Bud invited those he knew from a coach training school in Santa Barbara who were contributing significantly to their communities and society. After meeting for two years over the phone, we decided to meet in person for two days of brainstorming ideas and strategies with each other about the best approach to making a difference in the world using our individual expertise. Those two days were the most powerful experience I've ever had with brainstorming strategies.

Ann Connor was an expert in emotional intelligence. John Schuster had written a book, worked with several large clients, and done many speaking engagements. Mike Lindgren covered the non-profit arena. Bud and I were facilitating large-group conference calls in our consulting and executive coaching businesses. We all brought insights, ideas, and specialized expertise to our brainstorming session, as well as creative mind-sets.

We chose different topics to focus on during our two days together and then got down to the business of brainstorming. What I loved about our brainstorming sessions were the crazy ideas we came up with. Those ideas sparked some outside-the-box thinking that led to clear and concise, actionable items we committed to following through on. They were so crazy that we had to stop at times to regain our composure because we were laughing so hard, we were crying. It was often at those moments of total abandonment that someone's eyes would open wide, and they'd say, "I just realized something I never thought of before." We took notes, wrote on flip charts, and made commitments to each other about the future of our individual businesses.

As a result, Bud wrote a book on coaching, *Be More Productive—Slow Down: Design the Life and Work You Want,* and put a program together to teach companies how to have a coaching culture in their company. John and his wife wrote another book, *Answering Your Call: A Guide for Living Your Deepest Purpose,* and they are currently on the speaking circuit. Ann went

STEP 2: THINK—BRAINSTORM STRATEGIES

back to school for her doctorate, and is now teaching. I (with partners) put together a company called Conscious Choosing, LLC, developed the training Conscious Choosing for Flow, and wrote this book. I am confident that many of the things in our lives might never have happened if we didn't get together for our mountain-top brainstorming session.

BRAINSTORMING OCCURS WITHIN THE GAP

The coaching gap I mentioned earlier is between where you are and where you want to go, your goal. Once this gap has been identified, you now work within this gap to come up with new possibilities or strategies to reach your shared goal. The purpose of brainstorming is to identify new and different strategies than previously thought about. That is, if you truly brainstorm and think outside the box. My experience with most executive teams is that they limit their brainstorming by filtering their ideas through their own judgments of whether their idea is plausible rather than considering all options that are conceivable. Because of this, creativity and possibilities are stifled. The coaching model and where brainstorming fits in looks like this:

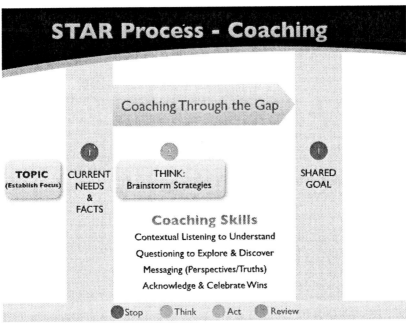

WHAT WE DON'T KNOW, WE DON'T KNOW

The magic about brainstorming is that we don't know what we don't know. If we are open to thinking outside the box, then new possibilities can arise that take us to new levels of productivity and influence in our world. Look at the following pie chart. When we think about all the knowledge in the world and then consider how much of that knowledge we actually know, the percentage might possibly be 0.5%. (I think this is generous, but then again, you may think you know more than that.) Then if we stop and acknowledge all the knowledge that we know we don't know, like brain surgery, speaking Mandarin, how our brain works, how to live in the Sahara desert, and so on, then we might come up with another 2.5% of all the knowledge. (Again, your percentages may vary according to the benefit you give yourself.) Ultimately, after we accumulate what we know and what we know we don't know, we can then speculate that the remainder of all the existing knowledge in the world is what we don't know we don't know. This might be around 97% of all the knowledge in the world. Therefore, if we really make it safe and respectful in brainstorming, it can open up our thinking to some of the things that we don't know we don't know as we explore and discover new possibilities.

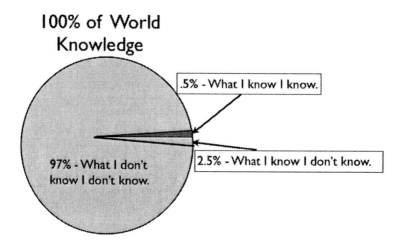

STEP 2: THINK—BRAINSTORM STRATEGIES

Curiosity Broke Through the Glass Ceiling

I was working with Paul Dunham of Dunham & Jones Law Offices, a law firm with offices in Austin and Ft. Worth, Texas. By his account, he had the largest criminal law practice in Texas dealing mostly with DWI cases. I would meet with him once a week at his office and work on challenges he was facing in his practice. One day he shared with me that, after 17 years, his firm was experiencing a glass ceiling in their ability to make money. You may be saying, "Ah, too bad!" Yet if you think about all of the attorneys, administrative staff and office buildings he managed, you could perhaps see his dilemma.

Sitting in a chair in front of Paul's desk, I said to him, "I'm going to teach you a skill that if you honestly use it, it will give you the ability to bust right through that ceiling you are experiencing."

His excitement was visible, and he prodded me to continue.

"The skill is to say, 'Mmmmm? I wonder . . .' and then let your mind think outside the box and truly get curious about what is possible that you have not yet thought of."

"This is a law office, Hayden." he responded. "We don't need any of your woo-woo stuff here. Give me something I can really use."

I asked him what he had tried to do to break through that ceiling. He responded that they sent out thousands of letters every month to those who had received DWIs. He even had his own postal center at his offices. He shared several other facts, ending by stating that he had done everything he could think of to increase their profits and yet he was still stuck.

"You are coming from a place of 'knowing' and need to get out of 'knowing' and into being curious." I responded. After some additional conversation, he asked me to close the door so the other attorneys wouldn't hear him saying it. He then jokingly said, "Mmmmm? I wonder . . . ?" and then looked at me sheepishly and said, "Now what?"

I asked him to rearrange his schedule for the next day by giving his appointments to some of the other attorneys. After some resistance, he reluctantly agreed. Then I asked him to stay in his office all morning

CONSCIOUS CHOOSING FOR FLOW

saying, "Mmmmm? I wonder . . ." and follow the prodding of his thought process. He said he would.

The following week he informed me that he did actually rearrange his schedule, sat in his office and said, "Mmmmm? I wonder . . ." For the first hour, he said he thought it was stupid and was wondering why he was following my ridiculous advice. Then after about an hour, he decided to take it seriously. He thought that since most of his business deals with DWI that perhaps he should have a website that has to do with DWI. So for the next hour he checked on various URL's that had to do with DWI, like DWIgetoff.com or DWIrelease.com, and so on. All of them were taken. Then a crazy idea occurred to him when he asked himself a wisdom access question, "What would be the very best website URL to have?" The answer was obvious to him—DWI.com.

He checked and found that the URL had been owned for many years by a company in Dorchester, England —Dorchester Workouts and Instruction— DWI.com. He called and got the owner on the phone and inquired if he would be willing to sell the URL to him. The owner said, "You're an attorney from the United States, aren't you? I get calls every day from you guys, and I'm not interested in selling it."

Paul continued to use the skill and said, "Mmmmm? I wonder if you mentioned a price and I said 'Sold,' what would that price be?"

The owner responded with, "You wouldn't be interested."

Paul replied, "Mmmmm? I wonder if you would take a chance and give me a try."

The owner said it would cost him several hundred thousands of dollars.

Paul said, "Sold." Two days later he owned the URL and put his technology team to work creating a website for it. They created a map of the United States with city names on it. An animated receptionist greeted you when you arrived at the site and asked you in which city you would like an attorney, to which you put in your request. The website generated hundreds of leads each day for those law firms in cities across the U.S.

STEP 2: THINK—BRAINSTORM STRATEGIES

Within six months, Paul had broken through that 17-year-old glass ceiling by three- to four-fold. Paul's comment to me was, "Hayden, I'm now making 'stupid money'." I think he was referring to what most of us would call 'plenty of mailbox money.'

Paul did his own brainstorming and then acted on it. For him, it was easy to come up with what needed to be done (call the guy in Dorchester, England), who was going to do it (he was), when it was going to be done (right away), and create a follow-up (an escrow account was set up to fulfill on the transaction).

When we get out of a mind-set of *knowing* and enter a mind-set of *curiosity*, new possibilities emerge that we can take action on to create the life we love and live it powerfully. Or as Tony Robbins, the motivational speaker and author, has said, "The only reason we don't have what we want in life is the reasons we create why we can't have them."[96]

STRATEGIES OFTEN VARY, SO MANAGE YOUR EXPECTATIONS

Strategies can vary based on the following:
- Generational differences
- Decision-making preferences
- Position and involvement
- Values, culture, and beliefs
- Past experiences

One of the most noticeable ways that strategies differ from one person to the next has to do with the generation we were born into and the worldview we have adopted because of this.[97]

For example, a Traditionalist, a person who has lived through a world war and the reality of combat, has learned to value the chain of command operational strategy. A Baby Boomer's frame of reference is entirely different. Born into the vast societal upheavals of the Civil Rights Movement and the Vietnam War, Boomers have learned how to embrace change. And so their operational strategy for meeting their needs is more Change of Command than Chain of Command. Generation X-ers provide another contrast. Many in this generation were latch-key kids, meaning they came home to an empty house because both their parents were working or because their single parent had to work to make ends meet. Therefore, these folks believe more in Self-Command. And insight into Millennials is still emerging.

Let's take a brief look at how generational influence might play out at work.

Your team is being led by a senior manager, someone who has been with the company for 30-plus years and is a Traditionalist. As a chain-of-command-style leader, he would likely expect any team member to check in with him before making any changes to the process in order to get the results agreed upon.

On the other hand, there are members on the team who are Generation X-ers, who value self-command, in part due to their latch-key upbringing in the '70s and '80s, when they learned independence while their Boomer parents were busy climbing the corporate ladder. Due to this very different worldview, X-ers likely assume that reaching the final results is more important than asking permission. They don't tend to seek approval for changes to the process.

Given these profound differences in life experience and worldview, we can easily imagine how these generational differences might cause a conflict in completing a project if participants do not discuss their different approaches or strategies. Each group has the same needs, but they employ very different strategies for meeting those needs. That is why speaking our expectations and coming up with clear agreements and commitments for follow-through are so important for keeping us out of the Regressive Cycle and in the Progressive Cycle.

STEP 2: THINK—BRAINSTORM STRATEGIES

MANAGING EXPECTATIONS

Progressive Cycle:	Regressive Cycle:
○ Spoken Expectations	○ Unspoken Expectations
○ Clear Agreements	○ Unclear Agreements
○ Shared Commitment	○ Lack of Commitment
○ Consistent Follow-through	○ Lack of Follow-through

LEADERS POISON THE WELL

The challenge that many leaders have when brainstorming with their teams or direct reports is poisoning the well. They short-circuit brainstorming before it actually gets started by contributing their own ideas before anyone else can share. This prevents others from contributing because they latch onto the leader's idea. Thus, the boss has poisoned the well, preventing others from dipping into it to gather the other 97% of "what they don't know they don't know."

So why did we go through the exercise of what we know, don't know, or don't know we don't know? To emphasize why brainstorming is so valuable for creativity and innovation. Without curiosity, we are accessing a very small percentage of awareness and consciousness in our world. With a little humility and respect for others, we may see something or think about something we may have never thought of unless we remain open to other's ideas.

In his book *Imagine*, Jonah Lehrer stresses the importance of gaining an outsider's perspective and encourages us to think outside the box on a regular basis in order to achieve new "awakenings" in our lives.[98] Since most of us approach life a bit more along the lines of coming from a place

CONSCIOUS CHOOSING FOR FLOW

of knowing, making brainstorming a part of our regular approach to problem solving is a great start. Someone once said, "When you learn how to learn, you have learned all you need to learn."

Staying Curious Leads to Simple Solutions

Juan Garza was the former city manager of Corpus Christi, Texas. He later went on to serve as the general manager for Austin Energy in Austin, Texas, and as the general manager for the Pedernales Electric Cooperative (PEC), the largest rural electric cooperative in the United States.

During his tenure in Corpus Christi, it came to his attention that the machine that cleaned the highway just before the lines got painted on the road was at the end of its life. The replacement cost was very high for the department's budget, around $200,000.

Juan knew that the money for this replacement machine was not there, and so he went to his staff and asked for alternatives. They came back with the option of mounting a large sweeping implement to the back of a pickup truck. The cost was far less, around $40,000.

Juan was pleased, but he believed that another option might still exist. And so he asked his team to keep thinking about it. Shortly thereafter, the man who actually drove the truck was cleaning the hose that delivered the paint to the road surface. He noticed that the water he used to clear the hose came out of pressurized sprayer with considerable force. **He became curious.**

After tinkering around with the equipment, he came back to Juan with his idea. He told Juan that this same type of pressurized hose could be directed at the spot to be painted just before the paint was delivered to the road surface. All that was needed was the hose and air tank attached to the truck.

The cost? About $12.00.

MAKE REQUESTS TO BRAINSTORM STRATEGIES

Sometimes as leaders, our worst enemy resides between our own two ears. When we brainstorm with others, as Juan did, new possibilities present themselves. Without asking those closest to the problem, we are cutting

STEP 2: THINK—BRAINSTORM STRATEGIES

ourselves off from valuable information. So, if you think any of the people you work with don't have something to contribute, think about what the Dalai Lama said: "If you think you are too small to make a difference, try sleeping with a mosquito."[99]

The Skill for Connection

Honestly Express (OFN-R)
Your **O**bservations
Your **F**eelings
Your **N**eeds

Curiously Investigate (OFN-R)
Their **O**bservations
Their **F**eelings
Their **N**eeds

CURIOUS REQUEST

Request for Brainstorming Strategies: "I'm curious, would you be willing to..."

HONESTLY EXPRESSING AND CURIOUSLY INVESTIGATING USING JUAN GARZA'S EXAMPLE:

OBSERVATIONS

Honestly Expressing: "I've checked in with several people about a solution to our problem and have gathered some ideas and estimates to minimize our expenses."

Curiously Investigating: "I'm curious—would you be willing to do some more brainstorming before we pull the trigger on this solution?"

FEELINGS

Honestly Expressing: "I'm feeling a bit uncomfortable right now about the solutions gathered so far. I think there might be more we could investigate or other people we should ask."

Curiously Investigating: "Are you feeling the same way?"

NEEDS

Honestly Expressing: "I have a need for discovery and effectiveness; that we have considered all possibilities and conferred with people, like the road crew, who are closest to the challenge."

Curiously Investigating: "I'm curious if you have the same need?"

Make a Curious Request: "Would you all be willing to check with the road crew and ask them to come up with some ideas of their own before we choose our strategy to solve this challenge?"

Using safety and respect in our interaction and brainstorming with each other will help us stay in the Progressive Cycle and come up new and inventive ideas for reaching our Shared Goal. Once we've generated possible strategies, then we need to agree on which ones we will use prior to acting on them. The best tool I have ever come across for collaborating and agreeing on strategies is the Consensus Tool.

CONSENSUS TOOL FOR COLLABORATION

After brainstorming to come up with so many ideas, it is often difficult to agree on which one to use that most can agree with and support while at the same time maintaining the human connection. In my work with a health care system, I learned of a tool that fits the bill. It's called the **Consensus Tool** and it has ground rules for collaboration and a hand signal scale for gauging support.

STEP 2: THINK—BRAINSTORM STRATEGIES

THE FOUNDATION OF COLLABORATION IS THAT IT IS:
- Safe and mutually respectful
- Inclusive
    - Values diversity and minority views
    - Discourages cliques
    - Targets un-discussable subjects and silo mind-sets
- Open and fact-based
    - Investigates thoroughly
    - Considers all ideas fairly
    - Bases decisions on facts and shared values
- Consensus seeking

COLLABORATION GROUND RULES INCLUDE:
1. We take off our individual hats and put on our team or organization hats.
2. All team members will speak freely and in turn as we:
    a. Listen attentively to others,
    b. View all members as equal,
    c. Give all members the opportunity to be heard,
    d. Take turns speaking, and
    e. Refrain from dominating or discounting other's opinions.
3. Problems, not people, will be discussed, analyzed, or critiqued.
4. We value honesty before cohesiveness—no artificial agreements.
5. The meeting is the time for diversity to be leveraged.
6. We form agreements by consensus, whereby each gets their say, not their way. Silence equals agreement.
7. Once agreement is reached, the team will speak with **one voice**—especially after leaving meetings.

WHAT IS CONSENSUS?
- Consensus is . . .
    - Finding a solution acceptable enough that all members can support it, and no members strongly oppose it.

- Gaining understanding through group curiosity using hand notifications. This provides more insight into each other's strength of opinion than a straight up or down vote indicates.
- Determined through use of hand voting.
- Willingness, a "choose to do it" heart- and mind-set (WALK the Talk).

♦ Consensus is **not**...
  - *A unanimous vote*—consensus may not represent everyone's first priorities.
  - *A majority vote*—in a majority vote, only the majority gets something they are happy with; people in the minority may get something they don't want at all.
  - *Everyone totally satisfied.*

HAND NOTIFICATIONS MEASURE SUPPORT

Hand notifications are used to gauge each person's support of a strategy. These hand signals provide more insight into the opinions of each person than a straight up or down vote.

STEP 2: THINK—BRAINSTORM STRATEGIES

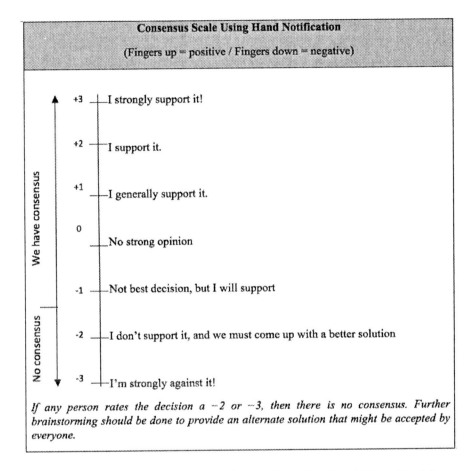

Consensus Tool. Used by permission from Regional West Healthcare Services, Scottsbluff, Nebraska

Consensus Tool Used to Get Engagement

I conducted an executive briefing over the phone with the executive team of a regional hospital in the Midwest. After a question and answer period, I asked if we would be working together. The CEO said they would

CONSCIOUS CHOOSING FOR FLOW

have to talk about it and get back to me at a later date. I briefly mentioned the consensus tool and the related hand signals and asked if he would be willing to give it a try with those in the room. He agreed. The hand signals went up, and the CEO said, "We have plus threes all the way around the room. I guess we're going to work together." By using the simple hand signals, the CEO was able to get a quick read on the entire group in the matter of a few seconds, making the decision process quicker and easier than a long discussion would have been.

The hand signals of the consensus tool are used to read each person's enthusiasm or hesitation about a strategy moving forward. In a quick look around the room, the hand signals gauge the positive, neutral, and negative feelings and thoughts about the strategy being talked about. It is simple and easy, and it can be done without talking. From this point, the leader or facilitator can see who has fingers pointing down and can then ask questions in order to gather new insights and ideas. While consensus doesn't mean that everyone must strongly support a strategy (+3 fingers up), strong lack of support (-2 or -3) means that consensus has not been established, and additional discussion and brainstorming is necessary. Consensus then means that regardless of each person's individual enthusiasm, everyone will support the strategy.

Quick Read Shifts Schedule

While conducting a strategy meeting with 18 executives of American YouthWorks who were deciding on whether to hold an additional meeting the following Friday to reach a decision on an issue they were facing, the leader asked for a show of consensus using the hand signals. There were plus two and plus three fingers all the way around the room except for one key person who held up negative three. The leader asked why he was against meeting next Friday. He responded that he had a critical meeting with fundraisers that day and couldn't come, but that he could meet on Saturday instead. The leader then asked for another show of consensus for a Saturday meeting and there were plus twos and plus threes throughout the entire room. By pausing and asking for hand signals, the leader was quickly able to identify a challenge and address it within minutes. This use of hand signals with the consensus tool is curiosity in action.

As you've seen, taking other's feelings and needs seriously doesn't require a lot of time. It does take giving them a chance to express themselves to the group in even a simple way. This provides a sense of safety and respect for each person, since they now have an opportunity to express their opinion, reflecting their feelings and needs. When this occurs, people feel a greater willingness to risk and openness to sharing their opinion. They also have the opportunity to bring new and different strategies or solutions to the group. When people are willing to take a risk, creativity and innovation begin to happen. When creativity and innovation happen, the group's morale increases, leading to exceptional results and on-going growth and development within the relationship, team and organization. This is the positive cascade effect of the Progressive Cycle.

RESPECT IS A CORE HUMAN NEED

> "**Respect** is to human relationships what **oil** is to a car's engine. Without Respect, relationships break down as quickly as an engine does without oil."
>
> — Conscious Choosing

I have used the word *respect* many times in this book. Conscious Choosing for Flow begins with this premise: All human beings, simply by virtue of being alive, deserve basic human dignity and respect. Respect is one of our meta-needs as human beings; something that each of us, no matter where we were raised or what our personality type is, holds very dear and precious to our lives.

So this is what I mean when I refer to Respect:
- **Respect** refers to our **basic humanness.**
- **Respect** does not require that you agree with the strategy people use to meet their needs.
- **Respect** acknowledges that others and you have feelings and needs.

CONSCIOUS CHOOSING FOR FLOW

Head Negotiator Uses Respect in Hostage Situations

My brother Phil retired from the FBI a few years ago, where he trained new agents and SWAT teams at the FBI headquarters in Quantico, Virginia. I would often visit him and watch some of the trainings before he and I would go over to the main building and work out at the gym together. He would often introduce me to other FBI agents.

On one occasion, he introduced me to the head negotiator for hostage situations. While shaking his hand, I asked him, "So what is it that has made you the head negotiator for hostage situations?" His reply surprised me.

"I was raised in a community where there was a profound level of respect for nature and for other human beings, no matter if they were like us or quite different. This has stuck with me throughout my life, and I am able to show that same level of respect to hostage takers, even though I completely disagree with their tactics. They can hear that respect in my voice and in the questions I ask them. I'm able to create a connection with them, while other negotiators create disconnection from them through the tone of their voice and their comments. Terrible things can happen when that occurs."

Every human being has the same basic human needs and the fundamental right to meet those needs in ways that do not infringe upon the ability of others meeting their own needs. You may disagree with the strategy another person or group uses to meet their needs, as did the FBI hostage negotiator. In fact, you may not have faith or *trust* in their strategy. To you, their strategy may just seem wrong! Respect does not require that you agree with the strategies others use to meet their needs. It does require you to acknowledge that we all have feelings and needs that should be taken seriously and to respect that we each have the right to choose strategies to meet our own needs.

Respect is about honoring the human being in front of you. It's a common, core need that all humans have on some level and will fight to defend. For some, you'll find that it's their dominant need.

How we interact with others, whether we're an FBI hostage negotiator or a project lead or a husband or wife, our voice, facial expressions, and the words we use telegraph respect (or lack of it). We can trigger others'

STEP 2: THINK—BRAINSTORM STRATEGIES

reptilian brains to react negatively to us, or we can trigger their higher reasoning center by being authentically curious and respectful. It's up to us.

When Respect or Safety is at Risk...

Our "Reptilian Brain" goes into **overdrive**...

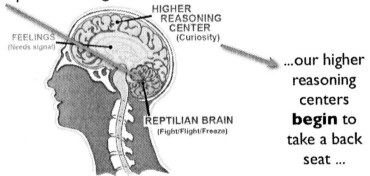

...our higher reasoning centers **begin** to take a back seat ...

...and we **instinctively** react with a Reptilian Reaction.

RESPECT AND TRUST

I've often heard people say, "You know, people have to earn my respect!"

With all due respect—pun intended—this statement confuses respect with trust.

What might be a more accurate statement is, "You know, people have to earn my trust." Trusting someone means that you have faith and belief in four things:

- Their **ability** to do what they say they will do
- Their **commitment** to follow through
- Positive **motivation** behind their actions
- A level of **communication** that will work for you.

Showing respect, even when there is a low level of trust, can provide enough safety to maintain or even transform interactions to establish or build a new level of trust. Curiosity is the respectful catalyst to transform

CONSCIOUS CHOOSING FOR FLOW

an interaction to a more empathic one, to transform disconnection to connection, and conflict to creativity.

Respectful Executive Builds Trust With Franchisee

Last year while conducting training in San Diego, an executive with an international company came up to me after our lunch break excited about a phone call he just had with a customer. His excitement stemmed from a breakthrough he had with this franchisee.

This customer purchased a franchise from his company and was initially quite excited about the possibilities. As the year progressed, her excitement turned into concern and then to anger that she wasn't getting the return on her investment that she expected. For the past three months, she had been calling this executive and yelling at him complaining about her return and blaming him for her financial failure.

He told me he used a very different approach with her this time that turned their "I versus you" conversation into a "we" conversation. He said his response to her complaining was, "I'm curious, what can we do to turn this around?" His curiosity and inclusion of himself in his question took her by surprise. He showed empathy for her situation and a willingness to help.

They then talked about possible strategies to meet her need for financial stability of her company. They came up with several possibilities that excited both of them, and agreed to put them into place right away. A new level of trust about his intentions and their ability to work together to reach a shared goal for a greater ROI was being established as they talked.

He shared that in the past he had typically justified his company's approach, but he hadn't been curious or shown empathy about what was going on with her. He said that this new approach of using curiosity and empathy for her seemed so simple, yet it had a profound effect on their interaction, turning their disconnection into connection for greater collaboration and partnership.

STEP 2: THINK—BRAINSTORM STRATEGIES

NEEDS BEFORE STRATEGIES

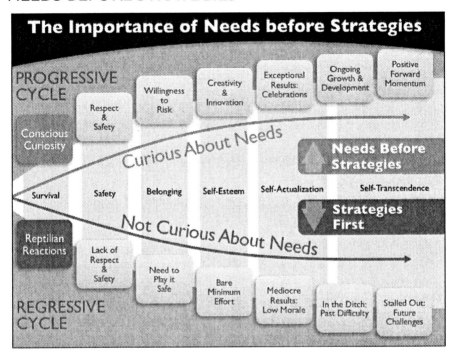

Progressive Cycle	Regressive Cycle
Needs before strategies	Strategies first
Create shared goal	No shared goal
Strategies to meet goal	Strategies that may or may not meet goal
Consensus on strategy	Buy-in unknown
Commitment	Uncertainty
Completion meets goal	Completion may not solve original need
On to solve the next challenge	Still trying to solve original challenge

CONSCIOUS CHOOSING FOR FLOW

Pat Requests Brainstorming for Better Solutions

Pat, a Senior VP of a large health care insurance company, reported to me that he had a employee under his direct supervision who was "quick with solutions and short on brainstorming." He said that when he went to her with a problem in her area, her immediate response was, "OK. This is what we'll do." He admitted that most of her solutions worked. After all, she was the company's resident expert in her field.

One day he decided to approach his conversations with her a little differently. He had a need to be seen as an innovative leader with new and different ideas. His strategy was to engage this woman by challenging her habit of "already always knowing" the answers. This time when he went to her with a problem, he prefaced his comments with, "When I tell you the challenge, I'd like us to think of at least three different ways we could handle this challenge before deciding on the solution." Initially, he was met with resistance, since she thought she had a handle on the best approach each and every time.

"It was a struggle at first," he reported. "But then it turned into a little game of coming up with some solutions outside of the proverbial box." Eventually, when he went to her with future problems, she would say, "I know, you want three possible solutions. Well, I think between the two of us, we can come up with five or six."

They began to have fun with this approach, and their work results continued to improve. The solutions they eventually came up with caught the watchful eyes of his peers and the CEO.

STEP 2: THINK—BRAINSTORM STRATEGIES

PERSONAL APPLICATION: BRAINSTORM STRATEGIES

Now, refer back to your personal challenge and brainstorm strategies that would meet your shared goal and would work for both you and person you are having a challenge with. You can write in the space here or in the full personal challenge worksheet at the end of the book.

Remember, the STAR Process for Results is interactive. You will likely generate additional strategies when working through it with another person.

The Key: Choose Curiosity

The key is to choose curiosity about all the strategies that could meet your needs and not just focus on one strategy, which would limit your possibilities.

PERSONAL CHALLENGE: TRANSFORM CONFLICT INTO CREATIVITY

STAR Process for Results

STOP ♦ THINK ♦ ACT ♦ REVIEW

2. THINK: Brainstorm Strategies

Think of possible strategies that would meet your shared goal and would work for both of you.

_____
_____
_____
_____
_____
_____
_____

Chapter 13

STEP 3: ACT—REQUESTS FOR COMMITMENTS

Roles and Responsibilities

"You may never know what results will come from your actions. But if you do nothing, there will be no result."

— Mahatma Gandhi[100]

ASSIGN ROLES AND RESPONSIBILITIES

After creating a shared goal and brainstorming strategies to use to reach that shared goal, step 3 in the STAR Process for Results is Act—assigning roles and responsibilities to those who will take actions to accomplish the goal. This involves making requests for commitments, forming clear agreements with those tasked with the multitude of activities in any project or initiative, and staying focused on the job at hand.

Often, teams are good at deciding what needs to be done but stop short of clearly identifying and getting commitments around who will be responsible for what and when it will be done and setting up a follow-up to make sure the task was done to the standards and quality expected. How roles and responsibilities are established will affect the level of commitment and attitude employed to complete the task.

WALK THE TALK TO BUILD ACCOUNTABILITY

We've all heard the expression "walk the talk." It generally means that our behavior is in alignment with our words. In Conscious Choosing, WALK the Talk stands for:

Willingness, an "I *choose* to do it" heart- and mind-set.

Alignment to shared goals and strategies

Loop back to the team with any challenges

Keep commitments as assigned and scheduled, and follow up

STEP 3: ACT—REQUESTS FOR COMMITMENTS

Walking the Talk is being absolutely clear around what is expected of each person, having clear agreements of who is going to do what and when it is going to be done, and scheduling a clear follow-up. This structure builds accountability, follow-through, and trust with those involved.

W: Willingness—the "I **choose** to do it" heart and mind-set

Willingness addresses "Why do you want people to do what you are asking them to do?" Because they choose to and not because they are being forced to do something. People are willing to commit when their internal conversation of "What's in it for me?" (WIIFM) has been satisfied. They will understand that their underlying needs will be met by taking the action. We'll get into the difference between requests and demands later.

A: Alignment to shared goals and strategies

In step 1, Stop, of the STAR Process for Results, we identified the current needs and the shared goal that we would all focus on meeting. Then we moved to step 2, Think, where we brainstormed strategies to meet our needs, using the consensus tool to align on the strategies we'll use to reach our shared goal. Now, in step 3, Act, we align the actions we will take to fulfill on the strategy we're using to reach the shared goal.

L: Loop back to the team with any challenges.

Challenges arise. Life happens. "Loop back to the team with any challenges" acknowledges disruptions and unforeseen roadblocks, keeps the team aware of any challenges, and allows those involved to make adjustments as needed to keep the team on track to reach the shared goal. One of the biggest frustrations in working as a team is finding out after the fact that a commitment has not been met. Communication manages expectations and maintains safety and respect for the team.

K: **K**eep commitments as assigned and scheduled, and follow up

Too often, action items are loosely committed to. We generally know what needs to be done but **who** does **what** by **when,** as well as how will we know it was done, is all vague. Keeping commitments by clearly assigning, scheduling, and creating a follow-up provides structure and accountability. A grid like this can be used to monitor commitments:

Commitment (What)	Assigned (Who)	Scheduled (When)	Follow-up (Date & Time)

Following Up Reduces Challenges

While working with the Livestrong Foundation (prior to Lance Armstrong's admission of doping), COO Betty Otter-Nickerson asked me to work with their challenge team. This team was the major fundraising arm of the foundation, arranging various cycling events around the country where participants got sponsors and contributed to the foundation. Each and every day, members of the team would visit her office or the

STEP 3: ACT—REQUESTS FOR COMMITMENTS

president's office six or seven times with problems they needed help with in dealing with vendors, volunteers, or municipalities for events.

During our two-day retreat, we talked about WALK the Talk and the importance of follow-up. We created follow-ups with many of their issues. After seeing the value of follow-ups, the team agreed that most of their problems stemmed from not making follow-ups with every individual or group they worked with, so they agreed to do so in the future prior to hanging up the phone or moving on to the next meeting. The team leader wrote their agreement on a piece of paper and passed it around the room for each person to sign.

Six months later, I ran into the president of the foundation, Doug Ulman. He asked me, "What did you do with the challenge team?" I got curious and asked him what he meant. He said, "Before your retreat with them, they would come into my office or Betty's office six or seven times a day. Now I'm lucky if I see them once a week. And I noticed that when I talk with them, and we agree to do something, their last question of me is, 'When would you like to set a follow-up to make sure we've gotten it done?'" He said he noticed himself getting a little angry over this last question, surprised that they would say that to the president. Then he looked at their numbers. They were bringing in two to three times more than the year before with far less hassle for him and others. He admitted that he is now asking that very same question, "When would you like to set a follow-up to make sure we complete on this agreement?"

FOLLOW UP TO ACHIEVE SPECIFIC RESULTS

Follow-ups create accountability if properly set because those involved know when they will meet to follow up on commitments made. The problem most people have is setting vague follow-ups that may happen, but most likely won't happen. When we say, "Let's meet next week sometime and talk about the project," we are actually setting false expectations by making vague commitments about meeting. The other person has no idea "when" and "what" will actually be talked about. All that's known is maybe there will be another meeting next week to talk about something concerning the project and maybe not.

A clear follow-up has three aspects:
1. Specific time
2. Specific place
3. Specific purpose

So, to restate the previous statement, I would say, "Let's meet next Wednesday morning for coffee at 8:00 to talk about the resources and personnel needed for our project." This has a clear date, time, and purpose. As Dr. Donald Berwick is famous for saying in his "Save 100,000 Lives" campaign, "Some is not a number. Soon is not a time."[101] Taking this further, I like to add:

"Some is not a number. Soon is not a time. And hope is not a plan."

If you want to achieve specific (not general) results, personally or professionally, make sure you are absolutely clear about **what** is being committed to and by **whom**, **when** it will be done, and the date and time of the follow-up. You can always physically or mentally fill out the WALK the Talk grid. In order to get predictable and sustainable results, we must have a plan and we must work it.

ACTIONS CLOSE THE GAP

Taking decisive and coordinated action is the last step in the coaching model to fill in the gap. It is this step that brings you from strategizing to achieving your shared goal. Without being absolutely clear on *who* is doing *what* by *when* with *follow-up* in the WALK the Talk grid and taking specific, concrete actions, there is no clarity towards or certainty of reaching your shared goal. If reaching your shared goal is important to you, make sure you complete this step. This is what it looks like in the coaching model:

STEP 3: ACT—REQUESTS FOR COMMITMENTS

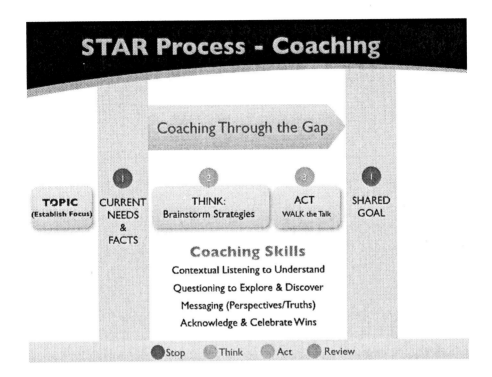

AGREEMENTS MANAGE EXPECTATIONS

When we speak our expectations, form clear agreements, and make firm commitments to follow up, we can limit the struggles and conflict in our lives. Alternatively, we can keep our mouths shut, expect others to know what we need from them (reading minds is a difficult skill set to master), and somehow believe they will act in a way that makes our life more wonderful. This is a great hope, but it is not grounded in reality. The choice of how we manage the existence of ourselves, and our interactions with others, is ours. We have the power to operate in the Progressive Cycle or the Regressive Cycle.

MANAGING EXPECTATIONS

Progressive Cycle:	Regressive Cycle:
○ Spoken Expectations	○ Unspoken Expectations
○ Clear Agreements	○ Unclear Agreements
○ Shared Commitment	○ Lack of Commitment
○ Consistent Follow-through	○ Lack of Follow-through

Not Having Clear Agreement Creates Tolerations

My wife and I have friends we get together with occasionally. Each time we see this couple, they complain about how their son and his wife have been living with them during their first year of marriage. They complain about how they don't contribute financially to the running of the house (electric, water, garbage, etc.) or even buy groceries, although the family eats together almost every night. They also complain that his son and his wife make no physical contributions, either, like helping with cooking and yard work or cleaning the house. "They're just freeloading off us!"

I've asked, "Have you talked with them about this, before they moved in or any time since?"

They looked at me with an incredulous look and said, "We shouldn't have to ask them; they're family. They should just know to help out."

"I hear that speaking our expectations and setting up agreements can really help relationships while keeping the friction between everyone to a minimum."

They reply, "Oh, Hayden. You just don't know our family."

(Obviously, I'm not making much of a difference here. Although their complaining is entertaining sometimes, it's difficult to see people live in their misery by blaming someone else for creating it by not clearly stating their expectations and making clear agreements.)

STEP 3: ACT—REQUESTS FOR COMMITMENTS

THE DIFFERENCE BETWEEN REQUESTS AND DEMANDS

I've talked a lot about managing expectations and following through on commitments. Now let's consider the ways that we ask, or request, others to perform tasks and take actions we've (individually or collectively) identified as necessary for achieving our shared goal. Assuming that we are actually speaking our expectations rather than just expecting others to know what they are, we can make requests or we can make demands. Requests have the power to recruit others and to incite passion and vision. On the other hand, demands have the power to squelch passion and bar vision.

Why do you want people to do what they are going to do? Because they feel pressure to do it as a "have-to" or because they "choose to do it?" Which approach do you think will provide you with the best results possible? If you make a demand and tell them what they have to do, they may go to a place of feeling like a victim or making you the villain. In that case, they will lack the passion and commitment to follow through on the task at hand. On the other hand, if they have choice in their decisions and have gotten in touch with the need it will satisfy in them, you probably will have buy-in.

So let's consider the differences between requests and demands.

Needs	Request	Demand
Attention	Attention is on the needs of others and myself	Attention is on the "have-to"
Intention	To get needs fulfilled and to fulfill the task at hand	To get others to do what I want
Appreciation	My appreciation for the other person does not change if the other one says no or counters.	I do not appreciate the other person as much if they say no.
Trust	I trust that my needs will be considered and satisfied.	I am scared that my needs do not count.

CONSCIOUS CHOOSING FOR FLOW

When we make requests of others, there are three possible answers—yes, no, and a counter. When we make demands of others, there is only one possible answer (for us)—yes. You know you are making a demand (possibly disguised as a request) when no or a counteroffer is not an acceptable answer. This is the classic "Do it because I said so" command. How many of us heard this as kids from the adults in our lives? Even as a child, did it feel respectful to you?

Examples of demands disguised as requests might be:
- "You should have finished that today, so would you please stay late and get the report to me by 8:00 a.m. tomorrow morning?"
- "You're supposed to be in charge of that, so will you take over the xyz project?"

Marshall Rosenberg makes the distinction between requests and demands when he says, "When the other person hears a **demand** of us, they see two options: to **submit** or to **rebel**."[102]

So, as an 18-year-old, I rebelled and drove my motorcycle through my parent's house. I didn't speak to them for a year as I traveled the U.S. on my motorcycle. Obviously, in the workplace, rebelling shows up in more discreet and subversive behavior. Earlier, I mentioned the Gallup poll that showed that 70% of employees are not engaged at work. This is worse than quitting, since those who stay are not engaged in propelling the company forward. What is even worse than not being engaged is quitting and staying. In other words, retiring in place.

REQUESTS ARE AN OPPORTUNITY TO CONNECT

The benefit of requests is that they keep respect and safety in place as we travel down the road to our destination in any project or shared goal we've created with others. One of our greatest needs as human beings is to have a say in our lives, to have autonomy in the way we choose to work and run our lives. Albert Bandura,[103] a professor emeritus of social science in psychology at Stanford University who is widely described in the U.S. as the greatest living psychologist, wrote that self-efficacy plays a critical role in "what people think, believe, and feel [which] affects how they behave."[104]

STEP 3: ACT—REQUESTS FOR COMMITMENTS

When we make requests of others, it allows them the autonomy to choose their response. What helps them choose in a way that works for them is to clearly understand what need of theirs will be met by consciously choosing to be enrolled in the actions necessary to fulfill the project, task, or endeavor. (We covered this earlier in the chapter 2 exercise of turning "I have to" into "I choose to.") There are consequences to our choices. If we are consciously aware of them, we will come from a place of personal choice.

What do we do if we receive a no or if someone counters our request? We may take these responses as a refusal to get the work done, but let's take a closer look at what is going on. Why would a person say no or counter our request? Usually it's because there is something that isn't working for them. Their needs are not being met through fulfillment of our request. This is an opportunity to use Conscious Curiosity, to connect with the person and uncover additional information that may ultimately provide a better solution rather than creating a crisis to overcome. By inquiring as to what is stopping them or what's preventing them from fulfilling your request and exploring and discovering through curiosity, you will find out more about what's going on with them—you'll learn their ideas and possibly a new way of completing the task. Or you may find out through further inquiry that they aren't engaged at all and that they want off the project, which is better to know at the start, rather than halfway through a project.

Sometimes you may have to go back to strategizing again because you become aware of roadblocks: unreasonable time frames, resource restrictions, or lack of manpower with the necessary expertise. Some roadblocks are easily removed, like American YouthWorks changing a meeting date. Other roadblocks may be more difficult to overcome, like ultimately accepting the resignation of a valued but misaligned employee. The bottom line is that any response to a request is an opportunity to create results through our human connection, rather than creating disconnection with others in conflict, stress, or confusion.

TWO TYPES OF REQUESTS

It's important to realize that we can make two types of requests—one for connection with others and one for results. We can combine them or keep

CONSCIOUS CHOOSING FOR FLOW

them separate. Requests begin with the words, "Would you be willing to...?" Or "What do you need from me...?"

Connection: These requests are about **people to people.** We want to fine-tune our relationships with others by connecting with them at a different level than perhaps we've done in the past.

> "**Would you be willing to** spend a few minutes talking with me about what we both really need in our working relationship for our work together to be successful?"

Requesting Connection Improves Relationship

Jennifer, a senior VP at a major health care insurance company, told me she has a direct report that calls herself a needs-based manager." When I asked what she meant by this, she related this story to me.

This manager had a direct report who butted heads with her on a regular basis. Getting results with her proved to be a struggle, and she wanted to change the dynamics. So she went to this direct report and said, "I'd like to have a better working relationship with you than we currently have. What do you need from me in order for that to take place?"

She admitted that what she thought her direct report would say is, "I'd like a raise or a promotion." But she didn't say those things. What she said was, "I'm in here every morning before you are. While sitting in my cubicle, I watch you come in and walk right past me without ever saying a word. All that I really want is for you to say hi to me when you come in."

What was the need that wasn't being met that drove the upsets in their interactions? She had a need for acknowledgement and perhaps gratitude that she was in there each morning earlier than most other employees. Three months later, I asked how the relationship was going now. She related that they really enjoyed working with each other, and their relationship had done a 180-degree turn around.

The request this needs-based manager made of her direct report was for connection. She asked directly, "What do you need from me in order for us to have a better working relationship?" Once we have created the

STEP 3: ACT—REQUESTS FOR COMMITMENTS

human connection and have entered into Flow, it's far easier to get results in our working relationship.

Results: These requests are about **people to tasks.** We have something to be accomplished, and we make a request of someone to complete it.

> **"Would you be willing to** spend a few minutes each Monday morning with me before our staff meeting (connection) to get clear on our priorities for the staff for the week (tasks)?"

THE POWER OF POSITIVE DOABLE REQUESTS (PDR)

Suppose I were to say to you, "Don't think about the pink rabbit!" It's only human nature to picture a pink rabbit in your mind. I have put the pink rabbit into your thinking, and you are now putting some energy into what you were asked not to do: "Don't think about the pink rabbit!" It is hard to do a "don't." That's why I like to say,

> **"Where focus goes, energy Flows."**

When we provide direction by using a negative, we are actually putting people's focus on exactly what we don't want them to put it on, and they will put their energy into trying not to do it. Unfortunately, this negative attention often causes the very thing we don't want to happen to be manifested.

Positive doable requests, on the other hand, focus on and direct energy toward the results we really want. When our entire focus is on what we want to do, we may find ourselves in the zone, as Mihaly Csikszentmihalyi found in his research. This creates Flow, removing resistance from our thinking and actions.

So let's put our energy where we really want to focus, on the task at hand.

> **Positive:** Ask for what you need rather than what you don't need. (It's hard to do a don't!)
>
> **Doable:** Ask for specific actions rather than vague behaviors like "fair," "reasonable" or "helpful."

Doable is the key is to making each request actionable, something that someone can actually do like, "**Would you be willing to** touch base with me each Monday morning to see if our goals for the week are in alignment?" This is positive and actionable. This is what we want to happen and it is something that the other person can actually do. Alternatively, I know the owner of a company who vehemently demands of his employees, "Don't ever be late to our meetings again!" Guess what? In the three years of running his business, he has never had a meeting where everyone was on time. He put their focus on—you guessed it—being late.

EXAMPLES OF NEGATIVE OR NOT DOABLE:
- "I want you to understand me." (Not doable—it's not actionable. The idea of "understanding" resides in your head, and no one else knows exactly what that means.)
- "Please don't be late to the meeting." (Not positive)
- "Don't forget to take out the garbage." (Not positive)
- "Please don't argue with me." (Not positive or doable. Again, what "argue" means to me might be very different than what it means to you.)
- "Don't sabotage the team." (Not positive or doable. "Sabotage" is a meaning.)
- "I want this negotiation to be fair and reasonable." (Not doable)

Try your hand at making **positive doable requests for connection and results** in this quick exercise.
1) Example: A co-worker is refusing to help you with a project that you both committed to working on.

   PDR for connection: "**Would you be willing to** meet with me to talk about how we work together and what commitments mean to us?"

   PDR for results: "Would you be willing to brainstorm with me to come up with some ideas for completing the project?"

STEP 3: ACT—REQUESTS FOR COMMITMENTS

2) Your son hasn't taken the garbage out and isn't responding to you while he's playing a video game.

   PDR for connection: _____

   PDR for results: _____

3) Your boss asked you to stay late at work today to get a report done.

   PDR for connection: _____

   PDR for results: _____

4) Your friend wants to use your house to throw a party.

   PDR for connection: _____

   PDR for results: _____

Here are some possible answers:
1) Example: A co-worker is refusing to help you with a project that you both committed to working on.

   PDR for connection: "**Would you be willing** to meet with me to talk about how we work together and what commitments mean to each of us?"

   PDR for results: "**Would you be willing** to brainstorm with me to come up with some ideas for completing the project?"

2) Your son hasn't taken the garbage out and isn't responding to you while he's playing a video game.

CONSCIOUS CHOOSING FOR FLOW

PDR for connection: "Son, **would you** please pause your video game long enough for us to talk?" (Some people have said they would pull the plug on the video game. I'm wondering how respectful you think the son would think that was when all his efforts have been erased.)

PDR for results: "Son, **would you** please put out the garbage after you are done playing your game and before 5:00?" (Again, some have said he's a kid, and he'd better do as I tell him he should do. Again, I'm wondering how respectful this kid will think that is and whether he will drive his motorcycle through the house when he's 18 (as I did) saying, "Hasta la vista!")

3) Your boss asked you to stay late at work today to get a report done.

PDR for connection: "Boss, **would you be willing to** meet with me this afternoon to talk about your request?"

PDR for results: "**Would you be willing to** talk about other ways I can get this report done without staying late, like taking the work home or letting me get help to complete it?"

4) Your friend wants to use your house to throw a party.

PDR for connection: "**Would you be willing to** meet with me and talk about how we are going to collaborate on this party?"

PDR for results: "**Would you be willing to** talk about other alternatives for throwing your party?"

STEP 3: ACT—REQUESTS FOR COMMITMENTS

MAKE REQUESTS FOR CONNECTION AND RESULTS

With the addition of making **positive doable requests,** we have some new distinctions that we can apply to the Skill for Connection. Let's see how it works.

The Skill for Connection

Honestly Express (OFN-R)	Curiously Investigate (OFN-R)
Your **O**bservations Your **F**eelings Your **N**eeds	Their **O**bservations Their **F**eelings Their **N**eeds

CURIOUS REQUEST

Request for Connection and Results: "I'm curious, would you be willing to..."

HONESTLY EXPRESSING AND CURIOUSLY INVESTIGATING WITH REQUESTS:

OBSERVATIONS

Honestly Expressing: "I've heard that you want us to get this project done by the first of the month with the current resources we have at our disposal."

Curiously Investigating: "Is that about right?"

FEELINGS

Honestly Expressing: "I'm feeling a bit nervous and anxious about fulfilling your request."

Curiously Investigating: "I'm wondering if you are feeling that way also or if you are feeling pretty confident?"

NEEDS

Curiously Investigating: "I need to confirm that the resources we have and the time frame is doable."

Curiously Investigating: "Would that be all right with you?"

Make a Curious Request: "Would you all be willing to meet with me tomorrow morning at 8:00 to talk about your request (connection) after I've had a chance to meet with my team to confirm we have the resources we require and the manpower to fulfill on your request by the first (results)?"

Honestly Expressing Yourself to the Boss

While bringing the executives of Data Tech through the Conscious Choosing for Flow training, the entire group had an aha moment during this section of the training. The aha centered around them not Honestly Expressing their needs to the two companies that owned them. The group of 32 executives realized that they focused on meeting their owners' needs without expressing what they needed in order for them to successfully meet their owners' needs and the shared goal.

What they needed was consideration and support for both themselves and the technology employed. The strategies they came up with were to update their technology platform, retain top technology engineers, rather than letting them be siphoned off by the new Microsoft office that opened in town, and to take the necessary time needed to fulfill their software needs.

STEP 3: ACT—REQUESTS FOR COMMITMENTS

They hadn't been Honestly Expressing themselves, and decided it was time. They realized as a group that there was some anger, fear of failure, and concern that they wouldn't meet the expectations of their owners. They needed to Honestly Express what they truly needed in order for all three companies to be successful as they moved into the new requirements of health care.

By Honestly Expressing their feelings and needs while making positive doable requests of their owners, they created an entirely new conversation about the three companies.

Let's look at what Data Tech did to Honestly Express themselves to the two companies that owned them.

> Data Tech met with one of their owner companies.
>
> They started off with: "We're wondering (curiosity) if we could talk with you about how to meet your objectives (request for connection and tasks)?"
>
> **Observations**: "We've been told by both of you (both owner companies) to limit cost by limiting spending on software and personnel and by taking less time on the software development. Is that about right?" The executives of their owner company agreed.
>
> **Feelings**: "We want to meet all your objectives, and yet we're feeling nervous about accomplishing that task without having our needs met as well."
>
> **Needs**: "We have a need for consideration and support concerning the strategies we've outlined to retain our top developers and upgrade our software, as well as a slightly different timeline for accomplishing your objectives. We think we all have the need to be successful in our interactions with each other."

CONSCIOUS CHOOSING FOR FLOW

Request: "**Would you be willing to** talk about these needs of ours with the other company to make sure we are all successful?"

The company agreed to talk with the other owner company to address their needs.

Of course, there were more words expressed in their meeting, but this was the gist of the conversation.

Making Requests to get commitments for action, getting absolute clarity on **what** was committed to, **who** is doing it, and **when** it will be done by, and setting a **follow-up** will help us stay in the Progressive Cycle.

MAKE REQUESTS INSTEAD OF DEMANDS

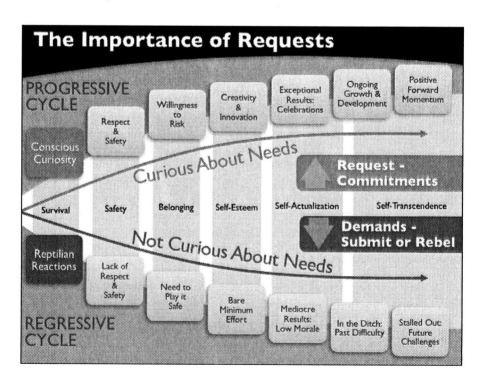

STEP 3: ACT—REQUESTS FOR COMMITMENTS

Progressive Cycle	**Regressive Cycle**
Request – Commitments	Demands – Submit or Rebel
Everyone's needs fulfilled	Autonomy challenged
Trust maintained	Trust undermined
I choose to do it mindset	Artificial agreements
Personal accountability	Lack of follow-through
No surprises or challenges	Last minute crisis
Actions completed	Actions reassigned

Failing to get curious in communication, brainstorm with the other members of a team or leadership group, and be absolutely clear on **who** is doing **what** by **when** with **follow-up** by making requests can have an adverse affect on our lives and businesses. When demands are placed on others, the resulting fear of punishment and retribution for questioning or not fulfilling the demand ultimately creates complacency and a go-along mentality. This perspective of "That's just the way we do things around here," creates conflict, stress, and confusion with others. I am reminded of a story someone shared with me that illustrates this in an experiment with monkeys where demands were made of them by spraying them with water if they didn't do what the experimenters wanted them to do.

> *A Culture of Demands Limits Creativity and Innovation* [105]
>
> Start with a cage containing five monkeys. Inside the cage, hang a banana on a string and place a set of stairs under it. Before long, a monkey will go to the stairs and start to climb toward the banana. As soon as he touches the stairs, spray all of the other monkeys with cold water. After a while, another monkey will makes an attempt and get the same result—all the other monkeys will be sprayed with cold water. Pretty soon, when another monkey tries to climb the stairs, the other monkeys will try to prevent him from doing it.
>
> Now, put away the cold water. Remove one monkey from the cage and replace it with a new one. The new monkey will see the banana and want to climb the stairs. To his surprise and horror, all of the other monkeys will attack him.

CONSCIOUS CHOOSING FOR FLOW

> After another attempt and attack, he will know that if he tries to climb the stairs, he will be assaulted.
>
> Next, remove another of the original five monkeys and replace it with a new one. The newcomer will go to the stairs and be attacked. The previous newcomer will take part in the punishment with enthusiasm! Likewise, replace a third original monkey with a new one, then a fourth, then the fifth.
>
> Every time the newest monkey takes to the stairs, he will be attacked. Most of the monkeys beating him will have no idea why they were not permitted to climb the stairs or why they are participating in the beating of the newest monkey.
>
> After replacing all the original monkeys, none of the remaining monkeys will have ever been sprayed with cold water. Nevertheless, no monkey will ever again approach the stairs to try for the banana.
>
> Why not? Because as far as they know, that's the way it's always been done around here. And that, my friends, is how company policy begins.
>
> By sharing this story, I'm hoping to make the point that often we live in reaction to what others do or say to us. Eventually we stop being curious. Instead, living in reaction to others becomes our way of simply getting along. As the experiment revealed, it's how company policy begins if no one is courageous enough to get curious and ask, "Why?"

PERSONAL APPLICATION: REQUESTS

Now, refer back to your personal challenge and make requests and commitments to fulfill on the strategies you have selected. You can write in the space here or in the full personal challenge worksheet at the end of the book.

Remember, the STAR Process for Results is interactive. Commitments are made only through requests and agreements.

STEP 3: ACT—REQUESTS FOR COMMITMENTS

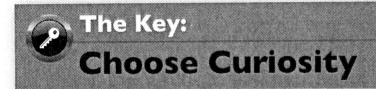

The key is to choose curiosity about **who** is doing **what** by **when** with **follow-up** to ensure accountability and commitment.

PERSONAL CHALLENGE: TRANSFORM CONFLICT INTO CREATIVITY

STAR Process for Results
STOP ◆ THINK ◆ ACT ◆ REVIEW

3. **ACT: Requests and Commitments**

What will you do?

_____

_____

What will you request of the other person for connection and results?

_____

_____

When will you do it?

_____

_____

How and when will you follow up to ensure the task was completed to the quality and standard you both agreed upon (date, time, and place)?

_____
_____

Chapter 14

STEP 4: REVIEW—STOP, MODIFY, OR START

Rest Stop!

"An error doesn't become a mistake until you refuse to correct it."

— Orlando A. Battista (1917–1995), Canadian-American chemist and author [106]

THE IMPORTANCE OF A REST STOP

Sometimes we need to slow down from our daily activity to take a rest stop and Review our progress in order to improve our relationships and the results we're getting. Review, the fourth and final step in the STAR Process for Results, may be the most important step because it reveals how the first three steps are working and whether we need to make any adjustments to reach our shared goal. In Review, we consider what we might need to Stop doing (something that isn't working), Modify (something that needs adjustment), or Start doing (something not yet present that would improve the situation) in order to get the very best results possible. It's a way of monitoring our relationships, teams, and operations to work toward the actual, measurable results we're committed to achieving.

REVIEW TO FINE-TUNE RELATIONSHIPS AND RESULTS

Review is an opportunity to check in with others, not just around tasks and work product, but also with respect to our relationships. It's a crucial aspect of Flow—taking the time to fine-tune the way we interact with others so that we can create the results we most want for those around us and ourselves, all while enjoying the process.

Review Maintains Flow in Relationship

Shortly after getting married 10 years ago, my wife Lani and I sat down and wrote out how we were committed to relating to each other

STEP 4: REVIEW—STOP, MODIFY, OR START

for respect, trust, and understanding, what we were committed to in our relationships, and what we each needed in our life together. We created a sheet with bullet points in these three categories that we called "our vows."

Once a month during morning coffee together, we look at this sheet and talk about whether there is anything we need to Stop doing, Modify, or Start doing in order to fulfill our vows and have the most awesome relationship any two people can have. It's our way of tracking how we're doing with each other.

Sometimes this review takes 10 minutes. Other times, there are things we really do need to talk about to keep our relationship clear of problems and to get the support and encouragement we need from each other. We write down what we need to Stop doing, Modify, or Start doing and then revisit it the following month to make sure we are continuing to improve in those areas and that we have truly done the things we agreed to. This review has given us some structure to consciously choose to keep the space between us clear and to exponentially capitalize on our differences.

REVIEW OFTEN TO KEEP SPACE CLEAR

When we first started our relationship reviews, I have to admit that Lani and I sometimes struggled with them. Too many times in our pasts, the phrase, "We need to talk about something" was a trigger for a painful conversation or the start to a fight. Feelings had been pent up, unmet needs accumulated, and a 'talk' meant the storm was about to be unleashed. In our relationship, we were and continue to be committed to keeping the space between us clear. To us, this means paying attention to our feelings as a guide to whether our needs are being met and speaking up before any challenges build enough steam to create conflict and disconnection between us.

The Skill for Connection

Honestly Express (OFN-R)
Your **O**bservations
Your **F**eelings
Your **N**eeds

Curiously Investigate (OFN-R)
Their **O**bservations
Their **F**eelings
Their **N**eeds

CURIOUS REQUEST

Request for Review: "I'm curious, would you be willing to..."

HONESTLY EXPRESSING AND CURIOUSLY INVESTIGATING USING MY RELATIONSHIP EXAMPLE:

OBSERVATIONS

Honestly Expressing (Lani): "I've really appreciated you cleaning up the kitchen by putting dishes in the dishwasher and washing the pans. I also noticed that each time you say you're done, the counters still have water and crumbs on them that haven't been wiped off."

Curiously Investigating: "I'm curious—have you noticed the same things?"

FEELINGS

Honestly Expressing (Lani): "I'm feeling a bit frustrated and annoyed with how the kitchen is looking after you say you're done cleaning up."

STEP 4: REVIEW—STOP, MODIFY, OR START

Curiously Investigating: "Do you have any feelings about this?"

NEEDS

Honestly Expressing (Lani): "I'm grateful for your contribution to the housework because I have a need for mutuality. Maybe I have a different standard around how I'd like the kitchen to look."

Curiously Investigating: "Does that make sense to you?"

Make a Curious Request: "Would you be willing to talk about our standards around cleaning the kitchen?"

REVIEW TO AFFECT THE FUTURE

While Review has a certain looking-back quality to it, its purpose isn't to judge the past, but to affect the future. Without Review, we will continue down the path we've chosen without course correction or improvement. John Foster Dulles, who served as U.S. Secretary of State under President Dwight D. Eisenhower and influenced U.S. politics during the Cold War, said,

"The measure of success is not whether you have a tough problem to deal with, but whether it's the same problem you had last year."[107]

When we Review, we address each problem as it arises rather than repeatedly fixing recurring problems. Reviews can take place at specific milestones on the path toward a shared goal and, most certainly, when problems or upsets arise.

At times, Review does catch errors by identifying and admitting them so that the course can be adjusted before we veer too far off track from the shared goals we have committed to. Without Review, errors are repeated, and there isn't continual improvement. Herbert V. Prochnow, noted U.S. banking executive and author, wrote, "To err may be human, but to admit it isn't."[108] Admitting errors, mistakes, misdirection, and failed strategies is challenging when one's job or livelihood is at stake. It's natural to hide our errors rather than fessing up, thinking that it's safer to just move on. Perhaps this comes from the punishments some of us received as children when we did confess and then had to endure the consequences. This protective mind-set inhibits personal and organizational growth and improvement. In contrast, an environment where people feel safe enough to speak up, be vulnerable, and admit their shortfalls will promote transparency and build organizational strength. So, is there a quick way to Review that doesn't zap all our time on rehashing the past?

Lightening Round Wrap-Up

Steve Martin, the CEO of Blue Cross and Blue Shield of Nebraska, realized the importance of Review in meetings. He also realized that the constant ebb and flow of meetings with loaded agendas didn't allow much time for Review in his organization. So, he met with his team of executive vice presidents (EVPs) and came up with a strategy for a "Lightening Round Wrap-Up" at the end of each meeting. This review would take five minutes and would give each leader a chance to improve on an ongoing basis by polling all those present in the meeting for their input.

The Lightening Round Wrap-Up requires each person in the meeting to rate themselves and the meeting on a scale of 1 to 10, with 10 being the very best, within these three criteria:

1. Motive for getting results and learning from each other rather than being right or winning
2. Staying in dialogue with others—not withholding information or being overly aggressive
3. Maintaining a positive perspective of all those in the meeting and not judging each other negatively

For the review, they would go around the room twice. The first time, they would rate the meeting and what they thought could be done to improve the meeting. That was it. No justification, no explanation or discussion. The second time, they would rate themselves, saying what they could do to improve—again, with no justification, explanation, or discussion. Since it is a Lightening Round Wrap-Up, each person audibly spoke to the group in rapid fire, moving right along without hesitation. Thus, they were able to take the pulse of the meeting. This provided the necessary input, highlighting what could be done better, for all to consider improving the interaction and function of future meetings.

Steve Martin said, "This type of review gave the entire organization a vision for how to improve while getting the results they all wanted."

When we communicate with each other in a way that guarantees safety and respect through Honestly Expressing or Curiously Investigating, we are far more likely to create an environment that we all enjoy working in while developing products that meet the needs of our customers and increasing our bottom-line revenues.

John Mackey, the CEO of Whole Foods Market, recently came out with a book called *Conscious Capitalism*. While listening to him speak at a book signing, it sounded to me as if he had gone through Conscious Choosing for Flow, since the principles he was espousing were so aligned with what I have written about in this book. One principle he talked about was the importance of having happy employees. He said, "When you have happy employees, you have happy customers because your employees provide them with an experience that pleases them. So, the customers are willing to come back time and time again, exchanging their hard-earned money for the quality products you provide for them. And when you have happy customers, you have happy investors because the stock price continues to climb and dividends flow." The consistent rise of Whole Foods stock confirms that this business walks the talk. They must be doing something right to grow from operating out of the back of John Mackey's truck into a multi-billion-dollar company.

HAVE YOU FILLED THE GAP?

Review evaluates whether you have closed the coaching gap for your goals. Considering what you should stop doing that isn't working, modify what needs adjustments and start doing that will help you get the results you truly want for your relationships and results is the final step in the

CONSCIOUS CHOOSING FOR FLOW

coaching process. Continual learning takes place from evaluating current and past performance in order to improve future outcomes.

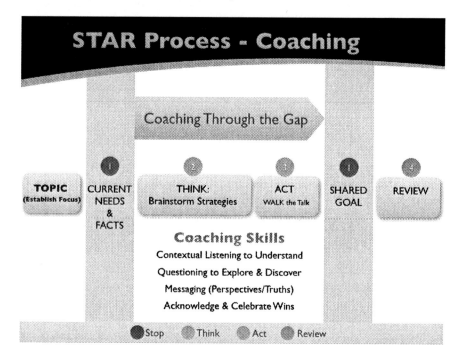

WE ARE WHAT WE REPEATEDLY DO

If you would like to change the effectiveness of your relationships, your teams, and your organization on a consistent and sustainable basis, then habitually understanding and taking people's feelings and needs seriously will help you elicit the response you seek far more quickly and consistently during times of conflict, stress, or confusion.

Will Durant talked about the power of practice while analyzing the work of Aristotle:

"We are what we repeatedly do. Excellence, then, is not an act, but a habit."[109]

STEP 4: REVIEW—STOP, MODIFY, OR START

If creating this new reality—transforming conflict into creativity, creating results through our human connection, and operating in Flow—is important to you, will you choose to be responsible for obtaining these results, rather than blaming or judging others for not producing them for you? If this is what you consciously choose to do in your life, you have taken the first necessary step to making it a reality. Remember, *you* get to say how your life goes. So, what are you saying?

When we first decide not to blame others, but rather to take responsibility for all that happens in our lives, including interactions with others and how they respond to us, then we have taken back our personal power. I came across a saying that made a significant difference in my mind-set and perspective on life. I put it on my mirror and looked at it each and every day for almost five years as a reminder (It has taken me a while to absorb some concepts in life.):

> "I am powerful, knowing that I alone am accountable for my actions and decisions."

By using the skills I've talked about in this book, of Consciously Choosing Curiosity and keeping your interactions with others safe and respectful, you will be able to Consciously Choose the life you love and to live it powerfully. Please take time on a regular basis to Review your life and determine if it is the life of your choosing, one that you love. Perhaps there are things you need to Stop doing, Modify, or Start doing in order to have that life and live it powerfully.

CONSCIOUS CHOOSING FOR FLOW

REVIEW TO REACH SHARED GOALS

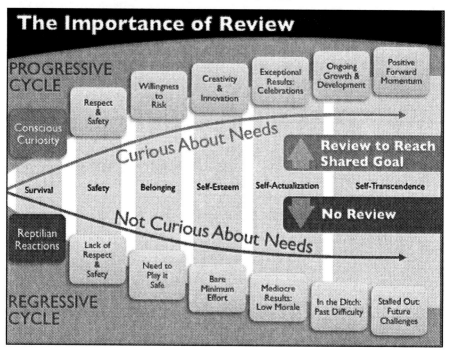

Progressive Cycle	Regressive Cycle
Review to reach shared goal	No Review
Look back and learn	Let it go and move on
Better informed to move forward	Potential for same errors, issues and challenges
Adjustments create momentum	Groundhog day with same problems
Project completed on time	Project delayed . . . again
Team in flow	Team in conflict
Happy people, happy organization	Grumpy people, not the place people want to work
On to solve the next challenge	Still trying to figure out "What happened?"

STEP 4: REVIEW—STOP, MODIFY, OR START

PERSONAL APPLICATION: REVIEW

Now, refer back to your personal challenge. After you have met with the person you are having a challenge with, set up a time to review what you need to Stop doing, Modify, or Start in order to fine-tune your relationship and the results you are getting. You can write in the space here or in the full personal challenge worksheet at the end of the book.

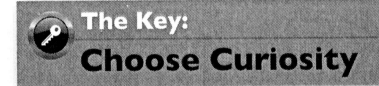

The key is to choose curiosity about your relationships and the results you are achieving and then decide if there is anything you need to stop doing, modify or start doing in order to have the life you love and live it powerfully.

PERSONAL CHALLENGE: TRANSFORM CONFLICT INTO CREATIVITY

STAR Process for Results

STOP ♦ THINK ♦ ACT ♦ REVIEW

CONSCIOUS CHOOSING FOR FLOW

4. **REVIEW: Stop, Modify, or Start**

   When you meet with the person you've had the difficulty with, set a time to get together to see how the resolution you agreed to is working. Perhaps there is something you both might need to **Stop doing, Modify, or Start** doing to make sure you fine-tune your relationship and results.

   _____
   _____
   _____
   _____

SECTION IV

PUTTING IT ALL TOGETHER WITH THE STAR PROCESS FOR RESULTS

Chapter 15

COMPANY APPLICATION

APPLICATION: SOFTWARE COMPANY

Data Tech is a 300-person company that develops software for large U.S. companies that handle customer claims. The executive and management teams have recently decided to re-organize the company, changing departments from role-focused teams, which shepherd a new product from inception to completion, to function-focused teams, which own a portion of the process and then hand it off to another group. This means taking people out of the larger groups in which they have been working for several years and putting them into new, smaller groups or teams.

The development and testing departments have always worked very closely together during project development. When a new software package was completed, it was then handed off to sales and customer relations. However, with the re-organization, each employee will now have a specific task in the process. The quality control team will review the final product before it is sent to sales and customer relations.

The management team has begun to share with the executive team that the employees are resisting this new work plan. The employees are saying things like:

"My full expertise isn't being used to its full extent—only a portion of it is being used now."

I've been with the same team for 3 years, and we really liked working with each other. Now I have to work on a new team with people I don't really know."

"I was on a career path that I liked and understood. Now I don't know what my path is."

The executive team is responding to this resistance with company-wide e-mails that have the following embedded talking points:

"This is going to help us move much more quickly and be more agile during the software development stage."

This is going to help us reduce stress and overload because team members only have to focus on one thing at a time."

Certainly, the results everyone would like to see for Data Tech are to become more agile and competitive, reduce employee stress and overload, break down departmental silos through greater collaboration, and experience higher morale. However, an impasse exists between management and the employees, and no one seems to know how to break down the barriers between the two groups.

STEP 1: STOP—CURRENT NEEDS OR CONCERNS

Ask: What are our current needs or concerns?

This question is **always** the beginning point for the STAR Process for Results. Some additional questions that help to generate greater clarity about the needs of everyone involved include the following:

- What is our present situation? (List facts.)
- What needs are being met, and what needs are not? (Make sure to separate needs from strategies. Only focus on needs. You'll get to the strategies in the step 2: Think.)

With these questions asked, you are now able to state the needs of those involved and the needs of the organization to determine places of common ground.

Group A: Employees	Group B: Managers
Career growth and development (self-esteem and self-actualization)—We are not sure now how this will be accomplished.	*Effectiveness*—We will develop software more quickly and become more agile as a company.
Belonging—We were taken out of teams that we had been working in for years.	*Efficiency*—Employees can now focus on one thing so there will be less stress and lowered workloads.
Safety and respect—We were not consulted on the re-org, and now wonder about our role in any future planning.	*Financial stability*—The company will do better financially and will create a more stable environment for our employees.

We can see by looking at the needs and concerns of both the employees and the managers that they are different. If the managers choose to ignore the needs of the employees, conflict or low morale may ensue. If the employees choose to ignore the needs of the leadership, the company may not survive, thereby costing everyone their jobs.

Step 1: Stop—Shared Goals

Ask: "What results would we ultimately like to attain? How can we shape these results into shared goals?" (Turn the rhetoric from an "I" conversation to a "we" conversation: "We are in this together! Let's focus on all the current needs.")

Determine the shared goals that will address the needs and concerns stated previously. Be careful to focus on common destinations, not on the path or on strategies to get there just yet. The path or strategy will be created in the next step of the STAR Process, where we Think to brainstorm strategies to reach our shared goal.

Example of shared goals. We'd all like the company to be stable financially, so we have job security. We'd like everyone working in the company to sense that they are developing and growing in their careers. We'd like to have greater efficiency for less stress and to decrease workloads. We'd like to create and sustain an atmosphere of partnership and collaboration with everyone for support and encouragement, thereby increasing morale.

CONSCIOUS CHOOSING FOR FLOW

Ask: "What is the current reality of our situation and keeping us in the Regressive Cycle?" Facts only! Identify all facts, what has actually been said and done. No evaluations.

The company went through the re-org three months ago. Here are some of the consequences of the re-org:
1. People were taken out of the work groups they had been in for years.
2. Individuals were now given specific tasks to complete rather than working on a project from beginning to end.
3. Financial considerations were taken into account with the re-organization by management.
4. Company clients were requiring the development of the software to go more quickly and efficiently, without work-arounds and fixes.
5. Clients threatened to take their business elsewhere if the company didn't meet their demands.

STEP 2: THINK—BRAINSTORM STRATEGIES

Ask: "What are the strategies we can use to remove our obstacles or barriers and to reach our shared goal?" (Take feelings and needs seriously.)

Employee's Feelings and Unmet Needs:		Manager's Feelings and Unmet Needs:	
1) Upset and angry	Career development	1) Scared and stressed	Financial stability of company
2) Discouraged and angry	Taken out of existing teams	2) Shocked and confused	Leadership not being acknowledged by employees
3) Frustrated and confused	Managers did a re-org that did not feel safe to employees because they were not consulted	3) Stressed and annoyed	Meeting client's demands of timelines
4) Concerned	Stable work environment	4) Exasperated and alarmed	Agility and flexibility of the company

COMPANY APPLICATION

Ask: "What will help us reach our shared goal and move us into in the Progressive Cycle?"

Brainstorm strategies that will meet each of the needs and concerns identified previously.

Examples of strategies for addressing roadblocks that have occurred since the re-org for employees and managers include the following:

Employee Career Development
- Employees could have the option of moving from one function to another after mastering their current function.
- Each section could meet once a week to share new insights within their functions to assist other team members in the learning process.
- When employees master all the functions in their section, they could apply to be transferred to a new section to learn a new set of functions and roles. This would signal advancement in their career and another opportunity for promotion or additional compensation.
- When employees master all the functions in their department, they could be eligible for promotion.
- Future supervisors could be picked from those who had mastered each function in their department.
- Future managers could be picked from those who had mastered each function in multiple departments.
- Succession planning for all future leadership roles could result from mastering the various functions of any department and demonstrating ability to work with and lead others through the creation of a safe and respectful environment (the Progressive Cycle).

Emotionally Safe Working Conditions for Employees
- Employee and manager representatives could meet monthly to talk about respect and safety, and would make changes as needed to shift teams out of the Regressive Cycle.

- Employees and members of leadership could make a commitment for collaboration and partnership prior to, during, and after any new company-wide changes.
- Employees could have a voice through surveys, meetings, and a dedicated e-mail box for complaints or suggestions.
- Employees from different departments could schedule social functions to get to know each other and have fun. Once a year, there would be a company-wide fun event for everyone and their families.

Manager's Need for Meeting Client's Timelines, for Greater Agility and Flexibility Within the Company
- Accounting could track income from each client with deliverables from each department and the overall impact with each client by surveying the client.

Leadership Acknowledgement
- Employees could include acknowledgments to leaders in messages sent to the new e-mail box dedicated for leadership, which would be collected and shared with the entire management group.
- During quarterly meetings, employees could have the opportunity to acknowledge management, and vice versa.

STEP 3: ACT—WALK THE TALK WITH REQUESTS AND COMMITMENTS

Each group will need to make requests of the other that will lead everyone to WALK the Talk, assuring that their words and actions match up.

WALK STANDS FOR:
- **W**illingness: An attitude of "I Choose to do it"
- **A**lignment to shared goals and strategies
- **L**ooping back to the team with any challenges
- **K**eeping commitments and priorities (assigned, scheduled, and follow-up)

Ask: "What actions that we can commit to will help us reach our shared goal?"

Commitment (What)	Assigned (Who)	Scheduled (When)	Follow-up (Date and time)

Ask: "What positive, doable requests (PDR) can we make of others to help us reach our shared goal?"

Examples of positive doable requests (PDRs) and committed actions include the following:

Employee Career Development
- Employees will meet with their supervisors within the next month to evaluate if the function they've been assigned is best for them and the company. The supervisor and employee will then create a scoreboard together for the employee to complete prior to applying for a new position. They will have a departmental meeting each quarter for the entire group to share their work and accomplishments with each other.
- Managers and an employee delegation will meet to collaborate on promotions and advancement criteria for future salary increases during the next three months. They will report their progress in each of the departmental meetings each quarter and address questions.
- Managers and employees will put a process in place for succession planning that meets the needs of leadership and employees alike. This will be accomplished through employee and leadership delegations. They will share their work in a survey throughout the company in three months to get feedback. They will take the feedback and incorporate any suggestions and ideas into the process and share it in a company-wide meeting in six months.

Emotionally Safe Working Conditions for Employees
- Emotional safety will be a regular agenda item in meetings conducted with employees and all leadership. This issue will also be addressed in the quarterly departmental meetings.
- An agreement for collaboration and partnership between employees and leadership will be part of the succession-planning meeting mentioned previously.
- A e-mail box dedicated for leadership will be set up within the next five days. Leaders will take weekly rotation of answering such e-mails. Leadership will be available at each departmental and company-wide meeting to field questions and concerns from employees about how this process is working.

Manager's Need for Meeting Client's Timelines and for Attaining Greater Agility and Flexibility Within the Company
- Accounting will set up a scorecard for each client to be shared with each department on a monthly basis. They will also conduct short verbal interviews with each client quarterly and provide feedback they have received from the client. These follow-ups will occur in the quarterly departmental meetings.
- Departments will create a social team to put together quarterly functions for their department to get together with another department for recreation and fun. HR will put together a company-wide event once per year.

Leadership Acknowledgement
- Employees will have the forum to acknowledge leadership in e-mails to the new dedicated e-mail box that will be collected and shared with the entire management group. This will be acknowledged in quarterly meetings.
- During quarterly meetings, employees will have the opportunity to acknowledge management and vice versa as part of the agenda for the meeting.

- HR will put together a one-page company newsletter that will be distributed through e-mail each month that shares the agreements and results obtained.

STEP 4: REVIEW—STOP, MODIFY, OR START

You have just read how a software company (name changed) used the STAR Process for Results to work through their challenge and came up with strategies and agreements for resolving their conflict. After following up with them after six months, the leadership reported that their clients were happy and well taken care of and that their employees had adjusted to the reorganization much more quickly than anyone previously thought possible. Morale is quite high at this company now.

One advantageous feature of the STAR Process for Results is that it is scalable. It works in large companies and organizations, as well as with smaller teams and even one-on-one, because it organizes the mind to think intentionally and logically toward putting a final plan in place. This process also has the added benefit of managing stress and anxiety, since each person knows what they are working on within a process whose express purpose is meeting individual and group needs. The underlying message here is that while the final outcome may not be utterly perfect, it will be fair and transparent.

Another key benefit of this process is the ability to sort out a multitude of issues in an orderly fashion. As a rule, in most of the executive or team meetings I've observed, multiple topics and ideas are thrown out to the group. Making sense of this overload of data and prioritizing it within these criteria greatly simplifies the process. Therefore, deal with one issue or agenda item at a time. Do not try to handle them all at once. That becomes confusing and lengthy, and the results will be sketchy.

Chapter 16

USING THE STAR PROCESS FOR RESULTS IN COACHING

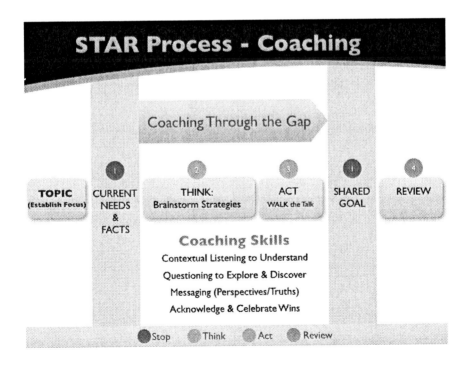

As an executive coach, I use the STAR Process for Results during all of my coaching calls. It is extremely reliable and effective because it seeks to first determine where people are currently located in relation to their problems and feelings, what their concerns are, and what is or isn't presently working for them.

Between the current needs or concerns and the shared goal lies the coaching gap—the space between where you are and where you'd like to be. Coaching, creating solutions, and dealing with problems all occur within this gap. An important aspect of defining the gap is the facts. Without facts, we are operating in a vacuum between reality and fantasy.

A client called me and said he had a real problem with how he believed his wife was treating his parents. (In particular, he was concerned about her relationship with his widowed father and his father's fiancée.) She seemed to experience real irritation when they were even mentioned. At least, this was his understanding of their present situation.

The coaching conversation went as follows:

STEP 1: STOP—UNMET NEEDS OR CONCERNS

Hayden: "It seems like you need some harmony and maybe even some level of partnership between your wife and father." (*Needs*)

Client: "Yes."

Hayden: "What would you ultimately like to see happen here?" (*Shared Goals*)

Client (quickly replying): "I'd like for us all to get along, to have fun together and to be supportive of each other. I'd like us to have family time together with my father and our kids." (This is the shared goal he'd like everyone to work on.)

Hayden (pressing forward): "What are the facts?" (*Facts*)

Client: "When my father calls, my wife immediately gives me the phone and refuses to talk with him.

"When my father invites us over, my wife says I can take the kids but she has other things she has to do.

"When we do get together with them, my wife doesn't talk much and makes comments that don't sit well with my father or his fiancée. They say so privately to me."

STEP 2: THINK—BRAINSTORM STRATEGIES

Hayden: "What are your hunches about the roadblocks you all are experiencing?"

Client: "It's my wife. I think she made up her mind not to like them, and I don't know what to do about it.

"My wife says she doesn't feel comfortable being around them.

"My father's fiancée is a bit pushy. She tries to convince us to do things even when we say we don't want to.

"My father and I don't know what to do. It seems like it's a woman thing. We don't get it."

Hayden: "What are some ideas that you haven't tried before that might get some results?" (*Brainstorm Strategies*)

Client: "Well, I guess that, instead of thinking my wife is wrong or trying to push her into getting together with them, I could talk with her and find out why she doesn't like to. I could talk about what needs of hers aren't being met when we get together.

"Maybe I could talk with my father and his fiancée about what needs of theirs aren't being met and ask them what they'd like to do about it.

"Maybe I could talk to both my wife and my father and his fiancée about what respect is and how we may be violating it with each other. Along the same lines, I could ask them about what does and doesn't feel safe for them when we get together with each other."

STEP 3: ACT—POSITIVE DOABLE REQUESTS AND COMMITTED ACTION

Hayden: "When will you talk with them?"

Client: "I'll talk with my wife this weekend on Sunday when we typically take some time to have coffee in the morning together. She's traveling this week, and it would be difficult for us to have some focused time together without the kids.

"I'll talk with my father and his fiancée on Wednesday night when the kids and I go over there for dinner. My wife will be out of town that night."

Hayden: "Let's talk next Monday during our coaching call about how the conversations went." (*PDR*)

STEP 4: REVIEW—STOP, MODIFY, OR START

During our next coaching call, the conversation went like this:

Hayden: "What did your wife say about why she doesn't like to get together with you father and his fiancée?"

Client: "She said that she can't stand it that my father's fiancée smokes, and she makes no qualms about doing it around the kids. It infuriates her. Also, all that his fiancée talks about is her real estate sales and listings. She said she is sick and tired of it and prefers not to be around them at all if my father's fiancée doesn't have something else to talk about."

At this point, it became clear that we needed to re-engage the process:

Step 1: Stop—Unmet Needs or Concerns

Hayden: "How about with your father's girlfriend? What is stopping her from enjoying getting together with your wife?"

Client: "She says it's really difficult for her to be around my wife because of the comments she makes. It's like they're digs at her. She can't stand my wife's attitude. She said something has to change or it could really affect their relationship big time when she and my father get married."

Hayden: "It sounds like she has a need for respect and safety. Is that what you think?"

Client: "Absolutely!"

Step 2: Think—Brainstorm Strategies

Hayden: "What ideas did they have about addressing it?"

Client: "None. They just blamed the other person and said when they change, everything will be all right."

Step 3: Act—Positive Doable Requests and Committed Actions

Hayden: "Would you be willing to get an agreement from your wife, your father, and his fiancée about meeting and working on a way to make it more agreeable and even enjoyable to get together?"

Client: "Yes. But what would I say or do once we get together?"

Hayden: **"Here are the needs that I hear from your wife:**
- A healthy environment for the kids (Strategy—no smoking around them)
- Interesting conversations when you get together (Strategy—topics other than real estate)

"Here are the needs that I hear from your father's fiancée:
- Positive atmosphere (Strategy—mutual consideration of each other's feelings and needs demonstrated by the things said)
- Mutual respect and safety (Strategy—Identify and write down some agreements that everyone will abide by. People could either do this exercise together or agree to do it on their own.)

"For instance, your father's fiancée could go outside for a smoke break when the kids or your wife are around. If that doesn't work, maybe they could agree on a deeper need they both have—to have a loving and compassionate environment when the family does get together. Maybe some people might put their other needs on hold for the time you're together in order to fulfill on the deeper need of creating a loving and a compassionate environment."

My client agreed to have his family get together and talk about how to address differing needs. We agreed to talk about it during our next coaching call two weeks later.

Step 4: Review—Stop, Modify, or Start

Two weeks later, my client said they had all been nervous about getting together and talking about their strained and stressful way of relating. When he shared with them the process they would use to address differing needs, they seemed to relax a bit, knowing that there was a structure to the STAR Process that would help them through the conversation.
- He shared what he thought their needs were.
- They agreed and added a few others.

CONSCIOUS CHOOSING FOR FLOW

- He said they were relieved to actually say to each other what they needed in the relationship. Identifying their needs took the juice out of the conflict. After that, they could more easily talk about addressing their needs (creativity).
- At times, both his wife and his father's fiancée seemed surprised at the need of the other and immediately agreed to do something about it, particularly the smoking thing. He said the conflict and tension soon turned into creative energy about how to meet each other's needs and that the idea of respect became a focal point of the conversation.
- They agreed that if it was consistently respectful and safe, they could actually have fun getting together. They wrote down their agreements and signed them. Then an amazing thing happened. His wife and his father's fiancée got together and created a fun evening out with the kids!

Appendix I

WORKSHEET FOR AGENDAS AND DECISIONS

CONSCIOUS CHOOSING FOR FLOW

THE STAR PROCESS FOR RESULTS - WORKSHEET

Topic: _____

1. STOP (Why?): Current Need/Shared Goal

Current Need: Identify the Needs of the individuals, team and organization.

Individual: _____
Team: _____
Organization: _____

Shared Goals: To meet the Needs, determine a Shared Goal that all can align on. Be careful to focus on the end result, not on the route or Strategies to get there.

_____

Facts: Gather data concerning this topic.

_____

2. THINK (How?): Brainstorm Strategies

Use people's diversity for different perspectives and ideas for meeting the Shared Goal.

_____

3. ACT (What?): Requests - Commitments

Make positive doable requests (PDR) of each other for the Strategies you choose to take action on from those above. Document - WALK the Talk!

Commitment (What)	Assigned (Who)	Scheduled (When)	Follow-up (date & time)

4. REVIEW (Now what?): Stop, Modify, Start

Set a time to review what you've set in motion in steps 1 – 3 to identify what is working, and what isn't working, in order to make corrections to reach your Shared Goal.

Stop: _____
Modify: _____
Start: _____

Appendix II

PERSONAL CHALLENGE WORKSHEET

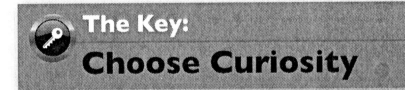

The key is to choose curiosity about what you and others are observing, feeling and needing as you work through the STAR Process for Results so that you can come up with a shared goal all are enthusiastic about, brainstorm strategies to reach the shared goal, establish actionable items of Who is going to What by When and when you'll Follow-up, and then review to fine-tune relationships and results.

PERSONAL CHALLENGE: TRANSFORM CONFLICT INTO CREATIVITY

State a challenge you are having with someone that you would like to resolve. It can be personal or professional. Choose someone you have access to talk to, preferably in person.

CONSCIOUS CHOOSING FOR FLOW

- Name of person: _____
- Relationship/position: _____
- What is the challenge? Give the challenge a name and write 3 sentences about it.
  Name: _____
  Description: _____
  _____
  _____
  _____
  _____
  _____
  _____

- What results would you like? In 1 or 2 sentences, describe what you imagine the best outcome could be.
  _____
  _____
  _____
  _____
  _____
  _____

- What do you think is preventing you from getting those results?
  _____
  _____
  _____
  _____
  _____
  _____
  _____

PERSONAL CHALLENGE WORKSHEET

The Skill for Connection	
Your observations:	**Their observations:**
Your feelings:	**Their feelings:**
Your needs:	**Their needs:**

STAR Process for Results

Stop ◆ Think ◆ Act ◆ Review

1. **STOP: Current Needs and Shared Goal**

   Facts: Refer to the observations you listed in the Skill for Connection and feel free to add more.

   Needs: Refer to the needs you listed in the Skill for Connection and feel free to add more.

   Shared Goal: Create a shared goal that you think you and the person you are having a challenge with could agree on and would feel enthusiastic about, one that addresses both of your needs.

   _____
   _____
   _____
   _____
   _____
   _____

2. **THINK: Brainstorm Strategies**

   Think of possible strategies for meeting your shared goal that would work for both of you.

   _____
   _____
   _____
   _____

PERSONAL CHALLENGE WORKSHEET

_____
_____
_____
_____
_____
_____

3. **ACT: Requests and Commitments**

    What will you do?

    _____
    _____
    _____
    _____
    _____
    _____

    What will you request of the other person for connection and results?

    _____
    _____
    _____
    _____
    _____
    _____

CONSCIOUS CHOOSING FOR FLOW

When will you do it?

_____
_____
_____
_____
_____
_____

How and when will you follow up to ensure your request was completed to the quality and standard you both agreed upon? (List a date, time, and place.)

_____
_____
_____
_____
_____
_____

4. **REVIEW: Stop, Modify, or Start**

When you meet with the person you've had the difficulty with, set a time to get together to see how the resolution you agreed to is working. Perhaps there is something you both might need to Stop doing, Modify, or Start doing to make sure you fine-tune your relationship and get results.

_____
_____
_____
_____

BIBLIOGRAPHY

Adiama. 2014. "Umuntu Ngumuntu Ngabantu: 'A person is a person because of people.'"Accessed March 20: http://adiama.com/ancestralconnections/2010/03/02/umuntu-ngumuntu-ngabantu-a-person-is-a-person-because-of-people/

American Presidency Project, the. 2014. "Speech of Senator John F. Kennedy, Raleigh, NC, Coliseum, September 17, 1960." Accessed March 20: www.presidency.ucsb.edu/ws/?pid=74076

Amundrud, Kjetil Johansen. 2009. *The phenomenology of interest-excitement*. PhD thesis, University of Oslo. www.duo.uio.no/bitstream/handle/10852/18475/ThePhenofInt-exc.pdf?sequence=2

ARVis Institute, LLC. 2012. *Conflict management in the workplace* [slideshow]. www.slideshare.net/ARVisInstitute/conflict-management-in-the-workplace-11949427

Bandura, Albert. 1986. Social foundations of thought and action: A social cognitive theory. Englewood Cliffs, NJ: Prentice Hall.

———. 1997. *Self-efficacy: The exercise of control*. Richmond, UK: Worth.

Berwick, Donald. 2014. "Overview of the 100,000 Lives Campaign." Accessed March 16: www.ihi.org/Engage/Initiatives/Completed/5MillionLivesCampaign/Documents/Overview%20of%20the%20100K%20Campaign.pdf

Bierce, Ambrose. 2003 (originally published in 1911). *The Devil's dictionary*. London: Bloomsbury.

Biography Channel. 2014. "Rob Reiner Biography." Accessed March 19: www.thebiographychannel.co.uk/biographies/rob-reiner/quotes.html;jsessionid=2D9E54EE860F669CC1EC4C5A7535E54D

Bradberry, Travis, and Lac Su. 2006. "Ability- versus skill-based assessment of emotional intelligence." *Psicothema* 18: S59–S66.

Brainy Quote. 2014. "Ezra Pound: 'Genius is the capacity to see ten things where the ordinary man sees one.'"Accessed March 20: www.brainyquote.com/quotes/quotes/e/ezrapound121459.html

Brown, Brené. 2012. *Daring greatly: How the courage to be vulnerable transforms the way we live, love, parent and lead*. New York: Gotham.

Burke, Kerry, and Bill Hutchinson. 2014. "Miracle on the Hudson survivors toast 5 years after Sullenberger's river landing of Flight 1549." *NY Daily News*, January 15. www.nydailynews.com/new-york/miracle-hudson-survivors-toast-5-years-article-1.1581358

Cherry, Kendra. 2014a. "Attribution: How We Explain Behavior." Accessed March 20: http://psychology.about.com/od/socialpsychology/a/attribution.htm

———. 2014b. "What is Self-Efficacy?" Accessed March 16: http://psychology.about.com/od/theoriesofpersonality/a/self_efficacy.htm

City Year. 2014. "Ubuntu." Accessed April 15: http://www.cityyear.org/about-us/culture-values/founding-stories/ubuntu

Conflict in Workplace. 2011. "Work place statistics—The cost of turnover, loss of productivity and absenteeism." www.conflictinworkplace.com/2011/07/31/work-place-statistics-the-cost-of-turnover-loss-of-productivity-and-absenteeism

CPP. 2008. *Workplace conflict and how businesses can harness it to thrive* [human capital report]. www.cpp.com/pdfs/CPP_Global_Human_Capital_Report_Workplace_Conflict.pdf

Csikszentmihalyi, Mihaly. 1990. *Flow—The psychology of optimal experience.* New York: Harper Collins.

———. 1997. *Finding flow.* New York: Basic Books.

Dana, Daniel. 2005. *Managing differences: How to build better relationships at work and home.* Prairie Village, KS: MTI Publications.

Davis, Nate. 2011. "NFL, players announce new 10-year labor agreement." *USA Today,* July 25.

Durant, Will. 1926. *The Story of philosophy: The lives and opinions of the world's greatest philosophers.* New York: Simon & Schuster.

Eichenwald, Kurt. 2012. "Microsoft's Lost Decade." *Vanity Fair,* July 8.

Eliot, George. 1996 (originally published in 1876). *Daniel Deronda.* Ware, Hertfordshire: Wordsworth.

Forbes. 2012. "12 Great Quotes from Gandhi on His Birthday." www.forbes.com/sites/ashoka/2012/10/02/12-great-quotes-from-gandhi-on-his-birthday/

Frankl, Viktor. 1997. *Man's search for meaning.* New York: Washing Square Press

Fritz, Robert. 1989. *The path of least resistance.* New York: Fawcett.

Fullagar, Clive J., and E. Kevin Kelloway. 2009. "Flow at work: An experience sampling approach." *Journal of Occupational and Organizational Psychology* 82, 3: 595–615.

Fullerton, Elaine. 2009. "The development of Nonviolent Communication in an early years setting to support conflict resolution and develop an emotional intelligence related to both self and others." *Behaviour4Learning* (GTC Scotland).

Gallup Organization. 2013. *2013 State of the American Workplace Report.* www.gallup.com/strategicconsulting/163007/state-american-workplace.aspx

Geirland, John. 1996. "Go with the Flow." *Wired* 4, 9: 160–161.

Goal Setting Help. 2014. "Thoughts Quotes and Beliefs Quotes." Accessed March 20: www.goal-setting-help.com/thoughts-quotes.html

Goodreads. 2014. "Albert Einstein Quotes." www.goodreads.com/quotes/330617-your-imagination-is-your-preview-of-life-s-coming-attractions

———. 2014. "Dalai Lama XIV Quotes." www.goodreads.com/quotes/7777-if-you-think-you-are-too-small-to-make-a

———. 2014. "Ernest Hemingway Quotes." www.goodreads.com/author/quotes/1455.Ernest_Hemingway

———. 2014. "George Eliot Quotes." www.goodreads.com/quotes/40245-our-deeds-determine-us-as-much-as-we-determine-our

———. 2014. "Helen Keller Quotes." www.goodreads.com/author/quotes/7275.Helen_Keller

———. 2014. "Johann Wolfgang von Goethe Quotes." www.goodreads.com/quotes/2326-things-which-matter-most-must-never-be-at-the-mercy

———. 2014. "Laozi Quotes." www.goodreads.com/quotes/753949-if-you-want-to-awaken-all-of-humanity-then-awaken

———. 2014. "Malachy McCourt Quotes." www.goodreads.com/quotes/40467-resentment-is-like-taking-poison-and-waiting-for-the-other

———. 2014. "O.A. Battista Quotes." www.goodreads.com/quotes/302234-an-error-doesn-t-become-a-mistake-until-you-refuse-to

———. 2014. "Ralph Waldo Emerson Quotes." www.goodreads.com/quotes/73656-the-only-person-you-are-destined-to-become-is-the

———. 2014. "Viktor E. Frankl Quotes." www.goodreads.com/author/quotes/2782.Viktor_E_Frankl

———. 2014. "Will Rogers Quotes." www.goodreads.com/quotes/881938-people-s-minds-are-changed-through-observation-and-not-through-argument

Good Therapy. 2013. "Maslow's hierarchy of needs." www.goodtherapy.org/blog/psychpedia/maslow-hierarchy-needs

Goodwin, Tai. 2011. "10 Quotes to Inspire You to Launch Your Business." www.launch-whileworking.com/10-quotes-to-inspire-you-to-launch-your-business

Google, Inc. n.d. "Google Corporate Information."Accessed February 14, 2010. www.google.com/about/company/

Haggbloom, Steven J., et al. 2002. "The 100 most eminent psychologists of the 20th century." *Review of General Psychology* 6, 2: 139–152.

Harley, Willard F. Jr. 2011. *His Needs, Her Needs — Building an Affair-Proof Marriage*. Grand Rapids, MI: Ravell.

Hashemi, Sahar, and Bobby Hashemi. 2004. *Anyone can do it: Building Coffee Republic from our kitchen table—57 real-life laws on entrepreneurship*. West Sussex, England, Capstone.

Hendricks, Gay. 2000. *Conscious living: Finding joy in the real world*. New York: Harper Collins

Hendricks, Gay, and Kathlyn Hendricks. 1990. *Conscious loving: The journey to co-commitment*. New York: Bantam.

Hertzfeld, Andy. 1982. "Creative Think." Accessed March 16, 2014: www.folklore.org/StoryView.py?project=Macintosh&story=Creative_Think.txt

Hill, Napoleon. 1928. *The law of success in 16 lessons*. Meriden, CT: Ralston University Press. www.bengtalvang.se/napoleonhill/law-of-success-napoleon-hill.pdf

Hoffman, Edward. 1988. *The right to be human: A biography of Abraham Maslow*. New York: St. Martin's.

Inc. 2010. "Review: Delivering Happiness." http://www.inc.com/articles/2010/07/book-review-delivering-happiness.html

Kashtan, Inbal, and Miki Kashtan. 2014. "Key Assumptions and Intentions of NVC." Accessed March 16: www.BayNVC.org

Kegan, Robert. 1982. *The evolving self.* Cambridge, MA: Harvard.

Khurana, Simran. 2014. "Get Motivated With These Earl Nightingale Quotes." http://quotations.about.com/od/stillmorefamouspeople/a/EarlNightingal2.htm

Kreisman, Barbara. 2002. *Insights into employee motivation, commitment and retention.* PhD thesis. Insights Denver.

Kremer, William, and Claudia Hammond. 2013. "Abraham Maslow and the pyramid that beguiled business." *BBC New Magazine,* 31 August.

Legend Advertising. 2014. "Kinds of People Archives." Accessed March 20: www.legend-inc.com/Pages/ArchivesCentral/QuoteArchives/TwoKindsOfPeople.html

Lehrer, Jonah. 2012. *Imagine: How creativity works.* New York: Houghton Mifflin Harcourt.

Maestripieri, Dario, 2012. "What monkeys can teach us about human behavior: From facts to fiction." *Psychology Today* [blog]: www.psychologytoday.com/blog/games-primates-play/201203/what-monkeys-can-teach-us-about-human-behavior-facts-fiction

Malanowski, Jamie. 2006. "The Loud Mouth: What Aristotle would like about Michael Moore." *The Washington Monthly,* November.

Mandela, Nelson. 2014. "Nelson Mandela Reflects on Working Toward Peace." Accessed March 16: www.scu.edu/ethics/architects-of-peace/Mandela/essay.html

Mayer, John D., and Peter Salovey. 1997. "What is emotional intelligence?" *Emotional development and emotional intelligence: Implications for educators,* edited by Peter Salovey and David Sluyter, 3–31. New York: Basic Books.

Merriam-Webster's collegiate dictionary (11th ed.). Available from www.merriam-webster.com

Milton, John. 1671. *Paradise Regained.* Full text of poem available at www.dartmouth.edu/~milton/reading_room/pr/book_2/

Mint Quotes. 2014. "Curiosity Quotes." Accessed March 16: www.mintquotes.com/quotes/curiosity/5/

Miyashiro, Marie, and Jerry Colonna. 2011. *The empathy factor: Your competitive advantage for persona, team and business success.* Encinitas, CA: PuddleDancer Press.

Moore, Thomas. 2004. *Dark nights of the soul: A guide to finding your way through life's ordeals.* New York: Penguin.

Oprah. 2014. "Quotes We Love: Marianne Williamson." Accessed March 19: www.oprah.com/finder/quote/quote_category.html?author_id=2683

Pajares, Frank. 2002. Overview of social cognitive theory and of self-efficacy. www.uky.edu/~eushe2/Pajares/eff.html

Peck, M. Scott. 1979. *The road less traveled: A new psychology of love, traditional values and spiritual growth.* New York: Simon and Schuster.

Pratkanis, Anthony R., and Elliot Aronson. 1992. *Age of propaganda.* New York: Owl.

Prochnow, Herbert V. 1955. *Speaker's handbook of epigrams and witticisms.* New York: Harper.

BIBLIOGRAPHY

PuddleDancer Press. 2014. "Marshall Rosenberg's NVC Quotes." Accessed March 19: www.nonviolentcommunication.com/freeresources/nvc_social_media_quotes.htm

Ringer, Robert. 1973. *Winning through intimidation*. New York: Ballantine Books.

Ronald Reagan Presidential Foundation and Library. 2014. "Talking 'to' people, not 'about' them." Accessed March 16: www.reaganfoundation.org/mikhail-gorbachev.aspx

Rosenberg, Marshall. 2003. *Nonviolent communication: A language of life* (2nd ed.). Encinitas, CA: PuddleDancer Press.

SAS. 2014. "Company Facts & Financials." Accessed April 15: http://www.sas.com/en_us/company-information.html#stats

Satir, Virginia. 1972. *Peoplemaking: Because you want to be a better parent*. Palo Alto, CA: Science and Behavior Books.

Singh, M.P. 2006. *Quote Unquote*. New Delhi: Lotus Press.

Stein, Joel. 2013. "Millennials: The Me Me Me Generation." *TIME*, May 20.

Stephen R. Covey. 2014. Books: The 7 Habits of Highly Effective People. Habit 5: Seek First to Understand, Then to Be Understood." Accessed March 20: www.stephencovey.com/7habits/7habits-habit5.php

University of Kentucky. 2014. "But They Did Not Give Up." Accessed March 19: www.uky.edu/~eushe2/Pajares/OnFailingG.html

US Airways. 2009. *US Airways flight 1549 initial report* [press release]. http://phx.corporate-ir.net/phoenix.zhtml?c=196799&p=irol-newsArticle&ID=1245239

Virgin Unite: Leadership and Advocacy. 2014. "Mandela's five strategies from Davos." Accessed March 16: www.virgin.com/unite/leadership-and-advocacy/mandela's-five-strategies-from-davos

Viscott, David. 1976. *The language of feelings*. New York: Arbor House.

Viscott, David S. 1993. *Finding your strength in difficult times*. New York: McGraw-Hill.

Vlad TV. 2012. "John Foster Dulles: The measure of success is not whether you have a tough problem to deal with, but whether it's the same problem you had last year." www.vladtv.com/blog/140957/john-foster-dulles-the-measure-of-success-is-not-whether-you-have-a-tough/

Walsch, Neal Donald. 1995. *Conversations with God: An uncommon dialogue*. New York: Putnam.

Weick, Karl E., and Kathleen M. Sutcliffe. 2007. *Managing the unexpected: Resilient performance in an age of uncertainty*. San Francisco: Jossey-Bass.

Wikipedia contributors. "Nonviolent Communication." Accessed March 18, 2014: http://en.wikipedia.org/wiki/Nonviolent_Communication

———. "SAS (software)." Accessed March 18, 2014: http://en.wikipedia.org/siki/SAS_(software)

———. "Triune brain." Accessed March 18, 2014: http://en.wikipedia.org/wiki/Reptilian_Brain

———. "US Airways flight 1549." Accessed March 20, 2014: http://en.wikipedia.org/wiki/US_Airways_Flight_1549

Wikiquote contributors. "Talk: Albert Einstein." Accessed March 19, 2014: http://en.wikiquote.org/wiki/Talk:Albert_Einstein

Wildmind Buddhist Meditation. 2007. "Lyman Abbott: Do not teach your children never to be angry; teach them how to be angry." www.wildmind.org/blogs/quote-of-the-month/quote-lyman-abott-on-anger

Witty, Bob. 2013. "Quotes Attributed to Deming." http://certspeak.com/2013/01/27/quotes-attributed-to-deming/

Witty, Marjorie C. 1990. *Life history studies of committed lives, volume 3*. Ann Arbor, MI: UMI Dissertation Information Service.

ENDNOTES

Introduction
1 Walsch 1995
2 CPP 2008; ARVis Institute 2008
3 Eichenwald 2012

Chapter 1
4 Ringer 1973
5 Two products of VitalSmarts, LC
6 Rosenberg 2003
7 June 6, 2011
8 Hendricks and Hendricks 1990
9 Hendricks 2000

Chapter 2
10 Oprah 2014
11 Daniel 2005; Kreisman 2002
12 Conflict in Workplace 2011
13 Mandela 2014
14 Ronald Reagan Presidential Foundation and Library 2014
15 Pratkanis and Aronson 1992, 214-223
16 Kegan 1982, 11
17 Fritz 1989, 4
18 Geirland 1996
19 Fullagar and Kelloway 2009
20 Csikszentmihalyi 1990
21 Csikszentmihalyi 1997
22 Grant, Richard, personal communication
23 Eliot 1996 (originally in 1876), 445
24 Frankl 1997, 86
25 Moore 2004
26 Attributed to Frankl, source unknown: Goodreads 2014
27 Virgin Unite: Leadership and Advocacy 2014

Chapter 3
28 Hill 1928, 52
29 Wikiquote 2014, "Talk: Albert Einstein"
30 SAS 2014, "Company Facts & Financials"
31 Gallup 2013
32 Wikipedia 2014, "Triune Brain"
33 Bierce 2003, originally published with this title In The Devil's Dictionary in 1911
34 Goodreads 2014, "Ernest Hemingway Quotes"
35 Biography Channel 2014
36 Singh 2006, 156
37 Attributed to Frankl, source unknown, see Goodreads 2014, "Viktor E. Frankl quotes"
38 Goodreads 2014, "Ralph Waldo Emerson Quotes"

Chapter 4
39 Mint Quotes 2014
40 University of Kentucky 2014
41 Merriam-Webster 2014
42 Goodreads 2014, "George Eliot quotes"

Chapter 5
43 Delivering Happiness at Work 2014
44 Witty 1990, chapter 7

Chapter 6
45 Goodreads 2014, "Laozi quotes"
46 City Year 2014, "Ubuntu"
47 Hoffmann 1988, 109
48 Haggbloom et al. 2002
49 Wikipedia 2014, "Nonviolent Communication"
50 Kashtan and Kashtan 2014
51 Fullerton 2009
52 Wikipedia 2014, "Nonviolent Communication"
53 Google 2010
54 Satir 1972, 30

Chapter 7
55 Kegan 1982, 11
56 Goodreads 2014, "Will Rogers quotes"
57 Hashemi and Hashemi 2004, 187

ENDNOTES

58 Goal Setting Help 2014
59 Legend Advertising 2014
60 Hertzfeld 1982
61 Brainy Quote 2014
62 Khurana 2014
63 Goodreads 2014, "Helen Keller quotes."
64 Goodreads 2014, "Malachy McCourt quotes."
65 Cherry 2014a

Chapter 8

66 Peck 1979
67 Viscott 1976, 11, as cited in Johansen 2009
68 Mayer and Salovey 1997, 3-31
69 Bradberry and Su 2003, 59-66.
70 Full text of poem available at www.dartmouth.edu/~milton/reading_room/pr/book_2/
71 Merriam-Webster 2014
72 Wildmind 2007
73 Brown 2012
74 Harley 2011
75 List contributed by Pat Siebert, student of Marshall Rosenberg and NVC practitioner
76 Miyashiro and Colonna 2011, 13
77 Miyashiro and Colonna 2011, 14
78 Attributed to Frankl, source unknown, Goodreads 2014 "Viktor E. Frankl quotes"

Chapter 9

79 William Arthur Ward (1921-1994), author of Fountains of Faith, wrote many of America's most quoted inspirational maxims (Orlando Sentinel, April 1, 1994).
80 Kremer and Hammond 2013
81 Good Therapy 2013
82 PuddleDancer Press 2014; see Rosenberg 2003 for more on the topic of needs
83 Ibid.
84 Malanowski 2006

Chapter 10

85 Kennedy made this speech on September 17, 1960 as a senator running for President; The American Presidency Project 2014
86 US Airways 2009
87 Burke and Hutchinson 2014

88 Wikipedia 2014, "US Airways flight 1549"
89 Witty 2013
90 Weick and Sutcliffe 2007

Chapter 11
91 Goodreads 2014, "Johann Wolfgang von Goethe quotes"
92 Rosenberg 2003, Introduction
93 Davis 2011
94 Stephen R. Covey, 2014

Chapter 12
95 Goodreads 2014, "Albert Einstein quotes"
96 Goodwin 2011
97 Stein 2013
98 Lehrer 2012
99 Goodreads 2014, "Dalai Lama XIV Quotes."

Chapter 13
100 Forbes 2012
101 Berwick 2014
102 Rosenberg 2003, 79
103 A 2002 survey ranked Bandura as the fourth most-frequently cited psychologist of all time, behind B.F. Skinner, Sigmund Freud, and Jean Piaget. He is described in the U.S. as one of the most influential psychologists of all time.
104 Bandura 1986, 25, as cited in Pajares 2002
105 Maestripieri 2012

Chapter 14
106 Goodreads 2014, "O.A. Battista quotes"
107 Vlad TV 2012
108 Prochnow 1955, 142
109 Durant 1926, 87